# The Deaf Population of the
# United States

# The Deaf Population of the United States

JEROME D. SCHEIN

*Director*

Deafness Research & Training Center

New York University

and

MARCUS T. DELK, JR.

*Coordinator of Survey Research*

Deafness Research & Training Center

New York University

NATIONAL ASSOCIATION OF THE DEAF

814 Thayer Avenue

Silver Spring, Maryland 20910

**ISBN #0-913072-16-8**
Library of Congress Catalog #74-18904
Copyright © 1974 by The National Association of the Deaf

To

Frederick C. Schreiber

and

Boyce R. Williams

For their Inspiration

and

Guidance

Throughout Our Research

On Deafness

This project was supported, in part, by a grant from the Rehabilitation Services Administration, Social and Rehabilitation Services, U.S. Department of Health, Education and Welfare

# Acknowledgments

The National Census of the Deaf Population (NCDP) from the outset required the assistance of many people. As a large-scale voluntary project lacking official leverage, the NCDP depended upon unselfish cooperation to accomplish its objectives. We want to acknowledge all the individuals and organizations whose support made whatever success the NCDP attains possible. At the same time, none of those named below are at fault for any inadequacies in design or execution or for errors in the text.

The Rehabilitation Services Administration, Social and Rehabilitation Service, U.S. Department of Health, Education and Welfare, provided a major share of the funds for the NCDP. Dr. L. Deno Reed served as the Project Officer. He and Drs. Donald A. Harrington, Sigmund Schor, and Boyce R. Williams made up the Liaison Committee which maintained contact between the agency and the project staff.

The National Association of the Deaf gave the NCDP its home in Washington, D.C. The project originated in the NAD's Research and Development Committee whose present members are Yerker Andersson, Leon Auerbach, Alan B. Crammatte, Marcus Delk, Augustine Gentile, Leo Jacobs, Donald Pettingill (ex officio), Peter Ries, Jerome D. Schein (chairman), Frederick C. Schreiber (ex officio) and McCay Vernon. The members of the Board of Directors during the project period were Gordon Allen, Samuel Block, Walter Brown, Jr., Byron Burnes, John Claveau, Charles Estes, Robert Lankenau, Helen Maddox, Donald Pettingill, Albert Pimentel, George Propp, Harold Ramger, Robert Sanderson, Lillian Skinner, Jess Smith, Frank Turk, Ralph White.

New York University also supported the NCDP through the Deafness Research & Training Center. The Deafness Center's Advisory Board consists of:

| | |
|---|---|
| Craig Mills, Chairman | Peter J. Salmon |
| Edward C. Carney | Frederick C. Schreiber |
| Anthony S. DeSimone | Arthur J. Sinclair, Jr. |
| Daniel Griffiths | Elmer W. Smith |
| Gladys Harrington | Roy M. Stelle |
| Marion Martin | Boyce R. Williams |

Dr. Joseph Fenton is the Project Officer in the Rehabilitation Services Administration who is responsible for monitoring the activities of the Deafness Center supported by RSA.

Wise counsel was given the NCDP by its distinguished National Advisory Council: Drs. Paul B. Cornely, Eldon L. Eagles, D. Robert Frisina, Wilson Grabill, E. C. Merrill, Jr., Mr. Theodore D. Woolsey and Dr. William M. Usdane.

Nineteen professional, religious and social organizations formally sponsored the NCDP, thereby giving it access to resources which might otherwise have been denied. The sponsoring organizations are:

American Academy of Ophthalmology and Otolaryngology
American Athletic Association of the Deaf
American Council of Otolaryngology
American Speech and Hearing Association
Board for Missions to the Deaf (Lutheran Church, Missouri Synod)
Conference of Church Workers Among the Deaf
Conference of Executives of American Schools for the Deaf
Council of Organizations Serving the Deaf
Convention of American Instructors of the Deaf
Gallaudet College Alumni Association
International Catholic Deaf Association
National Association of Hearing and Speech Agencies
National Congress of Jewish Deaf
National Fraternal Society of the Deaf
National Institute of Neurological Diseases and Stroke
National Rehabilitation Association
Professional Rehabilitation Workers with the Adult Deaf
Registry of Interpreters for the Deaf
Deafness Research Foundation.

Compiling the names of deaf persons could not have been accomplished without the aid of the thousands of groups and individuals who sent us their lists. Their names appear in Appendix A.

The persons who made up the staff of the NCDP were unusually dedicated. They knew when they joined the project that it was short-lived. Nonetheless, they worked with great energy and devotion.

| | |
|---|---|
| Miriam Aiken | Danny La Hood |
| Janet Barber | Judy Lee |
| Laura Bergan | Patricia Leon |
| Marie Bestul | Virginia Lewis |
| Stanley Bigman | Willis Mann |
| LaVerda Birchfield | Dorothy Murrell |
| Delores Bushong | Betty O'Rourke |
| Kathleen Cantrell | Carrell Parker |
| Kethryn Clark | Jane W. Parker |
| Diana K. Dawes | Wendy Pool |
| Patricia Di Battista | Mary Jane Rhodes |
| Rita Dodson | Peter Ries |
| Glenda Ennis | Barbara Riggs |
| Rochelle Field | Betty Roberts |
| Augustine Gentile | Carmen Schein |
| Nancy Gentile | Catherine Sehler |
| Susan Gruhner | John Spruill |
| Robert Herbold | Peter Soltesz |
| Christine Hiller | James Sutton |
| Elaine Hirsch | Angela Thames |
| Jerald Jordan | Vanessa Washington |
| Deborah Knight | Sharon Wilson |
| | Fanny Yeh |

From across the United States, we selected a group of interviewers, whose monetary recompense could not have been adequate reward for enormous efforts they made to fully and accurately collect the information which makes up the NCDP.

| | | |
|---|---|---|
| Ramona Banks | Carole Davis | Sheri Hirschenbein |
| Edward Born | Diana Dawes | Robert Hoffmeister |
| Marilyn Brasel | Joan Doughty | Sylvia Hoffmeister |
| Larry Brice | Dennis Downey | Elaine Horvath |
| Elizabeth Carlton | Jeremiah Germany | Patrick Johnson |
| Dwayne Carroll | Gabriel Grayson | Barbara Jones |
| Edgar Clark | Brenda Grjalva | Edna Jones |
| Ruth Cowart | Wilhelmina Hall | David Kennedy |
| Linda Crews | Norman Henwood | Irma Kleeb |
| Hugh Cusack | Celeste Herse | Gertha Kurtz |

| | | |
|---|---|---|
| Clark La Reau | Shirley Prok | Doris Stelle |
| Nellie Lee | Rex Purvis | Bobbie Thompson |
| Diana Lusker | Thomas Reed | Jodine Trout |
| Mary Martinez | David Richardson | Patricia Vivo |
| Ann Maselli | Ruth Saunders | Bernice Weadick |
| Marguerite Moore | John Schroedel | Jean Weinheimer |
| Maxcine Nance | Thama Schull | Robert White |
| Patsy Nelson | Carol Smith | Elvira Williams |
| Charles Patneaud | Helen Snipes | Jimmie Wilson |
| Marian Pharr | Hazel Steinmetz | Richard Zola |

The National Center for Health Statistics, led by Robert Fuchsberg, Kenneth Haase and Elijah White, played a vital role in the NCDP. We are also deeply indebted to the Annual Survey of Hearing Impaired Children and Youth for invaluable data and unlimited coorperation.

The National Fraternal Society of the Deaf's president, Frank B. Sullivan, graciously provided the mortality data. Mr. Emil Ladner, then head of the Registry of Interpreters for the Deaf, aided our search for interpreters, as did Mr. John Darby, Executive Director of the San Francisco Bay Area Hearing Society, Mr. Robert Lauritsen, St. Paul Technical-Vocational Institute, and the presidents of the State chapters of the National Association of the Deaf.

Special recognition is due to Mr. Reuben Cohen for his patience and acumen, to Mr. Augustine Gentile for contributing his vast experience while sacrificing his own interests, and to Dr. Peter Ries for his administration during the NCDP's early years and for his counsel during the later stages.

Finally, we want to thank the deaf community for opening its doors, welcoming us into its homes, and sharing its experiences. The NCDP has not merely been a count of deaf people, it has been about deaf people. But for it to be ultimately successful, it should be for deaf people.

# Table of Contents

# Tables and Figures

## Chapter II

## Chapter III

# Chapter IV

# Chapter V

# Chapter VI

# Chapter VII

## Chapter VIII

# Figures

## Chapter II

## Chapter IV

## CHAPTER I

# Introduction and Overview

IMPAIRMENT of hearing is the single most prevalent chronic physical disability in the United States. More persons suffer a hearing defect than have visual impairments, heart disease, or other chronic disabilities. Yet despite the frequency with which it occurs in the general population, hearing impairment receives far less attention than would be justified by the numbers of persons afflicted. Even basic data on the incidence and prevalence of various degrees of hearing impairment have not been gathered as often and as carefully as information on far less common health problems.

The last nationwide study of deafness—the extreme end of the impairment continuum—was conducted by the U.S. Bureau of the Census in 1930. Since that date, studies of deafness have been confined to a few states or have provided little more knowledge about the deaf population than its approximate size.

The National Census of the Deaf Population (NCDP) came into being because the forty-year gap in data made planning for social, educational and rehabilitation services tenuous. Administrators have depended upon outdated information, and to the extent the information proves false, the deaf community loses. The NCDP sought to determine the size, distribution and principal demographic, educational and vocational characteristics of the deaf population, in order to contribute current data which would improve programming and provide a baseline for the evaluation of present and future programs.

In 1969, The Social and Rehabilitation Service of the Department of Health, Education and Welfare awarded a grant to the National Association of the Deaf for the NCDP. The Deafness Research & Training Center at New York University assumed responsibility for the technical aspects of the project in 1970. During the last three years of the study, the two organizations cooperated fully in the NCDP's management—a productive blending of consumer and scientific interests with generous government support.

The NCDP's results appear in the seven chapters following this introduction. The purpose of this first chapter is to summarize the findings and to cast them into a comprehensive overview to make the intensive data on specific topics more meaningful. In developing the broader perspective, methodological details have been set aside. This critical factor receives extensive treatment in Chapter VIII, which the reader is urged to consult. Chapter I provides only a superficial treatment of the complex procedural issues encountered in the planning and execution of the NCDP.

Furthermore, in summarizing the various results, this chapter avoids details in favor of broad generalizations, eliminates most references to other pertinent literature, and brings together material from several chapters to bear upon particular points. The succeeding chapters aim to satisfy the scholarly need for fuller exposition and appropriate documentation.

## Delimiting the Target Population

The first decision faced by the NCDP was the definition of deafness. While hearing impairments of all degrees and types deserve attention, the NCDP focused on the extreme end of the impairment continuum. The population of interest consisted of those persons *who could not hear and understand speech and who had lost (or never had) that ability prior to 19 years of age.* For purposes of easy communication, we have labelled this group *prevocationally deaf.*

The definition of the target population takes into account the degree of impairment and the age at onset. Both factors are critical to explicating the effects of hearing impairment. Damage to hearing of the same extent occurring at different stages of ontogeny will have different psychological consequences. The NCDP concentrates on those persons whose loss occurred before adulthood.

## Design of the NCDP

Two projects merged to form the NCDP. The first was designed to determine the size of the deaf population and the geographical dispersion of deaf people. The second sought detailed information about the characteristic of deaf adults.

**Determining the Size of the Deaf Population.** To determine the number of prevocationally deaf people, the NCDP followed a model used to determine the size of rare groups embedded in large populations. First a national list of deaf persons was compiled. Then the persons on the list were contacted in order to establish that they met the NCDP criteria for prevocational deafness, were alive and residing at the given address. Next, a probability sample of 42,000 households in the United States was drawn and interviews conducted to locate all prevocationally deaf persons in the households. By comparing the prevocationally deaf persons in the households to those on the verified list, the completeness of the list could be estimated; i.e., the household survey provided an approximation to the size of the unlisted group. Adding the number probably not on the list to the actual number on the verified list yielded the total number of prevocationally deaf persons.

**Determining the Characteristics of Prevocationally Deaf Persons.** To gather detailed information about deaf persons, a national sample was drawn from the verified list. Specially trained interviewers were sent to question the listed persons and members of their households. Their responses were then weighted to reflect the verified deaf population. The results provide the bulk of the material on education, vocation, and related matters in the chapters which follow.

### The Size of the Deaf Population

For those experts accustomed to thinking of the prevalence rate for deafness as being about 1 per 1,000, the NCDP's findings will be shocking. The NCDP estimates prevocational deafness at 2 per 1,000—twice the old rate—or, more precisely, 203 per 100,000 population.

A discrepancy between expectation and result of this magnitude naturally raises questions about its accuracy. Statistically, the standard error for the estimate is 6.3 percent. This means that the "true" rate will fall between 190 and 216 per 100,000 in 2 of 3 instances affected by sampling errors only. Ninety-five out of 100 times the true rate will be between 177 and 229 per 100,000. If nonrandom errors intrude, then these calculations do not hold. The reader should, therefore, carefully review the methodological section (Chapter VIII) for evidences of bias. Our own appraisal is that the rate of 203 per 100,000 may be too low because of the lower rates for nonwhite persons. The statistical model used by the NCDP, however, has been well accepted and should produce a reasonable approximation of the actual figure.

Of course, the number of deaf persons has grown since 1930, simply because the United States has a greater population: 123,203,000, in 1930, and 203,212,000, in 1970. The rate for deafness is another matter. The Bureau of the Census counted 47 deaf persons per 100,000 in 1930; we now estimate 203 per 100,000. Why the increase? Is deafness occurring more frequently? Or have the earlier enumerations been so inaccurate? Or is some of the discrepancy due to different definitions?

The answers to each of the three questions would appear to be yes. Though we can only speculate as to the amount, there seems little doubt that there are proportionally, as well as actually, more deaf people today than 40 years ago. The lack of specificity as to the extent of growth arises from the nature of prevalence rates. Differences between two prevalence rates can be attributed to changes in the denominators as well as the numerators. Incidence data, not available in the United States, are needed to elucidate the observed trends. Nevertheless, the sheer size of the contrast between the 1930 and 1971 estimates of deafness argue for a true increase in deafness.

With respect to underenumeration, it must be noted that the Bureau of the Census itself declared its procedures in 1930 were inadequate. From 1830 to 1930 the Bureau's 11 decennial enumerations of the deaf population produced rates varying from 32 to 67 per 100,000. The range of those figures alone casts doubt on the techniques being used.

The biggest problem seemed to be the definition used. Each census taker made the determination of deafness. In the NCDP, deafness was defined by responses to a series of questions and not by the interviewer's judgment. The Bureau considered a person to be deaf if he lost the ability to hear before 8 years of age. The NCDP used a later upper age at onset, 18 years. When adjusted to the same age at onset as used in the 1930 census, the NCDP's rate is 160 per 100,000. The new rate is more than three times larger than the 1930 rate. That it reflects an actual growth in the relative prevalence of deafness, therefore, remains highly likely.

## Relation of Degrees of Hearing Impairment

When attention to the full range of hearing impairment replaces a focus solely on the severest degree, then the frequency of deafness in the population becomes more credible. The NCDP estimates that 13.4 million persons have an impairment of hearing. Of these, 1.8 million are deaf, and about 0.4 million became deaf before 19 years of age. Seen in these terms, the size of the prevocationally deaf population does not appear overly gross, occurring in about 3 percent of all hearing impaired persons.

Students of deafness are well advised to keep in mind the entire hearing impaired population. By doing so, their scientific perspective is enhanced. Effects attributable to near-total loss of hearing should also be demonstrable, though at reduced levels, in those who have less severe hearing losses. If such trends are not observed, any inferred causal relationship with deafness must be reexamined. Theories of the psychological consequences of deafness should be extensions of theories of hearing impairment.

Pragmatically, maintaining the cognitive intactness of the hearing continuum in considering health and welfare programs emphasizes the magnitude of the problem. Deafness is relatively rare; hearing impairment is not. Research on deafness can benefit those less severely afflicted. Programs to aid deaf people can be broadened to assist those who are only hard of hearing. Recognition of the relatedness of all degrees of hearing loss by legislators and administrators should be reflected in resource allocations and in the design of more efficient systems of service delivery. To always consider deafness, and more particularly prevocational deafness, in isolation unduly diminishes its importance.

## Age at Onset

Unlike definitions of blindness, definitions of deafness have tended to take the age at which the loss occurred into account. The reason probably involves the fact that the earlier hearing is lost the more severe are the consequences to speech and language development. Persons who become deaf after developing speech usually retain it, while prelingually deaf children have great difficulty acquiring speech. Language development also is more seriously disrupted by early childhood deafness than by deafness occurring in teenage.

These relationships translate directly into economic consequences. Personal earnings are lowest for those born deaf and highest for those deafened after 11 years of age, with proportional gradations between these two categories. Prelingually deaf persons do less well in the job market, holding fewer professional and technical positions than postlingually deaf persons. An interesting feature of the NCDP data deviates from this general finding and deserves being followed up: born-deaf workers held proportionally more higher-grade jobs than those who lost their hearing after birth but before age 3. The obtained difference may be due solely to sampling variability, but if it is not, it may prove psychologically valuable.

The consequences of early as opposed to later deafness are not independent of education. Educational preparation obviously differs for the two groups. The majority of prelingually deaf adults spent some of their academic tenure in residential schools. The majority of those whose deafness occurred between 12 and 18 years attended no schools for hearing impaired students. Since the amount, and probably the quality, of schooling bear a strong relationship to occupational status and personal income, the relationships between these outcomes and age at onset are likely to be some joint function of it and education. The kind

5

of education received depends, in part, on the age at onset of deafness. In turn, the economic factors associated with age at onset also depend upon education.

Demographically, the skewed distribution of ages at onset in the NCDP data arouse interest. The incidence of deafness may be inferred to be U-shaped. Deafness occurs most frequently in infancy and senectitude. Acquisition of deafness appears to decline rapidly from birth through five years of age, and to remain fairly constant until the fifth decade when it begins to increase markedly. Systematic incidence data would probably confirm the general pattern outlined; however, such data would also provide important epidemiological information now lacking in the United States.

### Regional Variations

Prevocational deafness is most common in the North Central region, least common in the Northeast. The South has a higher rate than the West. These findings argue strongly for more refined data to be used in state and regional planning. While Chapter II does contain estimates for individual states, it also holds a ·warning against overreliance on them. The sampling error for the national estimate of prevocational deafness is relatively small, but it rises sharply as the size of the population unit declines. Also, regional differences were found by the NCDP in educational attainment and occupational status. State surveys should be conducted to supplement the national data presented here.

### Age of the Prevocationally Deaf Population

Prevocational deafness is not uniformly distributed across all ages. Presently a greater prevalence rate appears in ages 6 to 24 than 25 to 44 years. The highest rate of prevocational deafness is in the 65-and-over category. These figures should concern administrators who base their plans for new facilities on their experience over the last decade. A wave of deaf clients seems about to crest in vocational rehabilitation agencies. The effects should also be evident in secondary and postsecondary programs for deaf students.

### Sex and Race

A higher percentage of men than women are prevocationally deaf—a long-standing fact repeated in every decennial census from 1830 to 1930. Deafness affects females more adversely than males. When deaf males and females are compared to like-sex persons in general rather than to each other, deaf females show higher unemployment rates, lower personal incomes, higher divorce rates, and lesser educational achievements.

As with sex, the less-favored deaf racial group does less well than its general-population counterpart. Nonwhites have a lower prevalence rate of prevocational deafness. This lower rate may be accounted for by medicosocial and genetic factors and by underenumeration. For those nonwhite deaf persons who have been identified, occupational conditions are poorer. Unemployment rates are higher and job levels poorer. Nonwhite males have the lowest median grade completed in school, but nonwhite females had a higher median grade than both white males and females—probably attributable to sampling error, since the overall distribution is peculiarly shaped suggesting unrepresentative drawing of high-school graduates. Personal earnings, however, for nonwhite males and females are substantially below those of white deaf persons.

The groups less favored by society—females and nonwhites—suffer more from early deafness than do white males. Deafness accentuates unfavorable differences.

## Family Composition

Most prevocationally deaf persons' parents have normal hearing. They are unprepared for their deaf child, and they frequently have great difficulty adjusting to their child's disability. When the deaf child becomes an adult and marries, the spouse will most likely be deaf, too. However, deaf persons marry less frequently than their age peers in the general population, and the deaf marriages tend to be somewhat less stable than marriages in general.

Fertility rates for deaf women are below those for the general population. The offspring tend to have normal hearing, varying from 81 percent for matings of congenitally deaf pairs to 92 percent for matings of an adventitiously deaf person with a normal-hearing person.

Reproduction in the deaf population appears to have fallen more rapidly than in the general population. There is a close relationship between number of children born to a deaf mother and the age at onset of her deafness. Birthrates are lowest for congenitally deaf mothers and highest for those deafened after 11 years of age. This fact suggests the possibility of eugenic practices in the deaf community.

## Education

The trend toward earlier entry of deaf children into formal instructional programs appears in the data for deaf adults whose education is considered to be completed; i.e., those 25 years of age and older. The change to younger age at first schooling has been slow, a reduction in average of one year in the four decades. The deaf children who were born since 1960 are expected to profit from federally supported programs which encourage the early education of handicapped children.

The average educational attainment of prevocationally deaf adults falls below that for the general population. This finding is particularly distressing in view of the likelihood that academic achievement of deaf students differs from students in general who have completed the same grade. The average deaf high-school graduate probably has not achieved as much academically as his or her nondeaf counterpart. The one-year median difference in educational attainment between deaf and general-population adults, then, probably reflects a much larger disadvantage.

The practical consequences of lesser education emerge from the data on occupation and income. In general, the higher the grade completed in school the larger the individual's personal income. Similarly, the positions higher in the occupational hierarchy tend to go to those with the most education. There are, however, numerous exceptions which deserve intensive review, as will be seen in Chapters IV and V.

With respect to the future, the NCDP projections of postsecondary school enrollments over the coming decade arouse grave concern about the nation's capacity to manage the numbers of students foreseen. Merely accepting these students in regular programs is not apt to provide them with an education. Most of the prevocationally deaf students require specialized instruction—an educational commodity in short supply. Swift, concerted action is called for, if the projected needs of these young deaf people are to be met successfully.

## Communication

Because deaf people constitute a small minority within the general population, they must accommodate to the larger group, rather than vice versa. The extent of the accommodation can be seen in the communication patterns adopted by deaf people. Most use speech, expressively, and lipreading, receptively, at least some of the time in their daily intercourse. But they also use fingerspelling, signing and writing in interpersonal contacts, depending upon the circumstances. In short, the majority of prevocational deaf persons are polymodal communicators.

Education and age at onset play key roles in determining communication skills. Self ratings of speaking ability correlate highly with amount of education. However, most prevocationally deaf adults rate their manual communication as good, regardless of educational level.

The relation between speaking ability and income does not emerge as might be expected. Those relying on speech alone at work average a lower income than those relying exclusively on writing. The manual-only and gesture-only groups earn the least. Better average earnings are associated with the speech-and-gesture and speech-and-manual groups. The figures suggest that other factors than communication skill have greater weight in determining personal income. Further investigations of this topic promise to be fruitful.

## Economic Impact

What is the cost of deafness? If one ignores the intangible social and emotional consequences, a rough answer can be calculated. First, consider the job market. White deaf males are employed somewhat more frequently than white males in general, but nonwhite deaf males and both white and nonwhite deaf females have far higher unemployment rates than their general population counterparts—differences of 1.5 to 5.3 percent.

Once on the job, deaf workers appear subject to considerable underemployment. Forty-three percent of those who completed some postsecondary education have jobs as clerks, operators, laborers, and service and household workers. Not every person with an educational level of attainment above the average for his occupational classification is underemployed; but the NCDP data, insofar as educational criteria alone are applied, indicates a sizable amount of underemployment among those who are prevocationally deaf.

The most clearcut measure of the penalty exacted by deafness is personal income. The average annual income for employed deaf persons fell $2,273 below the comparable figure for the general population—$5,915 versus $8,188. The prevocationally deaf worker's average income is 72 percent of the general population average. The nonwhite deaf worker earns, on the average, only 62 percent as much as nonwhite workers in general. For most of those who are afflicted, deafness is expensive.

## Occupation

Stereotypes of deaf workers receive little support from the NCDP. Prevocationally deaf persons work in every industry, performing a vast array of tasks. This is not to say that every occupation is open to deaf workers nor that all industries are equally hospitable. What should be emphasized is that deaf persons have demonstrated their capability to do almost any kind of work. Deafness per se should not bar a deaf person from employment in any occupation for which he qualifies by virtue of education and experience.

## Vocational Rehabilitation

No doubt that some of the achievements of deaf persons are attributable to government assistance. During the half century of their existence, the state Vocational Rehabilitation (VR) agencies have provided a variety of services to deaf persons. The allocation of resources by VR agencies, however, has not been made in proportion to the relative size of the deaf population nor to the expected benefits from service.

Deaf clients have a rehabilitation ratio above the average for all disability groups. Eighty-two of every 100 deaf clients accepted by VR agencies are successfully rehabilitated compared to the average of 78 for all disabilities. The comparison would be even more favorable if the data for all deaf persons were used instead of the data only for those who did not speak. The rehabilitation ratio for all hearing impaired clients, for example, is 8.21, or stated in another way, 89 percent of hearing impaired clients are rehabilitated.

Despite this favorable experience, the number of deaf persons served by VR agencies is low in contrast to blind persons. More blind persons receive VR support than deaf persons, yet deafness occurs nearly four times more frequently than blindness. This parallel is not drawn so as to imply that blind people or those with any other disability should receive less VR assistance. What does emerge from the contrast is the need for increased services for deaf VR clients.

## Morbidity and Mortality

The NCDP found that 1 of 3 prevocationally deaf persons sampled had an additional disability. This proportion assumes increased significance from the realization of how heavy a burden a second disability places upon a person already deaf. A recent study of health-care delivery reported: "In almost every area touched upon in the study the deaf seemed to experience greater difficulties than the blind in their dealings with the health worker. As anticipated, communication stands out as the most serious problem. Health workers seem satisfied that they can communicate adequately by crude unstandardized signs with the deaf, while the latter do not find this a satisfactory system."[1]

Studies of deaf children in elementary and secondary schools indicate that the next generation of deaf adults will also have a large proportion with multiple disabilities. Their health care, it is hoped, will be more congenial and effective as the result of attention directed toward present problems.

Mortality data do not reflect the morbidity picture. It is likely that, as with their deafness, many of the secondary disabilities to which prevocationally deaf persons fall victim are not life-threatening. Information

---

[1]Thomas J. Harte, Ann M. Douglas, Paul H. Furfey, and Mary Elizabeth Walsh, *Differentials in the health care of the sensory deprived.* Washington, D.C.: Bureau of Social Research, Department of Sociology, The Catholic University of America, 1973. We are indebted to Monsignor Furfey for graciously providing a copy of this document in advance of publication.

*10*

supplied by the National Fraternal Society of the Deaf suggest that longevity in the deaf population is equal to or greater than that in the general population. Recognizing the nonrepresentativeness of the Fraternity's membership, however, more must be learned before this conclusion can be accepted.

## Variability

An exclusive focus on averages can mislead the reader. An accurate picture of the deaf community must reveal its heterogeneity. Some deaf persons attain doctorates and distinguish themselves in professional callings, while others are illiterate and work at menial tasks, if at all. A few deaf people have substantial personal incomes and live in expensive surroundings, while others earn nothing and dwell in slums. The NCDP, taken in its entirety, illustrates the great variety among members of the prevocationally deaf population.

To speak of the extensive ranges of abilities and of accomplishments is to state the obvious. Yet the obvious often goes overlooked. We believe that investigations of extremes—of successes and failures—yield as much if not more valuable insight as concentration upon central tendencies. The NCDP could only point to the available extent of variations; it could not explicate tham.

In practical terms, we hope to avoid any contribution to the stereotyping of deaf individuals. Constant attention to averages without compensating glances at the deviations might create the false image of a population homogenized by their common feature, deafness. In many respects, deaf people differ as much from each other as they do from all other individuals.

## Trends

The day after the NCDP interviews were completed the facts they contained were outdated. In most instances, the lag between gathering and applying data does not diminish their usefulness as a measure of current status. When the interval is too great, however, serious questions arise about their validity. Certainly 40-year gaps between data are too gross for one of the purposes of surveying: establishing trends from which to project the future.

All planners work with the disadvantage of an uncertain future. Past performance must supply the key to predictions. Earlier data establish the foundation for anticipating later results. The NCDP has tried to assist those concerned with the welfare of the deaf community by pointing to aspects of the information at hand which augur important coming events. The age distribution of the present deaf population, for example, means that a heavy strain will be placed upon educational and rehabilitation facilities in the present decade and into the next one. Not only is the deaf population larger than prior estimates had shown it to be, but also a disproportionate share of the population is under 25 years of age.

With respect to occupations, the deaf population is not well placed for the anticipated shift in the economy. Too many deaf workers presently hold jobs in declining industries or occupational categories. Vocational preparation can aid new deaf workers by directing them toward occupations for which demand will be great.

Trends such as these cannot easily be detected from scant data. The planner's effectiveness increases with an increase in the amount and quality of information. This holds true especially for the formulation of social programs. Our society is dynamic. Interrelationships between groups in the community continuously flux. The deaf community in particular appears to be changing with respect to parameters defining its very composition—size, age at onset, etc.

## Proposal for a Continuing Survey

Having completed the NCDP, we find ourselves in the position of strongly recommending another study. But with a difference. What we urge is not another ad hoc survey but a continuous one.

No existing organization, governmental or voluntary, presently has the responsibility for routinely collecting information about the deaf population. Yet such information is essential to the planning and administration of services. Equally important is that data from successive years be uniformly defined and gathered so that they can be combined, trends determined and projections of future developments detected early.

A program for annually surveying the deaf population meets these specifications. What is more, it provides an economical approach to the information problem. By contrast, ad hoc surveys are expensive to mount. Personnel must be recruited, trained and then dispersed after a brief period of service. This waste by such once-only projects dismays anyone with the stewardship of research funds. Even more appalling is the lack of opportunity to profit from errors or from serendipity. A mistake in a one-time survey can be fatal; in a continuing survey it is corrected in the next sample drawn. An exciting lead gets lost in the ad hoc case, while it provides grist for the continuing survey.

A continuing survey also can provide knowledge about the incidence of deafness; i.e., about the number of new cases arising each year. At present we have little basis for estimating the rate at which deafness occurs. We depend upon differences between prevalences, a most unsatisfactory substitute for incidence.

Yet another advantage of the countinuing survey over the ad hoc survey is the adaptability of the former. Every year brings new questions, topics made important by recent events. New legislation, an epidemic, a new invention—these unforeseen events demand specific data not anticipated or only generated by the event itself. For the continuing survey such a demand can be met often by only dropping less valuable information from the next sampling. Indeed, the continuing survey takes advantage of the fact that much data may not be needed annually and others can be extrapolated from information maintained routinely.

In closing, then, we look forward to the data in the following chapters being quickly supplemented by more-current figures. Best of all would be the assurance of a continuous flow of information about the deaf community.

## CHAPTER II

# Size, Distribution, and Salient Characteristics of the Deaf Population

THE DESIGN OF THE National Census of the Deaf Population (NCDP) called for combining the results of list building with those from a stratified random sample of the civilian, noninstitutionalized population. The verified list, as will be noted in Chapter VIII, yielded a total of 98,448 prevocationally deaf persons. To this total was added the unduplicated estimate of prevocationally deaf persons from the Health Interview Survey (HIS) of the National Health Survey—312,074. The total of 410,522 when divided by the civilian noninstitutionalized population yields a prevalence rate for prevocational deafness of 203 per 100,000. The corresponding rates for hearing impairment and deafness at all ages are shown in Table II.1, which places the estimates in a context displaying the relations between degrees and ages at onset of impairment.

Interpretation of these data requires bearing in mind the definition of terms used and the method by which the information was derived (see Chapter VIII). The figure for total hearing impairments—about 6.6 percent—includes all persons who responded in an interview that they "had trouble hearing in one or both ears." Of this group, half reported difficulties in both ears. A little more than 13 percent of the hearing impaired group (0.87 percent of the population) indicated they could not hear and understand speech; i.e., were deaf.

When the deaf group is subdivided by age at onset, a little less than one fourth fall into the prevocational category (hearing ability lost before

# Table II.1

**Prevalence and Prevalence Rates for Hearing Impairments
in the Civilian Noninstitutionalized Population,
by Degree and Age at Onset: United States, 1971.**

| Degree[a] | Age at Onset | Number | Rate per 100,000 |
|---|---|---|---|
| All hearing impairment | All ages | 13,362,842 | 6,603 |
| Significant bilateral | All ages | 6,548,842 | 3,236 |
| Deafness | All ages | 1,767,046 | 873 |
|  | Prevocational[b] | 410,522 | 203 |
|  | Prelingual[c] | 201,626 | 100 |

[a]See text for definitions of terms.
[b]Prior to 19 years of age.
[c]Prior to 3 years of age.

19 years of age) and 11.4 percent in the prelingual category (hearing ability lost before 3 years of age).

**Reliability of the Estimates.** All rates based on samples contain error; i.e., they are larger or smaller than the rates which would be derived from a complete enumeration. The amount of expected variability—the standard error—expresses the likely limits within which the true rate can be found, provided that the sources of error are chance factors. The smaller the standard error the greater the reliability of the estimate. By adding one standard error to the rate one determines the upper limit of a range within which the "true" rate will be found 68 out of 100 times; subtracting one standard error from the rate provides the lower limit for this range. Thus, the range for the prevalence of prevocational deafness is 384,620 to 436,424: there is less than 1 chance in 3 that the "true" prevalence lies outside that range. The most likely number, of course, is 410,522.

Those who are statistically oriented will appreciate the value of the combined estimate (adding the deaf persons on the verified list to the NHS estimate) by noting the reduced standard error. The NHS estimate has a standard error of 8.3 percent (Gentile, Schein and Haase, 1967). Since the number on the verified list represents an actual count, not an estimate, it has no error. The result is a standard error for the combined estimate of 6.3 percent—a reduction of 24 percent. The increased reliability enhances the usefulness of the data.

The standard error for the estimate of deafness without regard to age at onset is 3.9 percent. In other words, in 68 out of 100 chances the true prevalence will be between 1,698,131 and 1,835,961. The standard error for the estimate of significant bilateral impairment is 2 percent. For hearing impairment, the standard error is 0.8 percent.

These standard errors apply when the sources of variability are random. Any constant bias would distort the estimates in a way, and to an extent, determinable only with knowledge of the bias. For that reason, every effort has been made to avoid such mistakes. The reader is referred to the procedures described in Chapter VIII to determine the adequacy of the precautions taken.

## Relation to Earlier Prevalence Rates

How do these rates compare to others calculated at different points in time and gathered by various methods? In order to answer that question, care must be given to the definitions underlying the terms used and to the means by which data were gathered. The studies reviewed below are presented so as to aid in the assessment of the NCDP's findings.

### The United States Census

From 1830 through 1930, the United States Bureau of the Census included an enumeration of deaf persons[1] in each decennial census. The prevalence rates from 11 decennials are shown in Table II.2, which reveals the extreme fluctuation from a low of 32.1 per 100,000, in 1900, to a high of 67.5, in 1880—the larger rate being more than twice the smaller rate. The erratic nature of these data caused the Bureau to conclude, "No high degree of accuracy is to be expected in a census of the blind and of deaf-mutes carried out by the methods which it has been necessary to use thus far in the United States" (U.S. Bureau of the Census, 1932). The Bureau gave up the enumeration of deafness and other disabilities after 1930, recommending to the government that a separate agency be established for that purpose. It is apparent that the last Census prevalence rate, 47 per 100,000, is far less than the rates from NCDP, including that for prelingual deafness. The Bureau's 1930 instructions limited deafness to those whose hearing loss occurred prior to 8 years of age. Using that same age at onset, the NCDP presently estimates deafness at 160 per 100,000 or 3.4 times as great a rate as reported in 1930.

### The National Health Survey

In 1956, the Congress appropriated funds for the National Health Survey (NHS), a division of the National Center for Vital and Health Statistics. NHS is charged with "determining the health of the nation"

---

[1]The Bureau used the then-acceptable term "deaf-mutes" to describe the population. For a discussion of terminology, see Chapter VIII.

# Table II.2

**Prevalence and Prevalence Rates per 100,000 Population
for Prelingual Deafness: United States, 1830-1930.**

| Year | Number | Rate per 100,000 |
|------|--------|------------------|
| 1930 | 57,084 | 46.5 |
| 1920 | 44,885 | 42.5 |
| 1910 | 44,708 | 48.6 |
| 1900 | 24,369 | 32.1 |
| 1890 | 40,592 | 64.8 |
| 1880 | 33,878 | 67.5 |
| 1870 | 16,205 | 42.0 |
| 1860 | 12,821 | 40.8 |
| 1850 | 9,803 | 42.3 |
| 1840 | 7,678 | 45.0 |
| 1830 | 6,106 | 47.5 |

Source: U.S. Bureau of the Census

(National Center for Health Statistics, 1965). Each year NHS interviews a stratified random sample of the United States population to inquire about various conditions affecting the physical well-being of the household members. Questions about hearing ability are routinely included in the annual Health Interview Survey (HIS). In 1962 and again in 1971, a more extensive series of questions about hearing were included. These data will be referred to as HIS '62 and HIS '71 respectively.

NHS also conducts physical examinations of samples of the population. In 1960-62 a sample of adults aged 18 to 79 years was given audiometric tests (Glorig and Roberts, 1965). Hearing ability of a sample of children 6 to 11 years of age was tested in 1963-65 (Roberts and Huber, 1970). Results from these audiometric examinations will be referred to as HES '60 and HES '63, respectively.

**HIS '62.** For HIS '62, degree of impairment was determined by a series of statements which will be referred to as Hearing Scale I (see Chapter VIII). The items making up Hearing Scale I form a hierarchy of hearing impairment such that once a person responds No to a statement he will respond No to all those succeeding it.

Persons reported in the household interviews to have a hearing problem were mailed a questionnaire which included Hearing Scale I.

# Table II.3

**Prevalence and Prevalence Rates for Persons Identified as
Having Trouble Hearing in the Health Interview Survey of 1962-63
(HIS '62) by Degree of Impairment: United States, 1962-63.**

| Degree of Hearing Impairment | All Ages at Onset | |
| --- | --- | --- |
| | Number | Rates per 100,000 |
| All persons[a] | 8,005,000 | 4,370 |
| Reported hearing good | 647,000 | 350 |
| Unilateral impairment only | 2,470,000 | 1,350 |
| Bilateral impairment | 4,085,000 | 2,230[b] |
| Unable to understand speech | 855,000 | 470 |
| Able to hear and understand a few words | 736,000 | 400 |
| Able to hear and understand most speech | 2,439,000 | 1,330 |
| Nonresponse | 804,000 | 440 |

[a]Does not include persons under 3 years of age.

[b]Includes 54,000 persons for whom degree of loss is unknown.

Source: Gentile, Schein, and Haase, 1967.

The estimates of hearing impairments are based on the responses to the mail questionnaire plus information gathered in the household interview. The survey design is explained fully in Gentile, Schein, and Haase (1967). Briefly, it involved a stratified random sample of the civilian, noninstitutionalized population of the United States, consisting of about 134,000 persons in 42,000 households which were visited between July 1962 and June 1963.

Table II.3 shows the estimates of hearing impairment from that survey. The category "unable to understand speech" includes those persons answering No to the fourth statement in Hearing Scale I ("I can hear and understand a little of what a person says without seeing his face and lips"), as well as those responding No to the previous statements. When age at onset is taken into account the categories are divided into those with onsets prior to 17 and those at or after 17 years of age (Table II.4).

# Table II.4

**Prevalence and Prevalence Rates for Persons Classified as Having
a Significant Bilateral Impairment of Hearing,
by Degree and Age at Onset: United States, 1962-63.**

| Degree of Impairment/<br>Age at Onset | Number[a] | Rate Per<br>100,000 |
|---|---|---|
| **All Ages at Onset** | | |
| Significant Bilateral Impairment | 4,085,000 | 2,230[b] |
| Unable to understand speech | 856,000 | 467 |
| Able to hear and understand a few words | 736,000 | 402 |
| Able to hear and understand most speech | 2,439,000 | 1,331 |
| **Onset before 17 years of age** | | |
| Significant Bilateral Impairment | 843,000 | 460 |
| Unable to understand speech | 231,000 | 126 |
| Able to hear and understand a few words | 157,000 | 86 |
| Able to hear and understand most speech | 450,000 | 246 |
| **Onset at or after 17 years of age** | | |
| Significant Bilateral Impairment | 2,799,000 | 1,528 |
| Unable to understand speech | 561,000 | 306 |
| Able to hear and understand a few words | 536,000 | 293 |
| Able to hear and understand most speech | 1,682,000 | 918 |
| **Age at Onset Unknown** | | |
| Significant Bilateral Impairment | 443,000 | 242 |
| Unable to understand speech | 64,000 | 35 |
| Able to hear and understand a few words | 43,000 | 23 |
| Able to hear and understand most speech | 307,000 | 167 |

[a]Does not include persons under 3 years of age.

[b]Includes 54,000 persons for whom degree of loss is unknown.

Source: Gentile, Schein and Haase, 1967.

If only those in the category "unable to hear and understand speech" are considered deaf, then the HIS '62 prevalence rate for prevocational deafness is 126 per 100,000 compared to NCDP's 203 per 100,000. Some increase in the HIS '62 rate should be made for the two-year differential in age at onset; but the adjustment would be small. Much larger adjustments are in order for the "unknowns"—54,000 for whom degree of impairment was not determined and 443,000 missing age at onset. Some number of these latter persons would be expected to fall into the prevocationally deaf category. Furthermore, Hearing Scales I and II are not precisely coordinated; hence some portion of the group classified as "able to hear and understand a few words" on Hearing Scale I might have fallen into the deaf category on Hearing Scale II. The combined rate for the two most severe categories of Hearing Scale I is 212 per 100,000 without adjustments for unknowns and lower age onset. This latter figure is well within one standard error of the NCDP rate for prevocational deafness.

**HES '60.** The Health Examination Survey (HES) provides an audiometric assessment of hearing in adults. As shown in Table II.5, the

## Table II.5

**Prevalence Rates per 100,000 for Better-Ear-Average Hearing Levels of Adults (18 to 79 Years of Age) by Age, Sex and Race: United States, 1960-63.**

| Sex/Age/Race | Rate per 100,000 by Better-Ear-Average Hearing Levels[a] | |
| --- | --- | --- |
| | 26 dB and Over | 76 dB and Over |
| Both Sexes | 7,309 | 414 |
| 18 to 44 Years | 1,770 | 136 |
| 45 to 64 | 6,942 | 240 |
| 65 and over | 32,269 | 2,073 |
| Males | 7,686 | 443 |
| Females | 6,969 | 389 |
| White | 7,400 | [b] |
| Black | 6,600 | [b] |

[a]Decibel level is converted to ISO.
[b]Not available.

Source: Glorig and Roberts, 1965; Roberts and Bayliss, 1967.

HIS '62 data probably underestimate significant bilateral hearing impairment when compared to HES '60. If a hearing level for speech of 25 dB is accepted as the point beyond which a hearing impairment is considered significant (e.g., Glorig and Roberts, 1965), then the prevalence rate is 7,309 per 100,000 compared to the HIS '62 estimate of approximately 4,000. The 1971 Health Interview Survey's estimate of significant bilateral hearing impairment is even less—3,236 per 100,000. The discrepancy may be accounted for by the relatively low audiometric threshold considered significant; persons with better-ear-average hearing levels between 26 and 39 dB usually have difficulty only with faint speech. An interview may fail in many instances to identify the problem, because it causes too little discomfort to the individual or because it is not readily apparent to a proxy respondent.

Persons with hearing levels at 76 dB have a sensorineural component which means that the speech signal they receive will be distorted. Usually they can hear and understand only shouted or greatly amplified speech, if at all. Beyond 90 dB little speech comprehension occurs, even with best available amplification. If persons with hearing levels greater than 75 dB are considered deaf, then the audiometric survey yields a prevalence rate less than half that found in the NCDP; i.e., 414 versus 873 per 100,000.

Apparently, more than sampling error is needed to explain the difference in obtained rates. The results suggest that most individuals find a hearing level of 26 dB less disruptive of communication and 76 dB more disruptive than has generally been assumed. Thus, in an interview, a person with a small, but medically significant, hearing loss would tend not to report it; while at the other end, a person with a loss medically considered only to be severe would describe it as profound. The development of Hearing Scale II (Schein, Gentile and Haase, 1970) corroborates this reasoning. Persons denying the ability to hear and understand speech had average hearing levels of 81.8 dB. This latter group includes persons who even stated they could not hear loud noises. The Health Examination Survey of 1974 (Miller, 1973) should provide additional evidence on the functional significance of the hearing levels.

An earlier attempt to reconcile the prevalence rates from HIS '62 and HES '60 led to the comparison shown in Table II.6. By making the adjustments at the mild and severe ends of the continuum, nearly identical rates are produced. That these independent studies yield such close estimates mutually supports their methodological adequacy.

**Surveys of Children.** Two national audiometric studies have been made of samples of children. The Health Examination Survey in 1963-65 (HES '63) tested 7,119 children representing the noninstitutionalized population aged 6 to 11 years (Roberts and Federico, 1972). In 1968-69,

# Table II.6

**Estimated Distribution of Hearing Impairment for Speech
Among the Adult Population as Determined by Audiometry (HES '60)
and Self-Estimate (HIS '62): United States, 1960-63.**

| | Rates per 100,000 | |
| Speech Comprehension Group[a] | HES '60 | HIS '62 |
| --- | --- | --- |
| Some difficulty (40 dB+) | 2,700 | 2,700 |
| Can hear and understand most spoken words (40 to 54 dB) | 1,600 | 1,700 |
| Can hear and understand a few spoken words or cannot hear and understand any (55 dB+) | 1,100 | 1,000 |

[a]The verbal descriptions are from HIS '62. The numerical values are hearing levels for speech in the better ear converted to ISO (original in ASA).

Sources: HES '60 from Glorig and Roberts (1965);
HIS '62 from Gentile et al. (1968).

the National Speech and Hearing Survey tested 38,568 students in a national sample of grades 1 to 12. Because of the small numbers involved, results from both studies show only those having a significant bilateral hearing impairment; i.e., a hearing level for speech greater than 25 dB (see Table II.7). The rates are reasonably close, the difference being accounted for by differences in age ranges and sampling error. What is also noteworthy are the relatively large numbers of children having a significant hearing loss. Both samples exclude children in residential settings. The National Survey excludes children in all special schools, day or residential. With these thoughts in mind, educators must view with great concern the serious extent of hearing problems among today's children, since special programs for such children accommodate less than half of them.

## Regional Variations

The geographic distribution of prevocational deafness does not occur evenly across the United States (Table II.8). When the United States is quartered regionally, the largest prevalence rate for prevocational deafness is found in the North Central region and the lowest in the Northeast, the former having a rate almost 29 percent larger than the latter.

# Table II.7

**Prevalence Rates for United States School Children**[a] **with Better-Ear-Average Hearing Levels Greater than 25 Decibels (ISO), from Two Audiometric Surveys.**

| Source of Rate | Rate per 100,000 |
|---|---|
| Health Examination Survey, 1963-65[a] | 887 |
| National Speech and Hearing Survey, 1968-69[b] | 730 |

[a]Excludes children in residential schools and other institutions for handicapped children.
[b]Includes children in grades 1-12.

The South and West have nearly identical rates, about 20 percent lower than that for the North Central region.

These rates differ from HIS '62 in which the South had a higher rate than the West which in turn had a higher rate than the North Central. The Northeast again had the lowest prevalence rate. These relationships hold for all three degrees of hearing impairment, though the magnitude of the differences varies widely.

The regional differences in rates for prevocational deafness are also found for hearing impairments, though the magnitude of the differences and their directions are at variance. The highest rate for hearing impairment occurs in the West, not in the North Central as is the case for prevocational deafness. This finding agrees with that of HIS '62. Similarly, the South has a higher rate for hearing impairment than the North Central region. The rates for the West, South and North Central regions, however, are fairly close—within a range of 7 percent.

The rates for deafness occurring at all ages have a different distribution than for hearing impairment and prevocational deafness. The North Central region has the highest rate for deafness, but the West has the second highest rate. However, for deafness the difference in the rates for the South and West is only 4 percent, and less than 1 percent for prevocational deafness. In short, the prevalence of deafness appears at a fairly uniform rate in the North Central, South and West, and it is decidedly lowest in the Northeast, when age at onset is not taken into account.

That the Northeast has the lowest rate for hearing impairment and deafness has held true for a number of years in several studies. The Bureau of the Census routinely found lower rates for deafness in the Northeast than in any other area. HIS '62 and '71 both noted the lowest rate for hearing impairment in the Northeast.

*24*

# Table II.8

### Distribution of Hearing Impaired Population by Regions:
### United States, 1971.

| United States and Regions[a] | Hearing Impaired | Deaf | Prevocationally Deaf |
|---|---|---|---|
| United States | 13,362,842 | 1,767,046 | 410,522 |
| Northeast | 2,891,380 | 337,022 | 83,909 |
| North Central | 3,683,226 | 541,465 | 135,653 |
| South | 4,280,177 | 562,756 | 123,260 |
| West | 2,508,059 | 325,803 | 67,700 |
| **Rate per 100,000 Population** | | | |
| United States | 6,603 | 873 | 203 |
| Northeast | 5,977 | 697 | 173 |
| North Central | 6,563 | 965 | 242 |
| South | 6,807 | 895 | 196 |
| West | 7,170 | 931 | 194 |

[a]Northeast: Connecticut, Maine, Massachusetts, New Hampshire, New Jersey, New York, Pennsylvania, Rhode Island, Vermont

North Central: Illinois, Indiana, Iowa, Kansas, Michigan, Minnesota, Missouri, Nebraska, North Dakota, Ohio, South Dakota, Wisconsin

South: Alabama, Arkansas, Delaware, District of Columbia, Florida, Georgia, Kentucky, Louisiana, Maryland, Mississippi, North Carolina, Oklahoma, South Carolina, Tennessee, Texas, Virginia, West Virginia

West: Alaska, Arizona, California, Colorado, Hawaii, Idaho, Montana, Nevada, New Mexico, Oregon, Utah, Washington, Wyoming

Do the new findings reflect population movements over the last decade? Or are the results attributable to sampling error? Or methodological refinements? The answer may involve all three possibilities. The available data does not provide the basis for a definitive explanation of these fascinating discrepancies. Incidence data are needed to supplement the prevalence data.

While the greatly accelerated mobility of the United States population—in 1970, 26 percent of the native population resided in a state other than the one in which they were born—reduces the epidemiological value of these prevalence rates, they are critical for planning purposes. Permanently fixed facilities, whether for education, rehabilitation or custodial care, obviously should be placed proximally to the population to be served. Projecting the probable geographic distribution of the prevocationally deaf population, then, has considerable value, and this operation would be enhanced by a knowledge of the previous rates and an understanding of the factors affecting them.

**State Estimates.** Table II.9 provides estimates for hearing impairment and deafness by states. The state estimates have very large standard errors; they should be treated as rough approximations only. In general, a figure for each state was developed by applying the appropriate regional prevalence rate to the noninstitutionalized civilian population of the state. This procedure ignores probable variations among the states in the same region, but our data do not justify more refined adjustments. The state figures are, therefore, presented with some reluctance. We recognize the heavy demand for this information, and we are concerned that by printing these estimates they will assume a greater air of precision than they deserve. The estimates are, of course, better than that which would be derived from application of a national rate or a crude rule of thumb.

*Sex and Age*

Deafness occurs more frequently among males than females. This finding holds true in the NCDP for all ages (Table II.10). Overall the male excess is very small, about 2 percent, which is far less than is generally found (Fraser, 1964; Schein, 1973). The actual number of deaf females is, of course, greater than that of deaf males, because the United States now has more females than males in the general population. It is

## Table II.9

**Distribution of the Hearing Impaired Population by States:
United States, 1971.**

| State | Hearing Impaired | Deaf | Prevocationally Deaf |
|-------|------------------|------|----------------------|
| Alabama | 234,498 | 30,832 | 6,753 |
| Alaska | 20,480 | 2,664 | 553 |
| Arizona | 130,613 | 16,986 | 3,530 |
| Arkansas | 131,577 | 17,299 | 3,789 |
| California | 1,427,928 | 185,708 | 38,595 |
| Colorado | 160,902 | 20,926 | 4,349 |
| Connecticut | 179,486 | 20,921 | 5,209 |
| Delaware | 37,506 | 4,931 | 1,080 |
| District of Columbia | 49,350 | 6,489 | 1,421 |
| Florida | 472,263 | 62,093 | 13,600 |

| State | Hearing Impaired | Deaf | Prevocationally Deaf |
|---|---|---|---|
| Georgia | 312,096 | 41,035 | 8,988 |
| Hawaii | 52,990 | 6,891 | 1,432 |
| Idaho | 52,274 | 6,798 | 1,413 |
| Illinois | 719,792 | 105,815 | 26,510 |
| Indiana | 340,011 | 49,985 | 12,522 |
| Iowa | 184,017 | 27,052 | 6,778 |
| Kansas | 143,395 | 21,080 | 5,281 |
| Kentucky | 220,203 | 28,952 | 6,342 |
| Louisiana | 247,499 | 32,541 | 7,128 |
| Maine | 58,036 | 6,765 | 1,685 |
| Maryland | 267,783 | 35,208 | 7,712 |
| Massachusetts | 335,423 | 39,097 | 9,734 |
| Michigan | 579,614 | 85,208 | 21,347 |
| Minnesota | 250,234 | 36,786 | 9,216 |
| Mississippi | 150,024 | 19,725 | 4,320 |
| Missouri | 303,982 | 44,688 | 11,196 |
| Montana | 53,706 | 6,566 | 1,364 |
| Nebraska | 96,799 | 14,231 | 3,565 |
| Nevada | 35,732 | 4,647 | 966 |
| New Hampshire | 44,408 | 5,177 | 1,288 |
| New Jersey | 423,821 | 49,401 | 12,299 |
| New Mexico | 72,753 | 9,462 | 1,966 |
| New York | 1,074,764 | 125,275 | 31,190 |
| North Carolina | 343,204 | 45,124 | 9,883 |
| North Dakota | 39,507 | 5,808 | 1,455 |
| Ohio | 694,198 | 102,053 | 25,567 |
| Oklahoma | 175,209 | 23,036 | 5,046 |
| Oregon | 154,815 | 20,174 | 4,184 |
| Pennsylvania | 694,455 | 80,946 | 20,153 |
| Rhode Island | 54,151 | 6,312 | 1,571 |
| South Carolina | 173,440 | 22,804 | 4,995 |
| South Dakota | 42,854 | 6,299 | 1,579 |
| Tennessee | 269,825 | 35,477 | 7,770 |
| Texas | 767,887 | 100,961 | 22,113 |
| Utah | 78,626 | 10,225 | 2,126 |
| Vermont | 26,836 | 3,128 | 780 |
| Virginia | 308,692 | 40,587 | 8,890 |
| Washington | 243,036 | 31,608 | 6,568 |
| West Virginia | 119,121 | 15,662 | 3,430 |
| Wisconsin | 288,823 | 42,460 | 10,637 |
| Wyoming | 24,204 | 3,148 | 654 |

# Table II.10

Prevalence and Prevalence Rates for Prevocational Deafness in the Civilian, Noninstitutionalized Population, by Age and Sex: United States, 1971.

| Sex/Age | Number | Rate per 100,000 |
|---|---|---|
| **Both Sexes** | | |
| All Ages | 410,522 | 203 |
| Under 6 | 8,071 | 38 |
| 6 to 16 | 86,278 | 191 |
| 17 to 24 | 46,154 | 169 |
| 25 to 44 | 56,865 | 119 |
| 45 to 64 | 93,839 | 225 |
| 65 and over | 119,315 | 617 |
| **Females** | | |
| All Ages | 210,727 | 201 |
| Under 6 | 3,796 | 36 |
| 6 to 16 | 40,844 | 184 |
| 17 to 24 | 23,530 | 163 |
| 25 to 44 | 28,424 | 116 |
| 45 to 64 | 47,539 | 218 |
| 65 and over | 66,594 | 597 |
| **Males** | | |
| All Ages | 199,795 | 205 |
| Under 6 | 4,274 | 39 |
| 6 to 16 | 45,434 | 198 |
| 17 to 24 | 22,624 | 176 |
| 25 to 44 | 28,441 | 125 |
| 45 to 64 | 46,300 | 233 |
| 65 and over | 52,722 | 644 |

the proportion of prevocationally deaf persons in each group which is larger for males than females.

When significant bilateral hearing impairment is considered (Table II.11), the male excess emerges more emphatically. Again, the higher prevalence rates are found for males at every age level, and the better-than 1.5:1 ratio resembles more closely the findings of earlier investiga-

*28*

# Table II.11

**Prevalence and Prevalence Rates for Significant, Bilateral Impairment
by Age and Sex: United States, 1971.**

| Sex/Age | Number | Rate per 100,000 |
|---|---|---|
| Both Sexes | 6,549,643 | 3,237 |
| Under 6 | 56,038 | 262 |
| 6 to 16 | 384,557 | 852 |
| 17 to 24 | 235,121 | 862 |
| 25 to 44 | 642,988 | 1,356 |
| 45 to 64 | 1,870,356 | 4,478 |
| 65 and over | 3,360,583 | 17,368 |
| Females | 2,706,124 | 2,583 |
| Under 6 | 23,771 | 227 |
| 6 to 16 | 155,738 | 701 |
| 17 to 24 | 81,923 | 568 |
| 25 to 44 | 243,403 | 990 |
| 45 to 64 | 610,741 | 2,783 |
| 65 and over | 1,590,818 | 14,257 |
| Males | 3,843,519 | 3,938 |
| Under 6 | 32,267 | 295 |
| 6 to 16 | 228,819 | 997 |
| 17 to 24 | 153,198 | 1,191 |
| 25 to 44 | 399,585 | 1,749 |
| 45 to 64 | 1,259,885 | 6,535 |
| 65 and over | 1,769,765 | 21,606 |

tions for deafness, suggesting that the smaller difference found for prevocational deafness may reflect sampling error.

The age distribution for prevocational deafness carries significant information for planners of vocational rehabilitation services. The 25-to-44 age group has a much lower prevalence rate than the 17-to-24 and 6-to16 groups. Facilities which project their future needs solely on the basis of their present experience will be critically short of personnel and facilities in the next decade. The 6-to-16-year category contains prevocationally deaf persons at a rate 38 percent greater than the 25-to-44 group and 12 percent greater than the 17-to-24 group, so that even if the general population remained constant, the proportion requiring special services would grow rapidly.

Equally impressive is the fivefold increase in the prevalence rate from 25-to-44 to the 65-and-over categories. Does this differential reflect some substantial epidemics in the period 1900 to 1920? That would, of course, swell the numerator in the prevalence ratio. Another possibility is that death rates are lower for the prevocationally deaf group, thus reducing the denominator disproportionately. (Mortality will be discussed in Chapter VII.) There is always the possibility that the obtained rates fluctuate largely on the basis of sampling variability.

HIS '62 obtained a similar, though less extreme, trend. For persons with age at onset before 17 years, the following prevalence rates appeared:

| Present Age | Prevalence/100,000 |
|---|---|
| Under 17 years | 135 |
| 17 to 44 | 198 |
| 45 to 64 | 287 |
| 65 and over | 397 |

While these earlier findings do not resolve the explanatory arguments, they at least suggest that the one which attributes the entire trend to sampling error is untenable. Clearly, more intensive studies of the age factor are called for.

### Race

The higher proportion of deafness in the United States among whites than nonwhites has appeared in every census from 1830 to 1930. The widest discrepancy was found in 1920 (42.5 white versus 18.0 nonwhite) and the narrowest in 1930 (46.5 white versus 35.2 nonwhite). Other studies have found the same tendency for higher prevalence rates for hearing impairment among whites than Negroes (Post, 1964; Roberts and Bayliss, 1967; Schein, 1973).

Findings with respect to mild hearing losses are complicated. Post's review (1964) noted more hearing losses among Negroes at the lower frequencies (440 and 880 Hz) and more hearing losses among whites at the higher frequencies (3,520 and 7,040 Hz). In HES '60, more whites than Negroes had BEA's in excess of 25 dB, and Negro adults' hearing acuity was superior in all frequencies from 500 to 6000 Hz, although the differential was greatest at the higher frequencies (see Figure II.1). All of these studies stress the tentative nature of their conclusions, as a function of small samples and the likelihood of some sampling bias. The preponderance of evidence, however, favors the view that hearing impairment occurs more frequently among whites.

*30*

# Figure II.1

**Rates for white and Negro adults having hearing levels (in decibels re audiometric zero)[1] better than "normal" and with some hearing handicap in the better ear at 500, 1000, 2000, 3000, 4000, and 6000 cycles per second.**

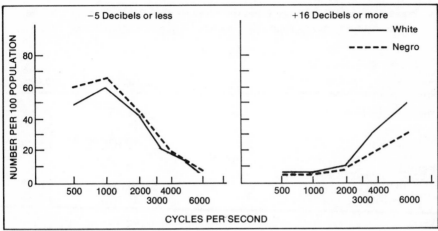

Source: Roberts and Bayliss, 1967.

[1]Figures in ASA rather than ISO

The NCDP found prevocational deafness to be much higher in the white population: 140 white to 100 nonwhite persons (Table II.12). The discrepancy is slightly greater for females than for males. The higher prevalence rate for prevocational deafness among whites is consistent with all previous data on deafness and hearing impairment (Schein, 1973). Nonetheless, many questions remain.

Might the observed differences be due to underenumeration? The U.S. Bureau of the Census believes that it probably counts only about 95 percent of the Black population. Is it possible that factors which contribute to underenumeration of the general Black population operate more vigorously in enumeration of the deaf Black population? Low socioeconomic status is one factor associated with underenumeration, and some evidence shows Black deaf persons earn at a rate less than Black persons in general (cf. Chapter VI). In the particular instance of the NCDP, there was heavy reliance on organizations to develop the name list. Despite special efforts to identify nonwhite deaf persons (see Appendix A), the name list may have been an inadequate source, because the nonwhite deaf community appears to be less well organized and nonwhite deaf persons have tended not to be affiliated with established organizations of deaf people. Other evidence cited in the following chapters suggests the likelihood of bias in the NCDP's nonwhite sample, as well as underenumeration.

## Table II.12

**Prevalences and Prevalence Rates for Prevocational Deafness in the Civilian, Noninstitutionalized Population, by Race and Sex: United States, 1971.**

| Sex/Race | Number | Rate per 100,000 |
|---|---|---|
| Both Sexes | 410,522 | 202 |
| White | 372,516 | 210 |
| Nonwhite | 38,006 | 150 |
| Female | 210,727 | 201 |
| White | 191,699 | 210 |
| Nonwhite | 19,028 | 143 |
| Male | 199,795 | 205 |
| White | 180,817 | 211 |
| Nonwhite | 18,978 | 159 |

Post (1964) argues for a genetic explanation of the lower prevalence rates for Blacks—"selection relaxation" is the term he uses. But he makes the case for hearing impairments, not deafness; and he feels his evidence is presently weak: "The evidence for selection relaxation is circumstantial and rests on assumptions for which there is no empiric demonstration as yet, but the case seems reasonable" (op. cit., page 75).

Associated with lower socioeconomic status are poor diets and inadequate medical care. It is likely that disadvantaged people succumb to diseases which better-fed and better-treated people survive—with attending deafness. Spinal meningitis, for example, not infrequently causes deafness. In those less able to resist its onslaught, the result would be death. Nonwhite persons, therefore, may have proportionally less deafness because they die from diseases which cause deafness.

From the above we conclude that most probably the white-nonwhite differences in rates for hearing impairment and deafness are the resultant of several factors—underenumeration, genetics, and socioeconomic conditions.

*Institutionalization*

The NCDP's target population was the civilian noninstitutionalized population. Residents of mental hospitals, prisons, institutions for mentally retarded persons, etc., were not included. Since there is some evidence indicative of a disproportionate number of prevocationally deaf persons in institutions (e.g., Webb et al., 1966), the likelihood is that the prevalence rate for deafness in the institutionalized population would exceed that for the noninstitutionalized population.

Surveys of institutionalized groups may prove particularly valuable, because of the suspicion that some inmates suffer from nothing but deafness. Deaf persons have been unjustly imprisoned, mistakenly diagnosed as psychotic, and incorrectly labelled mentally retarded. A study which aimed at determining the prevalence of hearing impairment in an institution might uncover some of these improperly incarcerated individuals, through serendipity if not design. In any event, the reader should bear in mind that the NCDP did not include institutionalized deaf persons.

*Trends*

One of the unfortunate consequences of the earlier lack of attention to statistics on deafness is the present inability to determine with any high degree of certainty the trend in prevalence. The 100 years of census data (Table II.2) yielded an eccentric series of rates. The eleven figures do not fall along any uniform trendline. It seems likely that a sizeable portion of the differences between decennial rates can be attributed to methodological factors—definitions, interviewers bias, etc.—rather than to true differences in the population.

How, then, do we respond to the important question, Has the prevalence of deafness in the United States increased or decreased? This question closely relates to the predictive query, Is deafness becoming more or less prevalent?

The NCDP prevalence rate for deafness acquired at or before age 8 exceeds the 1930 Census figure by more than 3 times: 160 to 48 per 100,000. We use the earlier age at onset for the NCDP estimate to conform to the definition used in the 1930 decennial. Even if the Bureau of the Census counted only half the deaf population—an unlikely event—there remains a substantial increase in prevalence. It appears highly likely that early deafness has become relatively, as well as actually, more prevalent over the last 40 years.

Better medical care has probably contributed to the increase. Diseases like meningitis need no longer cause death, but the high fevers and the destructive invasions of the meninges accompanying these diseases do cause deafness as a function of inner-ear damage. Paradoxically, further

*33*

improvements in health care may result in a lowering of the prevalence of deafness by preventing infections; yet some antibiotics which alleviate infections are ototoxic themselves, producing a minor counter-trend of iatrogenic deafness (Schein, 1973).

The available data, however, do not permit more than gross statements regarding prevalence rates over time. The necessary information on incidence has not been gathered. Present knowledge about causes is inadequate to identify significant factors which, it could be predicted, might contribute to fluctuations in the amount of deafness (cf. Chapter VII). However, the establishment of the Annual Survey of Hearing Impaired Children and Youth (Gentile and DiFrancesca, 1969) provides a source of data which will, in time, enable elucidation of trends among the student population. Another hopeful sign comes from the laws in New Jersey and Virginia mandating reporting systems for various conditions, including childhood deafness. When combined with appropriate survey techniques, the registers in these states will become valuable tools for epidemiologists, as well as for educational and rehabilitation administrators.

Turning to hearing impairment, several factors indicate a greater prevalence within the next few years. First of all, persons are living longer which allows for more presbycusis. Secondly, noise levels have continued to grow in our cities and our population has become more urbanized, therefore increasing hearing impairment due to acoustic trauma. Again, improved medical care in the short run will probably, as in the case of deafness, result in more hearing loss by saving from death persons assaulted by various diseases and injuries.

A significant counter factor has been the surgical treatment of conductive hearing impairment. While otosurgery is still relatively young and long-term assessments of its benefits are not yet concluded, the techniques have at least had spectacular short-term effects. Successful treatment of sensorineural impairment, however, remains for the future. It would appear, then, that the available data point to increasing prevalence rates for hearing impairment and deafness, though their magnitude and pace remain obscure.

## CHAPTER III

# Civil Status, Family Composition, and Fertility

THE FAMILY constitutes a basic social unit in our society; and marriage, divorce, and fertility rates measure, in a general way, the stability of these units and the social adjustment of the individuals within them. The NCDP probed for information about two families for each deaf adult in its sample: the family from which he came and the family he helped to establish. Both sets of data contribute to the current picture of the prevocationally deaf person and should stimulate, through the insights revealed, continuing studies of how deafness influences family life.

## Parents of Deaf Persons

Most deaf people have hearing parents. The NCDP data show that 91.7 percent of deaf adults' parents had normal hearing, the lowest percentage being for nonwhite females 88.4 percent and the highest for nonwhite males 93.4 percent (Table III.1). The remainder, from 4.8 to 8.4 percent, had parents who were either (a) both hearing impaired, (b) one hearing impaired and one hearing, or (c) of unknown hearing ability.

These findings in 1972 are similar to those reported for the 1910 and 1920 censuses of the population (Best, 1943). The 1920 census, for example, found 96.5 percent of native-born-white and 97.4 percent of Negro deaf persons did not have deaf parents. One or both parents were reported to be deaf by 2.2 percent of deaf persons in 1910, and 3.3

percent in 1920. The latter rate is nearly identical to the overall percent having both parents deaf in the NCDP.

## Table III.1

**Percent Distribution of Hearing Status of Respondents' Parents, by Sex and Race of Respondents: United States, 1972.**

| Respondent's Sex and Race | Total | Parents' Hearing | | | |
|---|---|---|---|---|---|
| | | Both Normal | Both Hearing Impaired | One Hearing Impaired | Unknown[a] |
| All Groups | 100.0 | 91.7 | 3.2 | .8 | 4.3 |
| Male | 100.0 | 91.7 | 3.0 | .8 | 4.5 |
| White | 100.0 | 91.6 | 3.3 | .8 | 4.3 |
| Nonwhite | 100.0 | 93.4 | — | — | 6.6 |
| Females | 100.0 | 91.6 | 3.4 | .9 | 4.1 |
| White | 100.0 | 92.0 | 3.4 | .9 | 3.7 |
| Nonwhite | 100.0 | 88.4 | 3.2 | 1.1 | 7.3 |

[a]Includes nonresponse and lack of knowledge of one or both parents' hearing ability.

The social and psychological consequences flowing from these findings have had less attention than they deserve. That 9 out of 10 deaf persons have parents lacking personal experience with deafness means the majority of parents are unprepared for the diagnosis of deafness in their children. Mindel and Vernon (1971) believe that such parents' reactions to a deaf child will be essentially negative: "Successful family adaptations to childhood deafness are rare today . . ." By contrast, consider: "Interestingly, deaf parents of deaf children appear to expect the diagnosis and to accept it at a much earlier age" (Schlesinger and Meadow, 1972, page 11.) These four authors agree that, in general, the deaf child of hearing parents faces more intrafamilial adjustment problems than the deaf child of deaf parents.

Mindel and Vernon counter their pessimistic assessment of hearing parents' ability to manage their deaf children by noting, "Those reactions which mire the family in bitterness and resentment can be prevented by early enlightened professional intervention" (op. cit., page 24). For rehabilitation and educational personnel this statement should

*36*

serve as admonition and exhortation in working with deaf clients and students. The deaf person's family background will most often be complicated by the difference in hearing between his parents and himself, a fact likely to have a bearing on his presenting adjustment.

What is involved in the hearing parent-deaf child interaction is more than empathy. True, similarly afflicted parents may better appreciate their deaf child's problems, but the deaf parents often have a more significant advantage—the ability to communicate readily. Several studies have uncovered a favorable relationship between language development and parental deafness. Deaf children of deaf parents seem to acquire language better than deaf children of hearing parents (Schlesinger and Meadow, 1972). Furthermore, the emotional upheaval attendant upon learning one's child is deaf should be less for the deaf person who, after all, knows that deafness need not be a handicap. Of course, acceptance of a physical disability is not equally well achieved by all deaf parents, nor is it impossible for hearing parents to adjust successfully to their deaf children. What the statistics on parental hearing status point out is the pervasive likelihood of maladjustment and the importance of vigorous educational programs which assist parents to adjust to their children's deafness.

## Marital Status

Table III.2 presents the statistics on current marital status for the NCDP sample, by sex and race. Of the males, 54.8 percent are married and 40.3 percent never married; the remainder are widowed, divorced or separated. The corresponding rates for females are: 62.8 percent married, 27.5 percent never married, 9.7 percent widowed, divorced or separated. When considered by race, however, these rates vary widely. White males are married more frequently than nonwhite males, and white females more than nonwhite females. The majority of these discrepancies are accounted for by the percentages of single persons rather than by divorce or widowhood. (In the discussions which follow, the term *single* means never married.)

**Age and Sex.** Marital status varies with age. As would be expected, single rates for both male and female deaf persons decline sharply through age 34, after which they remain fairly constant through 64 years of age (Table III.3). There are small upturns for both sexes in the rates for the 55 to 64 group. These deviations in the overall trend may be related to economic conditions which prevailed in the 1933-1942 period when this group's members were passing through their 25th year, the most favored year for marriage. A similar increment in percent singleness occurs at the same age for general population females, but not males.

# Table III.2

**Percent Distribution of Marital Status by Race and Sex,
Respondents 16 to 64 Years of Age: United States, 1972.**

| Respondents' Sex and Race | Total | Marital Status | | | | |
| --- | --- | --- | --- | --- | --- | --- |
| | | Single | Married | Widowed | Divorced | Separated |
| All Groups | 100.0 | 34.1 | 58.7 | 2.1 | 3.8 | 1.3 |
| Males | 100.0 | 40.3 | 54.8 | 1.0 | 3.0 | .9 |
| Whites | 100.0 | 38.1 | 57.4 | 1.0 | 2.9 | .7 |
| Nonwhites | 100.0 | 59.6 | 32.4 | 1.0 | 4.2 | 2.8 |
| Females | 100.0 | 27.5 | 62.8 | 3.3 | 4.7 | 1.7 |
| Whites | 100.0 | 25.0 | 65.6 | 3.6 | 4.8 | 1.0 |
| Nonwhites | 100.0 | 48.2 | 40.1 | 1.1 | 3.2 | 7.4 |

Deaf males marry at older ages than females. At ages 35 to 44, almost one fourth of the males remain single compared to 12 percent of the females. There is virtually no change in marriage rates for females in the next age category, while males drop to 16 percent single at ages 45 to 54.

Widowhood occurs more frequently among females than males, reflecting the well-established greater longevity of females. In the 55-to-64 age group, 10 percent of females and only 4 percent of males have lost their spouses. This difference accounts for the larger portion of males at those ages who are married.

The overall divorce rate is nearly 4 percent. The female again has a higher rate than the male: 4.7 percent divorced females to 3 percent males. (Persons who are separated remain in the married category for these tabulations.) In her later years, then, the deaf female more frequently than the deaf male must face the breaking of her marriage due to divorce or widowhood.

**Deaf vs. General Population.** Table III.3 also presents the comparable rates for the general population by age and sex. A greater proportion of persons in the general population marry than in the deaf population, and they marry at younger ages. By age 34, almost 8 in 10 males in the general population are married, compared to less than 6 in 10 deaf males. The same applies to females, though with a lesser difference: 84.7 percent of females in general as against 71.5 percent deaf females. The differences in the youngest age group may be accounted for by the fact that a large share of deaf students attended residential schools and were

*38*

closely supervised in their heterosexual relations. Pressures on them to postpone marriage may have been greater than on adolescents in general.

Females marry younger than males in both deaf and general populations. This fact increases the likelihood that they will outlive their husbands. However, widowhood is far less frequent among deaf than general females by nearly half. The rates for deaf and general males are equal overall in termination of marriage by death of spouse.

## Table III.3

**Percent Distribution of Marital Status of Deaf Population
Compared to General Population,[a] by Age and Sex: United States, 1972.**

| | Marital Status | | | | | | | |
| Respondents' Sex and Age | Single | | Married[b] | | Widowed | | Divorced | |
| | Deaf | General | Deaf | General | Deaf | General | Deaf | General |
|---|---|---|---|---|---|---|---|---|
| **Total** | 34.1 | 18.5 | 60.0 | 74.3 | 2.1 | 3.5 | 3.8 | 3.6 |
| 16 to 24[c] | 83.9 | 57.6 | 15.4 | 40.9 | 0.2 | 0.2 | 0.5 | 1.3 |
| 25 to 34 | 28.3 | 13.6 | 77.6 | 82.0 | 0.3 | 0.4 | 3.8 | 3.9 |
| 35 to 44 | 17.9 | 6.3 | 76.4 | 87.6 | — | 1.5 | 5.7 | 4.6 |
| 45 to 54 | 13.6 | 5.9 | 77.1 | 84.5 | 4.1 | 4.9 | 5.2 | 4.7 |
| 55 to 64 | 18.3 | 6.1 | 70.1 | 77.3 | 7.1 | 12.8 | 4.4 | 3.8 |
| **Male** | 40.3 | 21.8 | 55.7 | 74.3 | 1.0 | 1.0 | 3.0 | 2.9 |
| 16 to 24[c] | 88.4 | 67.3 | 10.6 | 31.9 | 0.4 | — | 0.4 | 0.7 |
| 25 to 34 | 38.3 | 17.6 | 58.5 | 79.2 | — | 0.1 | 3.2 | 3.0 |
| 35 to 44 | 22.8 | 7.5 | 72.0 | 88.5 | — | 0.5 | 5.2 | 3.5 |
| 45 to 54 | 16.3 | 7.3 | 77.5 | 87.2 | 1.1 | 1.5 | 5.1 | 4.0 |
| 55 to 64 | 20.8 | 5.8 | 73.7 | 87.4 | 4.2 | 3.5 | 1.4 | 3.3 |
| **Female** | 27.5 | 15.4 | 64.5 | 74.3 | 3.3 | 5.9 | 4.7 | 4.3 |
| 16 to 24[c] | 78.1 | 48.8 | 21.3 | 49.2 | — | 0.3 | 0.6 | 1.8 |
| 25 to 34 | 24.6 | 9.7 | 71.5 | 84.7 | 0.3 | 0.9 | 3.6 | 4.8 |
| 35 to 44 | 12.0 | 5.2 | 81.7 | 86.7 | — | 2.5 | 6.3 | 5.6 |
| 45 to 54 | 11.1 | 4.5 | 76.7 | 82.0 | 6.9 | 8.0 | 5.3 | 5.4 |
| 55 to 64 | 16.0 | 6.4 | 66.7 | 68.2 | 10.0 | 21.2 | 7.3 | 4.1 |

[a]Source: Statistical Abstract of the United States: 1972.

[b]Includes persons who are separated.

[c]General population rates do not include persons 16 and 17 years old.

*39*

Divorce rates for the deaf and general populations are similar: 3.6 percent for the general population vs. 3.8 percent for the deaf population. However, divorce appears to be more frequent per deaf marriage.

**Other Deaf Samples.** The percent of single persons in the NCDP is almost identical to that found in the New York State Survey (Rainer et al., 1963). It is far higher than the rate from the 1957 survey of some deaf adults (Lunde and Bigman, 1959) and the Metropolitan Washington sample (Schein, 1968). Both of the latter studies yielded 25 percent single deaf persons. These differences can be accounted for by the probable discrepancies in proportions of males and females and of persons at the different age levels. Representation of marital status by one distribution combining male and female data masks rather than highlights the actual pattern of relationships.

Historically, the lower marriage rates among deaf persons were noted in the 1910 and 1920 decennial censuses (Best, 1943). The differences were more marked than in recent surveys. For deaf males 15 years and over, the single rate was 68.2 percent in 1910 and 60.4 percent in 1920. The comparable rates for the general population were 38.9 and 35.2 percent, respectively. For deaf females the rates were 58.6 percent in 1910 and 45.4 percent in 1920 versus 29.8 and 27.4 percent, respectively. Thus, deaf persons have followed the century-long trend toward more marriages expressed by the general population, but they have only slightly reduced the gap in the extent to which they marry.

## Table III.4

Percent Distribution of Hearing Status of Spouse, by Sex and Race
of Married Respondents 16 to 64 Years of Age: United States, 1972.

| Respondents' Sex and Race | | Spouse's Hearing | | |
| --- | --- | --- | --- | --- |
| | Total | Deaf | Hard of Hearing | Normal |
| All Groups | 100.0 | 79.5 | 6.9 | 13.6 |
| Males | 100.0 | 80.7 | 6.7 | 12.6 |
| White | 100.0 | 81.4 | 6.9 | 11.7 |
| Nonwhite | 100.0 | 67.5 | 3.7 | 28.8 |
| Females | 100.0 | 78.5 | 7.1 | 14.4 |
| White | 100.0 | 78.4 | 7.2 | 14.4 |
| Nonwhite | 100.0 | 79.6 | 5.8 | 14.6 |

**Spouse's Hearing.** In choosing a marital partner, the majority of deaf persons favor deaf partners. Among married deaf persons in the current survey, most have deaf spouses (Table III.4). Nonwhite deaf males had 28.8 percent hearing wives, a deviation which may reflect a lessened opportunity to select a deaf partner or a secondary preference for a hearing spouse; 67.5 percent had deaf wives and 3.8 percent hard of hearing wives. The rate for nonwhite deaf females is nearly the same as for white deaf females: a little over 14 percent having hearing spouses. The overall rates are close to those reported for New York State and Washington, D.C. Rainer et al. asked their deaf sample about preference for spouse's hearing; 86 percent expressed a desire for a deaf mate. In Washington, D.C., hearing of spouse significantly related to age at onset: the earlier the onset of deafness, the greater the probability that a deaf partner will be selected. The NCDP data bear out this relationship, with deaf females exhibiting this tendency more than deaf males (Table III.5). The relationship is statistically significant in each case. Schein also noted that divorce rates are far higher for marriages in which one spouse is hearing than for those in which both are deaf.

## Table III.5

Percent Distribution of Hearing Status of Spouse, by Sex and Age of Onset
of Deafness for Married Respondents 16 to 64 Years of Age: United States, 1972.

| Respondents' Sex and Age at Onset of Deafness | Spouse's Hearing | | | |
|---|---|---|---|---|
| | Total | Deaf | Hard of Hearing | Normal |
| **Males** | | | | |
| All ages at onset | 100.0 | 81.5 | 6.5 | 12.0 |
| Under 3 years | 100.0 | 83.5 | 6.9 | 9.6 |
| 3 to 18 years | 100.0 | 77.3 | 5.7 | 11.0 |
| **Females** | | | | |
| All ages at onset | 100.0 | 78.9 | 6.9 | 14.2 |
| Under 3 years | 100.0 | 85.5 | 5.8 | 8.7 |
| 3 to 18 years | 100.0 | 64.9 | 9.3 | 25.8 |

**Age at Onset.** Congenitally deaf persons marry other congenitally deaf persons at a higher rate than do deaf persons in general (Table III.6). In our married sample, congenitally deaf persons of both sexes appeared at a ratio of 1:2 with persons acquiring deafness after birth, but only 28 percent of their wives and 26 percent of their husbands were congenitally deaf. About one third of congenitally deaf males and females married a congenitally deaf person, while one fourth or less of those who acquired deafness selected a congenitally deaf mate.

## Table III.6

**Age at Onset of Deafness for Married Respondents,
by Age at Onset of Spouse's Deafness: United States, 1972.**

| Respondents' Sex and Age at Onset | Age at Onset of Spouse's Deafness | | | |
|---|---|---|---|---|
| | Total | Congenital | Acquired | Not Deaf |
| **Both Sexes** | | | | |
| All ages at onset | 1,092 | 293 | 577 | 222 |
| Congenital | 358 | 118 | 175 | 65 |
| Acquired | 734 | 175 | 402 | 157 |
| **Males** | | | | |
| All ages at onset | 533 | 150 | 285 | 98 |
| Congenital | 174 | 59 | 84 | 31 |
| Acquired | 359 | 91 | 201 | 67 |
| **Females** | | | | |
| All ages at onset | 559 | 143 | 292 | 124 |
| Congenital | 184 | 59 | 91 | 34 |
| Acquired | 375 | 84 | 201 | 90 |

**Education.** There is a tendency for better-educated deaf persons to select normal-hearing mates (Table III.7). The trend is clearer for females than for males. In both instances, however, it should be noted that the majority of married respondents at all educational levels chose deaf partners.

# Table III.7

**Percent Distribution of Hearing of Spouse, by Sex and Highest Grade Completed for Married Respondents: United States, 1972.**

| Education | Total | Hearing of Spouse — Hearing Impaired | Hearing of Spouse — Normal |
|---|---|---|---|
| **Males** | | | |
| All Grades | 100.0 | 85.8 | 14.2 |
| 0 to 8 | 100.0 | 85.8 | 14.2 |
| 9 to 12 | 100.0 | 89.0 | 11.0 |
| 13+ | 100.0 | 71.9 | 28.1 |
| **Females** | | | |
| All Grades | 100.0 | 85.6 | 14.4 |
| 0 to 8 | 100.0 | 92.5 | 7.5 |
| 9 to 12 | 100.0 | 85.1 | 14.9 |
| 13+ | 100.0 | 73.6 | 26.4 |

## Fertility

The data on childbearing by deaf women appear in Table III.8. The overall rate for white deaf women ever married is 1.84 children ever born and for nonwhite deaf women 2.44 children ever born. The Metropolitan Washington Study reported 1.83 children for white and 3.4 children for nonwhite deaf women ever married. In New York State, Rainer et al. found an overall rate of 2.29 children per married deaf woman. The current rates are lower than for the general population, suggesting some restriction in family size, consciously or unconsciously, by the deaf population.

# Table III.8

**Distribution of Children by Mother's Age, Race and Number
of Children Ever Born: United States, 1972.**

| Age and Race of Women | Total Women | Single Women | Women Ever Married | Children Ever Born | | |
| --- | --- | --- | --- | --- | --- | --- |
| | | | | Total | Per Woman | Per Woman Ever Married |
| **White** | | | | | | |
| 18 to 44 | 1357 | 396 | 961 | 1770 | 1.30 | 1.84 |
| 18 to 19 | 117 | 108 | 9 | — | — | — |
| 20 to 24 | 252 | 159 | 93 | 54 | .21 | .58 |
| 25 to 29 | 321 | 66 | 255 | 351 | 1.09 | 1.38 |
| 30 to 34 | 219 | 21 | 198 | 390 | 1.78 | 1.97 |
| 35 to 39 | 214 | 33 | 181 | 459 | 2.14 | 2.54 |
| 40 to 44 | 234 | 9 | 225 | 516 | 2.21 | 2.29 |
| 45 to 49 | 250 | 18 | 240 | 537 | 2.08 | 2.24 |
| 50 and Over | 690 | 96 | 594 | 1110 | 1.61 | 1.87 |
| **Nonwhite** | | | | | | |
| 18 to 44 | 178 | 94 | 84 | 205 | 1.15 | 2.44 |
| 18 to 19 | 24 | 24 | — | — | — | — |
| 20 to 24 | 36 | 24 | 12 | 6 | .17 | .50 |
| 25 to 29 | 42 | 18 | 24 | 33 | .79 | 1.38 |
| 30 to 34 | 43 | 13 | 30 | 61 | 1.42 | 2.03 |
| 35 to 39 | 21 | 15 | 6 | 33 | 1.57 | 5.50 |
| 40 to 44 | 12 | — | 12 | 72 | 6.00 | 6.00 |
| 45 to 49 | 30 | 6 | 24 | 102 | 3.40 | 4.25 |
| 50 and Over | 49 | 12 | 37 | 145 | 2.96 | 3.92 |

Of the children born, 88 percent are normal-hearing. The comparable figure for the Metropolitan Washington study was 89.4 percent, and 90.4 percent for New York State. When data are analyzed by hearing of parents, the rates become progressively greater for combinations of congenitally deaf parents as opposed to those with acquired deafness (Table III.9). Where one parent had normal hearing and the other acquired deafness, 92.5 percent of the offspring were normal-hearing. Where both parents were congenitally deaf, 81.4 percent of the offspring were normal-hearing. Despite the dramatic differences in percentages of deaf children for the various categories, it should be noted that the expectation from all pairings is for normal-hearing children. Genetic counseling can specify more closely the expectations for deaf offspring in particular instances of prospective matings.

## Table III.9

**Percent Distribution of Hearing Status of Children, by Hearing Status and Age at Onset of Deafness Married Respondents: United States, 1972.**

| Hearing and Age at Onset of Parents | Hearing of Children | | | |
|---|---|---|---|---|
| | Total | Normal | Deaf | Hard of Hearing |
| All Marriages | 100.0 | 88.0 | 9.1 | 2.9 |
| Hearing & Deaf Acquired | 100.0 | 92.5 | 4.5 | 3.0 |
| Hard of Hearing & Deaf Acquired | 100.0 | 91.8 | 5.5 | 2.7 |
| Deaf Acquired & Deaf Acquired | 100.0 | 89.4 | 6.0 | 4.6 |
| Hearing & Deaf Congenital | 100.0 | 85.2 | 11.5 | 3.3 |
| Hard of Hearing & Deaf Congenital | 100.0 | 84.4 | 12.5 | 3.1 |
| Deaf Congenital Deaf Acquired | 100.0 | 84.8 | 14.0 | 1.2 |
| Deaf Congenital & Deaf Congenital | 100.0 | 81.4 | 17.4 | 1.2 |

Table III.10 presents median numbers of children ever born by age at onset of mother's deafness. There is a clear relationship between the two. As mothers' age at onset of deafness increases so do the number of children. This inclination toward reduced progeny among those who are prelingually and congenitally deaf may be a deliberate effort to avoid reproducing deafness. The extent of eugenic practices in the deaf community has not been investigated, though there appears to be evidence of their existence.

# Table III.10

**Median Number of Children Ever Born to Female Respondents
15 to 64 Years of Age, by Age at Onset of Deafness: United States, 1972.**

| Age at Onset of<br>Deafness | Median Number<br>of Children |
|---|---|
| All ages at onset | 1.0 |
| Born Deaf | .4 |
| Less than 1 year | .9 |
| 1 to 3 years | 1.2 |
| 3 to 5 years | 1.8 |
| 6 to 18 years | 2.3 |

## CHAPTER IV

# Education and Communication

THE EFFECTS OF DEAFNESS are most apparent on education and communication. Particularly for the prelingually deaf child, special educational facilities are required for efficient learning. Since education is largely an exchange of ideas, deafness's disruption of communication also influences the education of those whose loss occurs at any age prior to the end of schooling.

The United States, almost from its founding, has recognized the unique educational needs of deaf children. The first permanent public school for deaf children opened in 1817, in Hartford, Connecticut. Less than half a century afterward, the first college in the world for deaf students began in Washington, D.C. The United States maintains a benign position of international leadership in the education of the deaf citizen. Gallaudet College continues to be the world's only liberal arts college for deaf students, for example. Accordingly, one would expect the demographic picture of the deaf community in the United States to reflect this enlightened attitude toward the education of deaf citizens.

## Age at Entry into School

At one time, some pedagogues held that the deaf child should enter school at an older age than the normal-hearing child because his language development was slower! Incredible as it may now seem, the obvious necessity for early education of deaf children only recently gained widespread acceptance in this country.

Table IV.1 shows the ages at entry into school for deaf respondents 25 to 64 years of age. The trend toward earlier formal instruction is clear: a

# Table IV.1

**Percent Distribution of Age at Entry into School,
by Present Age for Respondents 25-64 Years of Age: United States, 1972.**

| Age at Entry in School | | Present Age of Respondent | | | |
|---|---|---|---|---|---|
| | Total | 25-34 | 35-44 | 45-54 | 55-64 |
| All Ages | 100.0 | 100.0 | 100.0 | 100.0 | 100.0 |
| Under 5 | 13.5 | 25.1 | 13.6 | 8.6 | 3.8 |
| 5 | 20.9 | 22.6 | 25.1 | 18.9 | 16.0 |
| 6 | 32.9 | 32.4 | 36.8 | 34.1 | 27.5 |
| 7 | 16.3 | 10.8 | 13.3 | 20.3 | 22.0 |
| 8 and Over | 16.4 | 9.1 | 11.2 | 18.1 | 30.7 |
| Median | 5.97 | 5.57 | 5.81 | 6.16 | 6.62 |

little over a fourth of those in the 25-to-34-year category started school before 5 years of age, while at the other extreme, less than 4 percent of those 55 to 64 years started school before 5. The rates for the age groups between these extremes follow the general pattern of progressively earlier initiation of schooling. The change has been slow, as illustrated by only a one-year shift in median age at entry from the 25-to-34 to the 55-to-64 age groups.

The data gathered for New York State (Rainer et al., 1963) shows a younger average age at entry: 45 percent began school before age 6. This rate compares with 34 percent of the NCDP's sample beginning school before 6 years of age. The difference most likely can be accounted for by two factors. First, a difference in the age distributions of the two samples. (The New York State data are based on 536 respondents whose age breakdown is not provided.) Forty-eight percent of the 25-to-34-year group in the NCDP began school before age 6, while the corresponding percentages for the remaining three age groups are 39, 28, and 20, which illustrates the relationship to present age. Secondly, the New York State sample is drawn from a state which has many excellent educational programs for deaf children and which was among the first states to encourage their early entry into school. Some of the difference between the two samples in the proportion entering school before 6 years of age, then, is likely to be attributable to educational policies in the various states.

## Types of Schools

Deaf children attend one of four types of schools: residential schools, day schools, day classes, regular classes. *Residential schools,* as the name suggests, provide living quarters for the students during the time they attend classes. In the last few years, most residential schools in the United States send their students home every weekend, to maximize family involvement, though this procedure is not always practicable for all students. *Day schools* have no living quarters for students. They differ from other day schools in that the entire student body is deaf. *Day classes* are classes of deaf children within a regular school. These three settings account for most public education for deaf students. However, some do manage successfully in a regular school, often with only the occasional assistance of an itinerant speech therapist or of a resource teacher (Brill, 1971).

The distribution of prevocationally deaf persons by type of school attended is displayed in Table IV.2. Half of the persons in the age group covered, 25 to 64 years, obtained all of their education in a residential school. Somewhat more than 1 in 5 attended both regular and special schools, and nearly 1 in 11 never attended a school or class for hearing impaired children.

**Age at Onset.** Examining the data by age at onset reveals some underlying relationships. Half or more of those who are born deaf or are prelingually deaf attended only residential schools. The proportion declines for those who are postlingually deaf, principally because for a portion of their educational years they had no need of a special school. Over half those whose hearing was lost when they were 12 to 18 years of age never attended a school for hearing impaired students. From another perspective, two thirds of those who never attended a school for hearing impaired students lost their hearing postlingually. Of the prelingually deaf group, less than 5 percent attended regular schools only, and less than 25 percent went to a combination of special and regular schools. For the deaf population in the 25 to 64 age bracket, the residential school predominates as the main educational facility.

**Other Samples.** The NCDP sample has a far larger proportion who never attended a special school for deaf students than was found by Rainer et al. Nine percent of the NCDP adults went only to regular schools versus 1.6 percent of the New York State sample. This difference may reflect differences in the availability of educational facilities in various states. Also, the New York State sample contains fewer persons who became deaf after age 8 than does the NCDP.

The Lunde and Bigman (1959) survey categorized responses somewhat differently than these other studies. They report three groups of

# Table IV.2

Percent Distribution of Type of School Attended, by Age at Onset of Deafness, for Respondents 25 to 64 Years of Age: United States, 1972.

| Type of School Attended | All Ages At Onset | Age at Onset of Deafness | | | | | |
| --- | --- | --- | --- | --- | --- | --- | --- |
| | | Born Deaf | Under 1 Year | Under 3 Years | Between 3-5 Years | Between 6-11 Years | Between 12-18 Years |
| All Types | 100.0 | 100.0 | 100.0 | 100.0 | 100.0 | 100.0 | 100.0 |
| Residential Only | 50.0 | 56.9 | 50.3 | 54.9 | 46.1 | 34.1 | 17.8 |
| Day School Only | 5.3 | 4.0 | 6.4 | 5.9 | 8.1 | 3.9 | — |
| Day Class Only | 3.3 | 3.8 | 5.2 | 3.0 | 3.3 | .8 | 1.8 |
| Combination of Schools for Hearing Impaired | 10.6 | 12.2 | 15.0 | 12.5 | 6.2 | 5.4 | 3.6 |
| Both Schools for Regular and Hearing Impaired | 21.8 | 18.5 | 17.9 | 20.1 | 24.9 | 35.6 | 25.0 |
| Never Attended School for Hearing Impaired | 9.0 | 4.6 | 5.2 | 3.6 | 11.4 | 20.2 | 51.8 |

schools: residential, day, and "hearing". However, if a person attended more than one type, he is included more than once in their tabulation. Thus, 91 percent attended residential schools, 13 percent day schools, and 16 percent regular schools. Slightly over 1 percent attended regular schools. The significance of the residential school in the education of this earlier sample is apparent. Selection of the deaf sample was by members of the National Association of the Deaf, who were asked to interview other deaf persons known to them. This method of sample selection, of course, tends to introduce some bias. Nonetheless, the general statement that the majority of prevocationally deaf students spend at least part of their educational years in residential schools still holds.

In studying the above data, the current emphasis on "mainstreaming" should be taken into account. Mainstreaming refers to placement of physically handicapped children into regular classes. There are many variations on this theme. The basic idea, nonetheless, is the same in each instance—to maximize contacts between normal and handicapped children in school. Aside from being more economical, such programs are thought to be better for the child's social and emotional development. As noted in Table IV.2, however, numbers of deaf students have been integrated in varying degrees in the past. A careful study of their experiences would seem worthwhile, in order to determine what factors are associated with success in integrated programs. It is unlikely that a single educational program will be optimal for all deaf students.

## Highest Grade Attained

For many older residential-school students, years in school and last grade attended are the same, because their schools were essentially ungraded. Highest grade completed generally provides an easily understood measure, with the additional virtue of comparability to other groups in the population.

Table IV.3 provides this information for the deaf population 25 to 64 years of age. Over one third of the deaf population have completed high school (12th grade), and 12 percent have gone to college for one or more years, half of whom have earned baccalaureate degrees. But more than half of the adult deaf population have not completed high school, and 28 percent have only an eighth-grade education or less. Considering the difficulties imposed by deafness, the lack of academic achievement looms ominously as a portent for the future well-being of at least half of the deaf population.

Educators have questioned the equivalence of grades, in terms of the inferred educational attainment. The Annual Survey of Hearing Im-

# Table IV.3

## Percent Distribution for Highest Grade of School Completed, by Sex and Race Respondents 25 to 64 Years of Age: United States, 1972.

| Sex & Race | Total | Highest Grade of School Completed | | | | | | Median | |
|---|---|---|---|---|---|---|---|---|---|
| | | 1-8 | 9-11 | 12 | 13-15 | 16 | 17+ | Deaf[a] | U.S.[b] Pop. |
| All Groups | 100 | 28.4 | 24.9 | 34.7 | 5.6 | 2.7 | 3.7 | 11.1 | 12.1 |
| Males | 100 | 30.9 | 22.5 | 33.1 | 5.5 | 3.2 | 4.7 | 11.0 | 12.1 |
| White | 100 | 30.4 | 22.6 | 34.3 | 4.9 | 3.3 | 4.4 | 11.1 | 12.1 |
| Nonwhite | 100 | 38.6 | 21.4 | 17.1 | 12.1 | 2.1 | 8.6 | 10.1 | 9.7 |
| Females | 100 | 25.9 | 27.3 | 36.2 | 5.8 | 2.3 | 2.6 | 11.1 | 12.1 |
| White | 100 | 25.9 | 27.4 | 35.6 | 6.0 | 2.5 | 2.5 | 11.1 | 12.1 |
| Nonwhite | 100 | 25.6 | 25.6 | 42.0 | 3.4 | — | 3.4 | 11.4 | 10.2 |

[a]Includes only persons 25-64 years of age.
[b]Includes all persons 25 years of age and over.

52

paired Children and Youth has gathered achievement-test data on large numbers of deaf students (Gentile and DiFrancesca, 1969; DiFrancesca, 1972). Grade equivalents based on these examinations place the average deaf student several years behind his normal-hearing peers.[1] These studies should be borne in mind when comparing deaf and general populations with respect to highest grade completed.

**Race and Sex.** The median grade attained is nearly identical for males and females. The distributions, however, differ significantly (see Figure IV.1). Fifty-two percent of both sexes did not complete 12th grade, but nearly 31 percent of males as opposed to only 26 percent of females did not complete 9th grade. Females completed one or more years of college at a rate of 10.7 percent compared to 13.4 percent for males.

---

[1]The reader is cautioned against the "tyranny of averages." While it is true the average deaf student scores below the average student on the Stanford Achievement Test, it is also true that some deaf students score better than average students. As with all summary measures presented throughout this and other chapters, the averages typify the distribution only as to their central tendencies. The dispersions of the data about the averages are of equal importance in understanding the subject being covered.

## Figure IV.1

**Highest Grade Completed in School by Deaf Adults
25-64 Years of Age, by Sex: United States, 1972.**

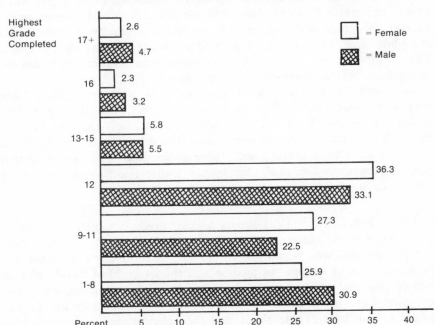

The nonwhite male sample has the lowest median grade (10.1) and its distribution is unusually shaped. Only 17 percent reported completing high school, with 60 percent below 12th grade. But nearly 23 percent completed one or more years of college. Thus, the nonwhite males had the highest proportions in the extreme categories: 38.6 percent with less than 9th grade education and 22.8 percent with one or more years of college. White males, by comparison, had only 12.6 percent who finished one or more years of college. Nonwhite females had the largest proportion that finished high school, but the smallest completing one or more years of college. The median grade attained by nonwhite females—11.4—was the highest for both white and nonwhite males and females.

These peculiar grade distributions probably arise from sampling bias. The techniques used in building the list from which the sample was drawn may have contributed to an overrepresentation of college males and female high-school graduates (see Chapter VIII). They obviously deserve further study than could be given by the NCDP, except as noted below.

**Deaf vs. General Population.** Reinforcing the preceding contention that the nonwhite sample may be unrepresentative are the comparisons with the general population. Overall the deaf sample is one year below the national educational level. This finding holds for males, females, white males and white females. Nonwhite deaf males, on the other hand, exceed the grade level of general nonwhite males by 0.4 year, and nonwhite deaf females exceed general nonwhite females by 1.2 years. The figures for the white deaf population meet earlier expectations, while those for the nonwhite deaf population do not.

As a spot check, a sample of nonwhite deaf residents of New York City was drawn. The results are shown in Table IV.4. Both nonwhite males and females have academic achievement levels close to national norms for the total nonwhite population. The relations to the white deaf averages are also in keeping with those anticipated. The likelihood that the national nonwhite deaf sample has a disproportionate number of better-educated deaf persons seems confirmed.

**Age at Entry.** Table IV.5 shows highest grade completed by age at entry into school. Those starting school earliest tend to go furthest. One out of 5 persons who began school before 5 years of age completed one or more years of college, as against less than 1 in 20 of those entering school after six years of age. Of course, age at entry and highest grade completed are both related to respondent's age. The older age groups began school later (Table IV.1), but they also tended to leave school

## Table IV.4

**Percent Distribution for Highest Grade of School Completed, by Race and Sex Respondents 25-64 Years of Age: New York City, 1973.**

Highest Grade of School Completed

| Race and Sex | Total | Elementary School | | | High School | | College | | Median Grade Completed |
|---|---|---|---|---|---|---|---|---|---|
| | | Less than 5 Grades | 5-7 Grades | 8 Grade | 9-11 Grades | 12 Grade | 1-3 Years | 4 Years or More | |
| All Races | 100 | 3.6 | 19.5 | 22.5 | 19.8 | 26.7 | 1.4 | 6.5 | 9.4 |
| Male | 100 | 3.2 | 17.1 | 23.2 | 25.2 | 24.2 | .6 | 6.5 | 9.5 |
| Female | 100 | 3.7 | 23.3 | 21.9 | 13.9 | 28.4 | 2.2 | 6.6 | 9.1 |
| White | 100 | 2.4 | 17.8 | 23.3 | 18.6 | 28.7 | 1.6 | 7.6 | 9.8 |
| Male | 100 | 1.6 | 13.6 | 24.8 | 23.2 | 28.8 | .8 | 7.2 | 9.9 |
| Female | 100 | 2.7 | 22.5 | 21.6 | 13.5 | 28.9 | 2.7 | 8.1 | 9.7 |
| Nonwhite | 100 | 8.9 | 26.7 | 19.9 | 25.0 | 17.8 | — | 1.7 | 8.6 |
| Male | 100 | 10.0 | 26.7 | 16.7 | 33.3 | 10.0 | — | 3.3 | 8.7 |
| Female | 100 | 7.6 | 26.8 | 23.3 | 15.4 | 26.9 | — | — | 8.5 |

## Table IV.5

**Percent Distribution of Age at Entry into School, by Highest Grade of School Completed for Respondents 25-64 Years of Age: United States, 1972.**

| Age at Entry in School | Highest Grade of School Completed | | | | | |
|---|---|---|---|---|---|---|
| | Total | 1-8 | 9-11 | 12 | 13+ | Median |
| All Ages | 100.0 | 28.4 | 24.7 | 34.9 | 12.0 | 11.1 |
| Under 5 | 100.0 | 20.5 | 20.5 | 38.4 | 20.6 | 11.7 |
| 5 | 100.0 | 20.6 | 23.5 | 39.0 | 16.8 | 11.7 |
| 6 | 100.0 | 25.6 | 25.4 | 35.7 | 13.3 | 11.4 |
| 7 | 100.0 | 31.6 | 29.2 | 35.8 | 3.3 | 10.4 |
| 8 and over | 100.0 | 47.1 | 23.8 | 24.3 | 4.9 | 8.9 |

sooner. The relation between age when schooling was initiated and highest grade completed is not necessarily causal.

**Regional Variations.** Like the general population, deaf persons in the West have the highest level of education. Those in the North Central region are closely behind, as is true for the general population. However, the Northeast has the lowest average educational level for deaf persons, with the South in third place rather than last, as it is for the general population.

With respect to highest grade completed, the New York State sample appears to have had superior schooling to the NCDP sample. Not only does it have a higher proportion of persons who began school at an early age, but it also has a larger proportion who graduated from high school (58.1 percent). However, only 6.7 percent went on to college versus 12 percent of the NCDP sample. The difference between those getting higher education does not compensate for the difference between those graduating from high school. The New York State sample is somewhat better-educated, probably reflecting the State's investment in education. It may also arise from sampling differences (vide supra).

Nearly one half of the Washington sample never attended a school for normal-hearing students. Just under 10 percent have ever been enrolled in a day class for the hearing impaired; about the same proportion spent some time in a day school for the deaf; while 71 percent spent one or more years in a residential school for the deaf. Of those who attended regular schools, 34 percent spent five or fewer years in such a setting.

About 14 percent of those who spent some time in a residential school stayed in it five or fewer years. The median number of years spent in a residential school by those ever attending such a school was 11.1 years.

The national sample of Lunde and Bigman also has a large proportion reporting some college attendance. For their 20-to-59-year group, 9 percent reported some college attendance. While the percent is the same as found by the NCDP, the interpretation is not. The Lunde-Bigman rate suggests a potentially better-educated group for its time, which precedes the NCDP by more than a decade. In the discussion of educational trends below, the sharp increase in proportion of deaf students obtaining higher education occurs in the 1960-1971 period. It is likely that Lunde and Bigman are correct, then, in their assumption of upward bias in their sampling.

The Washington, D.C. survey reported that almost 1 out of 3 deaf adults had attended college for one or more years. This rate compares favorably with national data for the general population, but the Capitol tends to attract a better-educated group of people. The major industry is government, and the area has few manufacturing jobs. Educational averages for the entire civilian population of Washington probably exceed the national averages by a considerable margin. Certainly the Washington deaf community contains a far higher proportion of college-educated persons than the national deaf population.

Judging from the two national and two regional samples, regional variations in educational attainment are apt to be fairly large. These differences in educational levels from place to place should prove of special interest to those planning continuing education for deaf adults.

**Income.** Does education pay? Table IV.7 shows the annual individual income for various grade levels. The differences between medians are substantial, ranging from 15 to 25 percent. Obviously, those with the most education earn most, on the average. The exceptions, nonetheless, are noteworthy. For example, 20 percent of deaf persons with 5 or more years of college had incomes of less than $5,000 in 1971. Some of these low earnings might be due to illness, early retirement, decisions not to work (e.g., housewife), etc., but some may be due to late entry into the labor market, underemployment and unemployment. Also note that almost 10 percent of those having no high school earned $10,000 or more in 1971.

Other studies of deaf samples have shown a similar pattern of income-education correlation. The Washington survey, Lunde and Bigman, Rosenstein and Lerman—all noted higher median earnings for higher educational groups. The amount of education does not completely determine income (see Chapter V). However, the relation between academic preparation and earnings is strong for the deaf population.

# Table IV.6

**Percent Distribution of Highest Grade of School Completed, by Regions for Respondents 25-64 Years of Age: United States, 1972.**

| United States and Regions | Total | Highest Grade of School Completed | | | | | | | Median | |
|---|---|---|---|---|---|---|---|---|---|---|
| | | 0-8 | 9-11 | 12 | 13-15 | 16 | 17+ | | Deaf | U.S. Pop.[a] |
| United States | 100.0 | 28.4 | 24.9 | 34.7 | 5.6 | 2.7 | 3.7 | | 11.1 | 12.1 |
| Northeast | 100.0 | 35.6 | 22.5 | 32.9 | 2.7 | 3.0 | 3.3 | | 10.4 | 12.1 |
| North Central | 100.0 | 26.2 | 23.9 | 38.6 | 6.3 | 2.7 | 2.3 | | 11.5 | 12.1 |
| South | 100.0 | 30.7 | 27.3 | 29.8 | 6.0 | 2.3 | 3.9 | | 10.6 | 11.3 |
| West | 100.0 | 19.4 | 26.4 | 37.0 | 7.4 | 3.2 | 6.5 | | 11.6 | 12.4 |

[a]Source: General Social and Economic Characteristics, Bureau of the Census, 1972.

# Table IV.7

Percent Distribution of Highest Grade of School Completed for Respondents 25 through 64 Years of Age, by Income: United States, 1971.

| Income | All | 1-8 | 9-12 | 13-16 | 17+ |
|---|---|---|---|---|---|
| | | | | Highest Grade of School Completed | |
| All amounts | 100.0 | 100.0 | 100.0 | 100.0 | 100.0 |
| Under $3,000 | 12.6 | 14.9 | 12.0 | 10.9 | 10.2 |
| 3,000-4,999 | 19.6 | 24.4 | 18.8 | 15.7 | 10.2 |
| 5,000-6,999 | 22.5 | 27.1 | 23.2 | 13.1 | 5.1 |
| 7,000-9,999 | 27.7 | 23.5 | 30.0 | 26.2 | 23.1 |
| 10,000-14,999 | 15.1 | 9.0 | 13.9 | 28.8 | 38.5 |
| 15,000 and over | 2.6 | .9 | 2.1 | 5.2 | 12.8 |
| Median | $6,584 | $5,788 | $6,655 | $8,199 | $10,222 |

## Postsecondary Education

Leadership roles in our society gravitate toward the best-educated persons. With more than 1 out of every 3 adults in the United States having had some college, the proportion of deaf adults who have attended college seems sparse. The actual numbers of college-educated deaf adults, distributed across regions, ages, races, and the sexes, cannot begin to fill the positions of authority in the organizations devoted to the welfare of the deaf community. Formal education, of course, is not the entire answer to developing leadership, but it has played, and will probably continue to play, an important part (Lloyd, 1973).

Oddly enough, deaf adults have not always suffered a disadvantage in higher education. Figure IV.2 illustrates the numbers of deaf persons in college as a ratio to the number of deaf students in school compared to the same data for the general population. These figures, updated to 1972, are taken from an earlier study of higher education (Schein and Bushnaq, 1962). At the turn of the century, the deaf and general populations are at parity. In the next five decades, however, the general population rates explode, while those for the deaf population remain fairly constant until 1960.

Thanks to vigorous action in the Sixties, the situation has changed somewhat. The proportion of deaf students known to be attending

## Figure IV.2

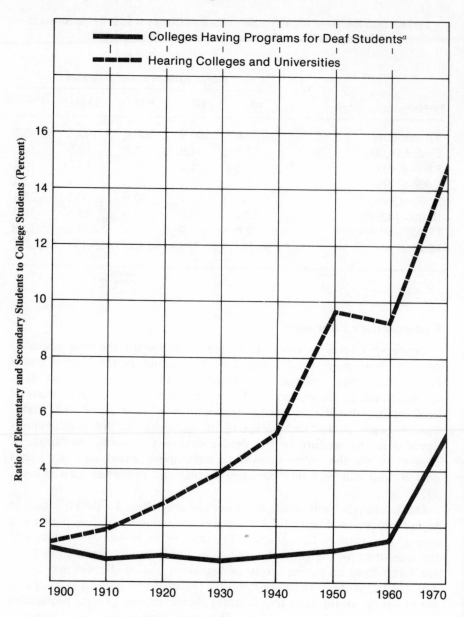

$^a$1900-1960 Gallaudet College only.

institutions of higher education in 1970 has grown appreciably (Schein, 1972)—more than triple the 1960 rate for deaf persons (see Figure IV.2). It remains, nonetheless, comparatively low.

## Projections of Postsecondary Needs.

The growing size of the prevocationally deaf population does not appear to have been met adequately by a growth in facilities. Table IV.8 contains projections of the 19-year-old deaf population for the years 1971-1990, divided into three educational groups. The first group contains those for whom higher education is feasible (College). The second (Technical) includes those for whom technical-vocational training or junior-college preparation would be most favored. Those in the third

## Table IV.8

**Projected Distribution of Nineteen-Year-Old Deaf Population by Most Suitable Postsecondary Educational Placement: 1972-1990.**

| | | Postsecondary Educational Placement | | |
|---|---|---|---|---|
| Year | All | College | Technical | Comprehensive |
| 1972 | 7,734 | 619 | 4,640 | 2,475 |
| 1973 | 7,938 | 635 | 4,763 | 2,540 |
| 1974 | 8,070 | 646 | 4,842 | 2,582 |
| 1975 | 8,172 | 654 | 4,903 | 2,615 |
| 1976 | 8,494 | 934 | 5,521 | 2,039 |
| 1977 | 8,452 | 930 | 5,494 | 2,028 |
| 1978 | 8,458 | 931 | 5,498 | 2,029 |
| 1979 | 8,358 | 919 | 5,433 | 2,006 |
| 1980 | 8,428 | 927 | 5,478 | 2,023 |
| 1981 | 8,252 | 1,238 | 5,694 | 1,320 |
| 1982 | 8,138 | 1,221 | 5,615 | 1,302 |
| 1983 | 7,982 | 1,197 | 5,508 | 1,277 |
| 1984 | 7,626 | 1,144 | 5,262 | 1,220 |
| 1985 | 7,244 | 1,087 | 4,998 | 1,159 |
| 1986 | 7,034 | 1,477 | 4,854 | 703 |
| 1987 | 6,858 | 1,440 | 4,732 | 686 |
| 1988 | 7,198 | 1,512 | 4,967 | 719 |
| 1989 | 7,022 | 1,475 | 4,845 | 702 |
| 1990 | 7,582 | 1,592 | 5,232 | 758 |

group (Comprehensive) require specialized training facilities—extended evaluation, personal and work adjustment, sheltered workshops —because of their very low educational potential. The projections are based on a number of assumptions and predictions which may or may not prove to be correct over the time period. The reader is urged to consult the original document, in order to determine the extent to which the underlying premises can be accepted (Schein, 1972).

The sobering conclusion from the predicted distribution of this single deaf age group is that educational and rehabilitation facilities to accommodate these young adults are not adequate. A number of universities have begun to make the arrangements deaf students require. The technical-vocational schools, led by the "Triangle" institutions (Craig, 1973), have made giant strides. The Rehabilitation Act of 1973 enables substantial government intervention on behalf of the severely disabled deaf adult and will provide for a number of comprehensive rehabilitation facilities. It can only be hoped that action will be swift at each of these levels of education.

### Communication[2]

Deafness has been characterized as a disorder of communication, in the same sense that blindness has been called a disorder of mobility. The interference with communication pervades all aspects of a deaf person's life. Since communication is a learned behavior, there should be a relationship between it and education. The data in Table IV.9 explicates that relationship for the NCDP sample.

In all aspects of communication, the two most educated groups tended to rate themselves higher than or equal to the less-educated groups. Half of those with some college education rated their speech "good" and less than 6 percent reported they did not speak. Only 17 percent of the group which completed less than 9 grades and 31 percent of those completing 9 to 12 grades rated their speech "good", and nearly 16 percent of the former and 9 percent of the latter reported no speaking ability. With respect to lipreading, the pattern is similar: the better-educated groups have the higher ratings.

More than half of the college-educated groups give their manual communication skills—receptive and expressive signing and fingerspelling—the top rating. But this holds true for the two noncollege groups. The majority of the prevocationally deaf population regards its manual communication skills highly. However, the college groups have the largest proportions of those claiming no ability to read or use sign language and/or fingerspelling: 20 percent in some categories, compared to less than 10 percent for those completing only the first 12 grades.

---

[2]For discussion of hearing aids and their use, see Chapter VII.

*62*

# Table IV.9

**Percent Distribution of Communication Ability as Judged by Respondent, by Highest Grade Completed for Respondents 25-64 Years of Age: United States, 1972.**

| Communication Mode/Rating | Highest Grade Completed | | | |
|---|---|---|---|---|
| | 1-8 | 9-12 | 13-16 | 17+ |
| **Speech** | 100.0 | 100.0 | 100.0 | 100.0 |
| Good | 17.5 | 31.2 | 47.4 | 54.2 |
| Fair | 41.5 | 41.3 | 39.0 | 27.1 |
| Poor | 25.1 | 18.5 | 11.8 | 12.5 |
| None | 15.8 | 9.0 | 1.9 | 6.3 |
| **Lipreading** | 100.0 | 100.0 | 100.0 | 100.0 |
| Good | 23.7 | 41.2 | 55.2 | 54.2 |
| Fair | 40.1 | 37.4 | 36.8 | 33.3 |
| Poor | 25.6 | 14.8 | 3.7 | 10.4 |
| None | 10.6 | 6.6 | 4.3 | 2.1 |
| **Signing** | 100.0 | 100.0 | 100.0 | 100.0 |
| Good | 65.8 | 69.6 | 58.9 | 64.6 |
| Fair | 21.6 | 16.8 | 17.5 | 10.4 |
| Poor | 6.7 | 5.6 | 3.7 | 6.3 |
| None | 5.9 | 8.0 | 19.9 | 18.8 |
| **Reading Signs** | 100.0 | 100.0 | 100.0 | 100.0 |
| Good | 64.4 | 71.1 | 61.7 | 66.7 |
| Fair | 21.8 | 15.3 | 15.6 | 8.3 |
| Poor | 6.7 | 5.2 | 1.8 | 4.2 |
| None | 7.0 | 8.4 | 20.9 | 20.8 |
| **Fingerspelling** | 100.0 | 100.0 | 100.0 | 100.0 |
| Good | 63.7 | 68.9 | 61.7 | 60.4 |
| Fair | 19.0 | 17.7 | 17.5 | 18.8 |
| Poor | 9.0 | 4.7 | 4.3 | 4.2 |
| None | 8.1 | 8.7 | 16.6 | 16.7 |
| **Reading Fingerspelling** | 100.0 | 100.0 | 100.0 | 100.0 |
| Good | 57.6 | 66.1 | 52.5 | 62.5 |
| Fair | 23.9 | 19.1 | 24.8 | 8.3 |
| Poor | 11.0 | 5.6 | 4.6 | 8.3 |
| None | 7.6 | 9.3 | 18.1 | 20.8 |

Choice of communication mode depends upon circumstances as well as upon ability. Seven out of 10 persons in the NCDP sample rated their speech "good" or "fair", yet only about 3 in 10 used speech alone in making a purchase in a store (Table IV.10). Being unable to estimate surrounding noise levels, the deaf customer may speak too loudly or too softly. The clerk, unaccustomed to the deaf person's voice, may have considerable difficulty comprehending him. Stories about misunderstandings arising in making purchases are the basis for many jokes told by deaf people (see "Humor Among the Deaf", a monthly feature in the *Deaf American*). For those reasons, writing, alone or in combination with speech, predominates in communication with clerks in stores. The Washington study's results were similar, though the sample had a higher proportion who rated their speech "good": half wrote only or wrote and spoke to sales clerks, while 44 percent spoke only (Schein, 1968).

**Communication on the Job.** At work, the deaf employee's communication varies with circumstances. To his supervisor, he speaks about as often as he writes. The supervisor tends to reply in the same mode; about half either speak only or write only. The Washington sample responded similarly. For the small number of deaf supervisors, the role of speech increases and writing decreases. Again, the subordinate's responses parallel in frequency the deaf supervisor's own choice of modes. To his colleagues, the deaf person speaks, unless his fellow workers are also deaf, in which case manual language predominates. Lunde and Bigman found that 2 out of 3 deaf persons at work used writing compared to 1 in 3 who used speech. These results varied considerably, however, by occupational groups. Professional and technical persons used speech more often than any other form. For the remaining occupational categories, writing predominated.

Crammatte (1968) compared his group of deaf professionals to those of Lunde and Bigman, and he noted his group had reported far more communication skills; e.g., 90 percent using speech with hearing colleagues at work versus 62 percent in Lunde-Bigman. However, Crammatte's monograph also permits a direct comparison with the NCDP (Table IV.11). Eighty-five percent of the NCDP professional and technical personnel used speech at work, either alone or in combination with writing and/or gestures. As was true for Crammatte's sample, more than 60 percent used speech only. The present importance of speaking ability for professional and management personnel seems clear; however, the fact that almost 15 percent of professionals and administrators in the NCDP sample and 10 percent in Crammatte's sample did not use speech is important to the nonvocal deaf person. Some of the professional and managerial personnel who do not use speech probably work largely with other deaf persons, but not all do. This means, then, that in

## Table IV.10

**Percent Distribution of Methods of Communication Used by Respondents with Various Persons: United States, 1972.**

| Method of Communication | To Sales Clerk | To Supervisor | By Supervisor | To Subordinates | By Subordinates | To Others At Work | By Others At Work |
|---|---|---|---|---|---|---|---|
| All Methods | 100.0 | 100.0 | 100.0 | 100.0 | 100.0 | 100.0 | 100.0 |
| Speech | 31.8 | 26.4 | 26.2 | 41.8 | 39.7 | 28.2 | 27.0 |
| Manual | .8 | 2.3 | 2.4 | 2.0 | 1.5 | 2.8 | 2.7 |
| Writing | 36.8 | 25.3 | 22.3 | 13.7 | 10.4 | 17.7 | 15.5 |
| Gesture | 4.1 | 3.5 | 4.1 | 3.0 | 4.5 | 3.4 | 3.8 |
| Speech and Manual | .2 | 1.7 | 2.7 | 5.3 | 6.0 | 5.0 | 4.9 |
| Speech and Writing | 12.7 | 11.1 | 12.8 | 13.7 | 17.9 | 9.5 | 11.2 |
| Speech and Gesture | 3.1 | 2.2 | 3.8 | 2.3 | 1.5 | 2.6 | 3.2 |
| Writing and Gesture | 4.8 | 3.6 | 6.2 | 3.0 | 3.7 | 4.6 | 5.5 |
| Speech, Manual and Writing | — | .5 | 1.1 | 1.5 | .7 | 1.3 | 1.5 |
| Other Combinations | 5.8 | 11.5 | 18.5 | 13.7 | 14.1 | 29.9 | 24.8 |

# Table IV.11

**Percent Distribution of Principal Occupation of Employed Respondents 16-64 Years of Age, by Method of Communication Used at Work: United States, 1972.**

| Principal Occupations | Total | Method of Communications Used at Work | | | | | | | |
|---|---|---|---|---|---|---|---|---|---|
| | | Speech | Manual | Writing | Gesture | Speech & Manual | Speech & Writing | Speech & Gestures | Writing & Gestures |
| All Occupations | 100.0 | 39.4 | 4.0 | 25.0 | 4.7 | 2.9 | 13.4 | 3.7 | 6.3 |
| Prof. & Tech. | 100.0 | 62.7 | 2.7 | 12.0 | — | 9.3 | 12.0 | 1.3 | — |
| Mgr. & Adm. (Nonfarm) | 100.0 | 71.4 | — | 14.3 | — | — | — | 14.3 | — |
| Sales | 100.0 | 80.0 | — | — | — | 20.0 | — | — | — |
| Clerical | 100.0 | 48.7 | 7.8 | 23.5 | .9 | 4.3 | 12.2 | .9 | 1.7 |
| Craftsmen | 100.0 | 26.3 | 2.9 | 30.6 | 5.8 | 2.3 | 16.4 | 4.7 | 11.1 |
| Operatives (Nontrans.) | 100.0 | 31.5 | 4.6 | 29.6 | 4.8 | 1.8 | 15.9 | 4.1 | 7.4 |
| Operatives (Trans.) | 100.0 | 75.0 | — | 8.3 | — | — | 8.3 | — | 8.3 |
| Laborers Nonfarm | 100.0 | 38.1 | 4.8 | 23.8 | 9.8 | 2.4 | 9.5 | 7.1 | 4.8 |
| Farmers & Farm Mgrs. | 100.0 | 40.0 | — | — | — | — | — | 20.0 | — |
| Farm Labor | 100.0 | 33.3 | — | 16.7 | 16.7 | — | 16.7 | 16.7 | — |
| Service and Private H.H. Workers | 100.0 | 50.2 | 1.4 | 19.4 | 11.1 | — | 6.9 | 2.8 | 6.9 |

a few instances employers, subordinates, and/or patrons must accustom themselves to nonvocal communication—an unusual circumstance in our society. That speaking ability is an advantage in most employment cannot be doubted, but it is not inevitably a necessity to occupational adjustment.

One third of clerical employees report using no speech at work. Similarly, one half of craftsmen and nontransit operatives report using no speech. While speech alone did not predominate, most other occupational groups did use speech in their work most of the time. Almost 2 out of 3 service workers used some speech, as did the same proportion of farm laborers and over half the nonfarm laborers. It is likely that, for those possessing exceptional skills and other high qualifications, employers will be less insistent upon speech. Ironically, those with least education and associated reduction in speaking ability may encounter greatest resistance to their communication handicap.

**Communication and Income.** The relation of income to communication at work is not clear-cut (Table IV.12). Of those using a single mode at work, writers have the highest median earnings, followed by speakers. Those using only manual communication or gestures do the worst financially of all the groups. The highest average earnings occur in the speech-gesture group which is dominated by craftsmen and nontransit operatives. Similarly, craftsmen and nontransit operatives make up the majority of the writing-only group. As noted above, the tendency of employers may be to accommodate the least to employees with lesser skills, hence lower earnings would tend to be associated with speech largely because laborers and other poorly paid occupational groups reportedly depend on speech more frequently than some of those in better-paying positions.

Inspection of the groups earning $10,000 or more per year tends to confirm this speculation. Almost half of the best earners use speech in some combination, and more than one third use it exclusively. Of those in the $10,000-and-over category who use only manual communication at work, most if not all are probably employed by schools for deaf students or by organizations such as the National Association of the Deaf and the National Fraternal Society of the Deaf.

**Communication Training.** Deaf adults do not see themselves in need of further communication training. The majority responded negatively to the question about the desire for further assistance in developing communication skills (Table IV.13). For the 1 out of 3 who did wish for more

# Table IV.12

**Percent Distribution of Personal Income by Method of Communication Used at Work, Respondents 16-64 Years of Age: United States, 1971.**

| Method Of Communication | Total | Income | | | | | | Median |
| --- | --- | --- | --- | --- | --- | --- | --- | --- |
| | | Under 3000 | 3000-4999 | 5000-6999 | 7000-9999 | 10,000-14,999 | 15,000 And Over | |
| All Methods | 100.0 | 19.5 | 20.1 | 21.6 | 24.2 | 12.7 | 1.9 | $5,970 |
| Speech | 100.0 | 25.3 | 17.7 | 18.7 | 21.0 | 14.0 | 3.3 | 5,750 |
| Manual | 100.0 | 31.8 | 22.7 | 4.5 | 22.7 | 13.6 | 4.5 | 4,599 |
| Writing | 100.0 | 14.1 | 20.2 | 24.4 | 27.6 | 12.8 | 1.0 | 6,289 |
| Gesture | 100.0 | 32.5 | 20.0 | 27.5 | 5.0 | 15.0 | — | 4,750 |
| Speech and Manual | 100.0 | 19.0 | 19.0 | 14.3 | 23.8 | 19.0 | 4.8 | 6,666 |
| Speech and Writing | 100.0 | 17.1 | 24.1 | 23.4 | 25.6 | 8.3 | 1.5 | 5,752 |
| Speech and Gesture | 100.0 | 8.7 | 13.0 | 26.1 | 30.4 | 21.7 | — | 7,214 |
| Writing and Gesture | 100.0 | 16.7 | 14.3 | 21.4 | 38.1 | 9.5 | — | 6,777 |
| Speech, Manual and Writing | 100.0 | 16.7 | 16.7 | 33.3 | 33.3 | — | — | 5,999 |
| Other Combinations | 100.0 | 18.1 | 23.9 | 21.0 | 22.5 | 12.3 | 2.2 | 5,758 |

training, the modal number wanted help with sign language. Since sign language has rarely been taught to deaf children in school—most acquire signs from other deaf children and adults—the need for formal instruction is not surprising. Recognition of the need, however, is unusual. The next most frequent request was for speechreading instruction, followed by speech and auditory training. Nearly 20 percent of the sample wanted more than one kind of instruction.

The nonwhite sample significantly more frequently than the white sample saw the need for communication training. Nearly 6 out of 10 nonwhite males and more than 5 out of 10 nonwhite females said they would like some form of instruction in communication. Most wished for two or more kinds. Speechreading headed the list for both nonwhite males and females. The next choice for nonwhite females was sign language and for males it was speech. Fourth choice for both was training in use of hearing aids.

In view of the ratings of their own speaking and speechreading abilities, the majority's lack of interest in further instruction seems to express resignation. Most deaf students spend a large part of their early school years attempting to develop speech and studying speechreading. They may regard further instruction as having little chance of being successful. Programs of continuing education for this group should be aware of these attitudes. Many programs have been directed at the educators' perceptions of deaf persons' motivation for additional training. In those cases where such programs have failed, the reason may have been selection of a curriculum which deaf adults regard as inappropriate (Friedman and Hall, 1971).

**Telecommunications.** The technological advances which will enable deaf persons to share in our heavily mediated culture are only beginning to become available. Television in its present form cannot be understood by most deaf people most of the time (Schein et al., 1972). In a short time, several changes are anticipated in telecommunications. Selective captioning is now being tested to determine its feasibility. Through use of the vertical interval, a signal can be sent which will be seen as captions on the television screen of those sets equipped with a special decoder. Thus, those wishing the captions can have them without inconveniencing those who may find them disturbing. Additionally, more television stations are providing simultaneous interpreting in the language of signs, and more programs especially for deaf audiences are being planned for cable television (Freebairn, 1974).

The telephone, originally inspired by the hope of aiding deaf people, has placed them at an economic disadvantage. Now that the teletype (TTY) has been adapted to transmission via the telephone, deaf persons

# Table IV.13

**Percent Distribution of Selected Communication Training Needed and/or Desired, by Sex and Race of Respondents 16 to 64 Years of Age: United States, 1972.**

| Training | Both Sexes | Male | | | Female | | |
|---|---|---|---|---|---|---|---|
| | | Total | White | Nonwhite | Total | White | Nonwhite |
| All Training | 100.0 | 100.0 | 100.0 | 100.0 | 100.0 | 100.0 | 100.0 |
| Speechreading | 4.2 | 3.8 | 3.3 | 7.9 | 4.7 | 4.0 | 10.3 |
| Speaking | 2.8 | 3.1 | 3.0 | 4.3 | 2.4 | 2.6 | 1.0 |
| Using Signs | 6.0 | 5.8 | 6.1 | 3.3 | 6.2 | 6.3 | 5.5 |
| Using Hearing Aid | 1.3 | 1.3 | 1.1 | 3.0 | 1.4 | 1.4 | 1.0 |
| Two of Above | 10.7 | 10.4 | 9.6 | 18.0 | 11.0 | 10.0 | 18.8 |
| Three of Above | 5.1 | 4.6 | 4.0 | 9.8 | 5.7 | 5.0 | 11.6 |
| All of Above | 4.0 | 4.9 | 4.3 | 9.8 | 3.1 | 3.1 | 3.1 |
| None | 64.9 | 64.6 | 67.7 | 37.7 | 65.1 | 67.5 | 44.5 |
| Don't Know | .8 | 1.0 | .8 | 2.9 | .5 | .1 | 4.1 |

can enjoy communications at a distance. Unfortunately, the TTY in any of its versions is not inexpensive, costing at a minimum about $250 to purchase. Upkeep is fairly expensive, and the relatively slow transmission speed results in high user chargers by the telephone companies. As noted in Table IV.14, nearly 6 out of 10 homes in which a deaf person is head of the household do have a telephone, but only 13 percent have a TTY. Steps are presently underway to develop a less expensive device. Until it appears, deaf persons will continue to be penalized by the inaccessibility of telecommunications.

## Table IV.14

**Percent of Deaf Heads of Households Reporting
Telephones and TTY's: United States, 1972.**

| Total | Number | Percent |
|---|---|---|
| All Responses | 2123 | 100.0 |
| No Phone | 874 | 41.1 |
| Phone Only | 1081 | 50.9 |
| TTY's | 168 | 8.0 |

## CHAPTER V

# Occupation

HOW DOES INABILITY to hear affect a person's competitive standing in the marketplace? What kind of work do deaf people do? How well do they perform on the job? Do deaf workers receive equal treatment from industry in hiring, retention and promotion?

These questions could not all be directly dealt with by the NCDP, but an attempt has been made to at least provide tangential answers to them. This chapter should be read, however, with the nationwide economic conditions prevailing at the time of the survey kept in mind. Without careful longitudinal studies, the influences of fluctuations in market circumstances can only be guessed at. It is important to anticipate how "depression-proof" are deaf workers' jobs, for example. The following material only offers hints in response to such queries.

## Labor Force Status

The United States Bureau of Labor Statistics defines employed, unemployed and labor force as follows:

**Employed.**—Employed persons comprise all civilians 16 years old and over who were either (a) 'at work'—those who did any work at all as paid employees or in their own business or profession, or on their own farm, or who worked 15 hours or more as unpaid workers on a family farm or in a family business; or (b) were 'with a job but not at work'—those who did not work during the reference week but had jobs or businesses from which they were temporarily absent due to illness, bad weather, industrial dispute, vacation, or other personal reasons.

**Unemployed.**—Persons are classified as unemployed if they were civilians 16 years old and over and: (a) were neither 'at work' nor 'with a job, but not at work' during the reference week, (b) were looking for work during the past 4 weeks, and (c) were available to accept a job. Also included as unemployed are persons who did not work at all during the reference week and were waiting to be called back to a job from which they had been laid off.

**Civilian labor force.** The civilian labor force consists of persons classified as employed or unemployed in accordance with the criteria described above.[1]

These definitions are critical to understanding the concepts of employment and unemployment. A person who is not in the labor force is not unemployed. The definition of "not in labor force" as defined by the Bureau "consists mainly of students, housewives, retired workers, seasonal workers enumerated in an 'off' season who were not looking for work, inmates of institutions, disabled persons, and persons doing only incidental unpaid family work (less than 15 hours during the reference week)."

The distribution of prevocationally deaf adults by labor force status is given in Table V.1. Two thirds are in the labor force; 83 percent of males and slightly less than half of females. These proportions are somewhat higher than for the general population. Of general population males 79.7 percent are in the labor force, as are 43.9 percent of females. These differences can be accounted for by variations in the age-sex-race composition of the two populations. As will be seen, these factors have an influence on labor force status.

## Unemployment

**Sex.** Less than 3 percent of deaf males were unemployed in 1972. This rate compared favorably to the unemployment rate for all males—4.9 percent. Deaf females are more frequently unemployed than females in general: 1 out of 10 deaf females are out of work as against about 1 in 15 general population females.

**Race.** When viewed from the nonwhite deaf person's point of view, the situation changes markedly. Nonwhite deaf males have an unemployment rate nearly 5 times that of white deaf males. Similarly, nonwhite deaf females have nearly double the unemployment of white deaf females. Nonwhites in the general population fare less well, also. The differences between white and nonwhite deaf persons, however, is larger than in the general population. Whereas 16.5 percent of nonwhite deaf females are unemployed, 11.3 percent of nonwhite females in general are unemployed. Similarly for males, the unemployment rate is 10.4 percent for those who are deaf versus 8.9 percent for the total. As is also true of income, being a member of two minority groups—nonwhite and deaf —tends to multiply the disadvantages.

---

[1]U.S. Bureau of the Census. *Census of Population, 1970, General Social and Economic Characteristics, Final Report. PC (1)-C1 U.S. Summary,* U.S. Government Printing Office, Washington, D.C.: 1972.

# Table V.1

**Percent Distribution of Labor Force Status by Race and Sex, Respondents 16-64 Years of Age: United States, 1972.**

| Respondents' Sex and Race | N | Labor Force Status | | | | Employment Status | | |
| --- | --- | --- | --- | --- | --- | --- | --- | --- |
| | | Total | Not In Labor Force | In Labor Force | | Employed | Unemployed | |
| | | | | Deaf | Gen'l Pop.[a] | | Deaf | Gen'l Pop.[a] |
| Males | 2707 | 100.0 | 17.3 | 82.7 | 79.7 | 97.1 | 2.9 | 4.9 |
| White | 2427 | 100.0 | 16.1 | 83.9 | 79.6 | 97.8 | 2.2 | 4.5 |
| Nonwhite | 280 | 100.0 | 28.2 | 71.8 | 73.7 | 89.6 | 10.4 | 8.9 |
| Females | 2552 | 100.0 | 50.6 | 49.4 | 43.9 | 89.8 | 10.2 | 6.6 |
| White | 2286 | 100.0 | 50.4 | 49.6 | 43.2 | 90.5 | 9.5 | 5.9 |
| Nonwhite | 266 | 100.0 | 52.3 | 47.7 | 48.7 | 83.5 | 16.5 | 11.3 |

[a]Source: Employment and Earnings, U.S. Department of Labor, Bureau of Labor Statistics (Vol. 20 #9), March 1974.

**Age.** Young deaf adults have the greatest problem obtaining employment (Table V.2). In 1972, 1 in 11 males and almost 1 in 4 females 16 to 24 years of age were out of work. These rates drop sharply for both sexes through the middle ages to the oldest age group studied, 55 to 64 years.

**Other Deaf Samples.** Some of the findings regarding unemployment appear consistent over time and across geographical boundaries. Best (1942) reviewed the 1910 and 1920 Census data and found nonwhite deaf persons employed less frequently than whites. He was unable to compare the deaf and general populations on unemployment in those two decennials, because the concept of labor force had not been introduced. However, during the Great Depression in the Thirties, several studies showed deaf workers suffered about the same as the general population. The apparent imprecision in defining the conditions of employment-unemployment led Best to the peculiar conclusion: "The proportion of the deaf who are without employment in 'hard times' differs appreciably, but not greatly, from that of the population at large" (op. cit., page 223). The intra-deaf comparisons favored those with the greatest and earliest losses of hearing. For example, 43 percent of deaf males who had been previously employed were out of work in 1935; for those born deaf, the comparable rate was 39.8 percent.

## Table V.2

**Unemployment Rates for Deaf and General Population[a] in the Labor Force, by Sex and Age: United States, 1972.**

|  | Males | | Females | |
|---|---|---|---|---|
|  | Deaf | General | Deaf | General |
| All ages | 2.9 | 4.9 | 10.2 | 6.6 |
| 16 to 24 | 8.9 | 12.6 | 23.1 | 13.0 |
| 25 to 34 | 4.8 | 3.7 | 11.3 | 6.2 |
| 35 to 44 | — | 2.7 | 4.5 | 4.9 |
| 45 to 54 | 1.3 | 2.6 | 6.9 | 3.6 |
| 55 to 64 | — | 3.2 | 5.6 | 3.3 |

[a]Extrapolated from Bureau of Labor Statistics, 1974.

# Table V.3

**Unemployment Rates for Deaf and General Population
of Metropolitan Washington, D.C., by Sex and Race: 1962.**

| | Unemployment Rate | |
| --- | --- | --- |
| **Race and Sex** | **Deaf Population** | **General Population** |
| White | | |
|   Male | 4.3 | 3.1 |
|   Female | 7.4 | 1.9 |
| Nonwhite | | |
|   Male | 16.9 | 5.6 |
|   Female | 41.2 | 5.7 |

Source: Schein, 1968.

Lunde and Bigman (1959) were unable to calculate an unemployment rate from their data, because of ambiguous wording in their questionnaire. However, an upper limit of unemployment can be determined—6.3 percent. Some portion of that figure represents persons not in the labor force (students, sick and crippled persons, and other not seeking employment). The gross figure does not deviate far from the unemployment rate of 5 percent for the general population at the time of the survey. It seems reasonable that had these data been gathered according to present methods the results would, like those of the NCDP, show the deaf population to be employed about as frequently as, or more frequently than, the general population. The Lunde-Bigman sample, however, consisted of almost 97 percent white persons. As noted above, the unemployment rates for whites are far lower than those for nonwhites.

In Metropolitan Washington, D.C., in 1962, the deaf population was not doing as well as the general population (see Table V.3). Again the differences between the deaf and general populations are most marked for the nonwhite groups.

Berger et al. (1972) reported an unemployment rate of 21 percent for a cluster of deaf adults in Oregon versus the unemployment rate for that state of 4.3 percent. The difficulty in interpreting this startlingly high disparity in these rates arises from the definition of "employable" used to classify those in the deaf work force. The criteria may have overincluded deaf persons whose counterparts in the general population would not be considered to be part of the labor force. The Oregon group did not ask if the person was working or seeking work in a defined period of time, as the Bureau of Labor Statistics does. It is also possible that, by gathering these data over three years, Berger et al. unwittingly established conditions tending to overestimate their sample's unemployment. No mention is made of its racial composition. Nonetheless, this extreme deviation from previous studies should alert rehabilitators to the possibilities of conditions varying sharply by region and over time.

The Texas School for the Deaf (1971) sent follow-up questionnaires to 410 former students who were 14 years of age or older when they left school and who departed the school between September, 1965 and May, 1970. The results are summarized in Table V.4. For those who completed questionnaires and indicated they were in the labor force, the unemployment rate is 21 percent. Unfortunately, Texas youth in the same age brackets are also experiencing unemployment at rates between 18 and 25 percent. This young deaf sample appears to be the victim of its youth more than its deafness.

## Table V.4

**Labor Force Status of Former Students of the Texas School for the Deaf Who Were 14 Years of Age and Older at the Time of Departure from School and Who Left School between September, 1965 and May, 1970: Texas, 1971.**

|  | Number | Percent |
|---|---|---|
| Total | 410 | 100 |
| Respondents | 331 | 81 |
| Nonrespondents | 79 | 19 |
| In Labor Force | 229 | 69[a] |
| Employed | 180 | (79)[b] |
| Unemployed | 49 | (21)[b] |
| Not in Labor Force | 102 | 31[a] |

Source: Texas School, 1972.

[a]Labor force participation rate
[b]Employment status

# Table V.5

Percent Distribution of Type of Employer for Present Jobs Held by Prevocationally Deaf Workers 16-64 Years of Age, by Sex and Race: United States, 1972.

| Type of Employer | Male | | | Female | | |
|---|---|---|---|---|---|---|
| | Total | White | Nonwhite | Total | White | Nonwhite |
| All Employers | 100.0 | 100.0 | 100.0 | 100.0 | 100.0 | 100.0 |
| Government | 15.8 | 14.6 | 26.5 | 24.4 | 23.9 | 30.0 |
| Private Company | 78.6 | 78.7 | 65.6 | 70.4 | 71.6 | 58.0 |
| Own Business | 2.3 | 2.1 | 3.2 | 2.1 | 2.3 | — |
| Paid Family | .7 | .8 | — | — | — | — |
| Unpaid Family | 1.3 | 1.4 | — | 1.6 | 1.1 | 6.0 |
| Other | 1.3 | .9 | 4.8 | 1.6 | 1.1 | 6.0 |

## Employment

The obverse of the labor-force coin is employment. As shown in Table V.1, the face of the coin presented in 1972 was relatively pleasant. The overwhelming majority of the prevocationally deaf sample is employed, though far less so for nonwhites than whites and less for women than men. This section will take up the types of employers, the types of jobs, and some characteristics related to occupation.

**Type of Employer.** Most prevocationally deaf people work for private companies (Table V.5). The rate for employment by government —federal, state or local—is somewhat less than for the population in general. Government employment does not include the Armed Services; the data in Table V.5 are for civilian workers. The small proportion of deaf persons in government service arises from the few white males so employed. Female and nonwhite deaf persons work for the government at a higher rate than for the general population—about 1 in 4 vs. about 1 in 5 for the general population. The implications of this distribution for the future are discussed at the end of this chapter.

**Industry.** The import of the information in Table V.6 is that prevocationally deaf people have positions in all industries. The heaviest concentration is in the manufacture of nondurable goods, nearly 3 out of 10 deaf workers. The lowest are in mining and personal service. As will be discussed at the conclusion of this chapter, the underrepresentation of deaf persons in the personal services threatens their long-term job security, for that category has substantial relative growth, while other industrial categories have a predicted relative diminution of workers.

*79*

# Table V.6

**Percent Distribution of Employed Deaf Persons, by Industry, Sex and Race: United States, 1972.**

Respondents' Sex and Race

| Industry | Both Sexes | Male Total | Male White | Male Nonwhite | Female Total | Female White | Female Nonwhite |
|---|---|---|---|---|---|---|---|
| All Industries | 100.0 | 100.0 | 100.0 | 100.0 | 100.0 | 100.0 | 100.0 |
| Agriculture, Forestry and Fisheries | 2.1 | 3.0 | 3.3 | — | .5 | .5 | — |
| Mining | .3 | .4 | .4 | — | .2 | .3 | — |
| Construction | 2.5 | 3.8 | 3.6 | 5.9 | .2 | .3 | — |
| Manufacturing Durable Goods | 16.4 | 19.4 | 20.1 | 11.9 | 11.0 | 11.8 | 4.7 |
| Manufacturing Nondurable Goods | 29.7 | 30.0 | 31.8 | 11.9 | 29.2 | 29.3 | 28.1 |
| Transportation, Communication and Other Public Utilities | 2.0 | 2.4 | 2.1 | 5.9 | 1.2 | 1.1 | 2.3 |
| Wholesale Trade | 3.7 | 4.1 | 3.7 | 7.4 | 2.9 | 3.0 | 2.3 |
| Retail Trade | 10.2 | 9.6 | 9.3 | 13.4 | 11.3 | 10.7 | 16.4 |
| Finance, Insurance, and Real Estate | 3.4 | 2.1 | 1.9 | 4.0 | 5.6 | 6.3 | — |
| Business and Repair Service | 3.8 | 4.3 | 4.2 | 5.9 | 2.9 | 3.3 | — |
| Personal Service | 3.3 | 2.8 | 7.4 | 7.4 | 7.0 | 6.3 | 13.3 |
| Entertainment and Recreation Services | .4 | .7 | .4 | 3.0 | — | — | — |
| Professional and Related Services | 14.5 | 11.2 | 10.4 | 18.8 | 20.4 | 20.3 | 21.1 |
| Public Administration | 6.3 | 5.7 | 5.8 | 4.5 | 7.4 | 6.8 | 11.7 |

The industrial data gathered by the NCDP contrasts sharply with that of Lunde and Bigman. Over half of their deaf sample (52.7 percent) were in manufacturing, compared to 46.1 percent in the NCDP (Lunde and Bigman did not break down their manufacturing category by durable-nondurable products). They found 7.1 percent of their sample in personal service industries; e.g., laundries, shoe repair, barber shops, etc. By contrast the NCDP found only 3.3 percent of its sample in these industries. Recognizing the difficulties in gathering this information and the intricate problems in coding responses, these differences should not be given undue weight. However, if they do represent a trend within the deaf community, then it is worth careful attention, because the trend runs contrary to the projected United States employment picture (vide infra).

**Principal Occupations.** Table V.7 illustrates that deafness need not hinder employability. Deaf persons are employed in all principal occupations from professional to domestic. The largest proportion are nontransit operators; i.e., they run machines of various kinds. Craftsmen make up almost as large a group. Professional and technical jobs are next most frequent. Of course, these gross categories do not contain numbers of deaf persons in the specific occupations proportional to the general public. There are fewer deaf lawyers, doctors and dentists—though there are some of each—than would be expected from their numbers in the general population. That there are even a few successful deaf persons in these professions demonstrates that such employment is feasible.

**Sex and Race.** Nonwhite deaf males have a higher rate of employment as service workers and a lower rate as craftsmen when compared to white males. About 1 out of 7 nonwhite deaf males are nonfarm laborers and only about 1 out of 14 white deaf males.

Among deaf females, more nonwhites than whites are in professional and technical positions. Whites have a higher rate of clerical and craftsman positions and far fewer nonfarm laboring jobs. In other categories the differences are small.

**Geographic Distribution.** More of the deaf population in the West —greater than 1 in 5—holds a professional or technical position than in the other three regions (Table V.8). On the other hand, the West has the lowest rate of clerks and craftsmen. It is possible that local usage of occupational terms may have contributed to these observed differences. In most other categories, the differences in rates between regions are small, except that the South has the lowest proportion of service workers.

# Table V.7

**Percent Distribution of Principal Occupations of Employed Respondents 16 to 64 Years of Age, by Sex and Race: United States, 1972.**

| | Male | | | Female | | |
|---|---|---|---|---|---|---|
| | Total | White | Nonwhite | Total | White | Nonwhite |
| All occupations | 100.0 | 100.0 | 100.0 | 100.0 | 100.0 | 100.0 |
| Professional and Technical | 9.2 | 9.5 | 6.1 | 8.1 | 7.6 | 12.1 |
| Nonfarm Manager and Administrators | 1.9 | 1.8 | 3.0 | .5 | .5 | — |
| Sales | .3 | .3 | — | 1.0 | 1.1 | — |
| Clerical | 8.1 | 8.3 | 6.1 | 27.7 | 28.6 | 19.4 |
| Craftsmen | 29.0 | 30.5 | 13.7 | 7.3 | 7.9 | 2.4 |
| Operatives Nontransit | 31.1 | 30.6 | 35.5 | 41.2 | 40.6 | 46.8 |
| Operatives Transit | 1.9 | 1.9 | 1.5 | — | — | — |
| Laborers Nonfarm | 8.2 | 7.5 | 15.2 | 2.4 | 1.9 | 7.3 |
| Farmers and Farm Manager | 1.2 | 1.3 | — | — | — | — |
| Farm Laborers | 1.1 | 1.2 | — | .2 | .3 | — |
| Service Workers | 8.0 | 6.9 | 18.8 | 11.3 | 11.2 | 12.1 |
| Private Household Workers | .1 | .1 | — | .2 | .3 | — |

**Education.** The expected relationship between education and occupation occurs (Table V.9). The professional and technical occupations have the highest average education (14 years). The small group in sales have completed high school in half or more instances. The remaining groups have an average education below high school graduation, with nonfarm managers and administrators coming close to that educational attainment. The lowest averages are for farm workers and nonfarm laborers.

**Age at Onset of Deafness.** The born-deaf group have a more favorable occupational distribution than the remainder of those who are prelingually deaf (Table V.10). A greater proportion are in professional and technical, and nonfarm manager and administrator positions. They have fewer clerks and craftsmen and about an equal proportion of nontransit operators. The highest rate for professional and technical employment is among those deafened after age 6. This group also has the highest rate for service workers and transit operators.

## Underemployment

While employment is not as high among the deaf population as would be desirable, it does not arouse as much concern as underemployment—employment in positions incompatible with the workers' intelligence, skills, and education. Williams and Sussman (1971) in discussing the employment picture state,

This glowing picture nonetheless has three serious flaws. The first is that employed deaf people are very often seriously *underemployed*. The deaf college graduate linotype operator or pressman is quite common, for example. Everywhere we find deaf men and women of normal or above abilities operating automatic machines, performing simple assembly line operations, or otherwise occupied in unchallenging routines. This stereotyping illustrates the inadvertent discriminatory attitudes toward deaf job applicants that are inevitable among slightly informed professionals when relating this or another small minority that has very complex characteristics.

An official in the U.S. Department of Labor expressed a similar viewpoint:

In an economy where the rate of unemployment is one of the lowest in modern history and *the* lowest in over 15 years, where over a million and a half additional workers are absorbed every year in our labor market, the deaf should find employment quite readily—but too often it is at a level greatly below their true capacities. They quickly reach a plateau, and there they remain. As a result, underemployment is so prevalent as to become a major problem for most deaf people who are capable and interested in working (Stahler, 1969).

## Table V.8

**Percent Distribution of Principal Occupations of Employed Respondents 16 to 64 Years of Age, by Regions: United States, 1972.**

| Principal Occupations | United States and Geographic Regions | | | | |
|---|---|---|---|---|---|
| | United States | Northeast | North Central | South | West |
| All occupations | 100.0 | 100.0 | 100.0 | 100.0 | 100.0 |
| Professional and Technical | 8.8 | 8.8 | 6.8 | 9.0 | 21.3 |
| Nonfarm Manager and Administrators | 1.4 | 1.5 | 1.0 | 1.9 | 1.0 |
| Sales | .5 | .8 | .8 | .3 | — |
| Clerical | 15.0 | 12.6 | 15.6 | 19.6 | 8.4 |
| Craftsmen | 21.3 | 22.6 | 21.6 | 22.0 | 15.8 |
| Operatives Nontransit | 34.7 | 37.5 | 34.8 | 31.3 | 32.7 |
| Operatives Transit | 1.2 | 1.5 | 1.6 | .9 | .5 |
| Laborers Nonfarm | 6.2 | 5.4 | 5.2 | 6.8 | 7.4 |
| Farmer and Farm Managers | .8 | .4 | .5 | .9 | 1.5 |
| Farm Laborers | .8 | .8 | .5 | 1.2 | .5 |
| Service Workers | 9.2 | 8.0 | 11.7 | 6.0 | 9.9 |
| Private Household Workers | .2 | — | — | — | 1.0 |

A clue to quantifying the extent of underemployment may be found in Table V.9. While education as a single criterion for underemployment is inadequate, it does provide a gross indication. For example, almost 43 percent of deaf adults who have completed 13 years or more of school (i.e., have one or more years of higher education) have principal occupations in the following categories: clerical, transit and nontransit operatives, farm and nonfarm laborers, and service and household workers. Underemployment certainly describes many of these job placements, though not necessarily all. Of those who completed one or more years of secondary education, 6 percent are employed as laborers. Again, all may not be underemployed, but some portion are likely to be. For older deaf persons, higher education was far less frequent than it now is, and many positions to which they aspired did not require as much education as they presently do. Thus, it should be noted that small proportions of the Professional and Technical and of the Nonfarm Manager and Administrator categories contain deaf persons with less than high-school diplomas.

Another way of viewing the possible underemployment is to note the median educational levels. The most startling in this respect is the 10.2 year average education for service and household workers. Craftsmen only have a median of 9.9 years. Otherwise, the averages seem somewhat high for some occupational groups, but not extremely so.


## Vocational Rehabilitation

Half a century has passed since Congress first legislated the establishment of vocational rehabilitation (VR) services. Designed to assist physically and mentally disabled individuals to become self-supporting, the original law has now been greatly expanded by the Rehabilitation Act of 1973 which assigns a high priority to severely disabled persons, among whom are many deaf persons. The law is administered at the federal level by the Rehabilitation Services Administration (RSA). Within RSA is the Office of Deafness and Communicative Disorders, headed by Dr. Boyce R. Williams. This office has the responsibility for monitoring VR programs assisting deaf and hearing impaired persons.

RSA properly concerns itself with how effectively the state VR agencies are serving all disability groups. It regularly publishes the number of persons rehabilitated by type of disability. Examination of such a table reveals some interesting information about the standing of deafness relative to other disabilities.

The rehabilitation ratios shown in Table V.11 are derived by dividing the number not rehabilitated into the number rehabilitated. Thus, for all disabilities, the ratio of not rehabilitated to rehabilitated was 3.52, or

# Table V.9

**Percent Distribution of Principal Occupations of Respondents 16 to 64 Years of Age, by Highest Grade Completed: United States, 1972.**

| Principal Occupations | Total | Highest Grade Completed | | | | |
| --- | --- | --- | --- | --- | --- | --- |
| | | 0-8 | 9-12 | 13-16 | 17+ | Median |
| All occupations | 100.0 | 23.2 | 62.6 | 10.5 | 3.7 | 10.3 |
| Professional and Technical | 100.0 | 2.0 | 33.7 | 38.6 | 25.7 | 14.0 |
| Nonfarm Manager and Administrators | 100.0 | 20.0 | 40.0 | 13.3 | 26.7 | 11.5 |
| Sales | 100.0 | — | 50.0 | 33.3 | 16.7 | 12.5 |
| Clerical | 100.0 | 11.1 | 73.1 | 13.5 | 2.3 | 10.6 |
| Craftsmen | 100.0 | 25.5 | 68.5 | 4.7 | 1.3 | 9.9 |
| Operatives Nontransit | 100.0 | 32.4 | 61.6 | 5.5 | .5 | 9.6 |
| Operatives Transit | 100.0 | 23.1 | 61.5 | 15.4 | — | 10.2 |
| Laborers Nonfarm | 100.0 | 34.3 | 56.7 | 9.0 | — | 9.6 |
| Farmer and Farm Managers | 100.0 | 33.3 | 66.7 | — | — | 9.5 |
| Farm Laborers | 100.0 | 33.3 | 50.0 | 16.7 | — | 9.8 |
| Service Workers and Private Household Workers | 100.0 | 19.4 | 72.4 | 8.2 | — | 10.2 |

stated in other words, for every failure to rehabilitate a person, 3.52 persons were successfully rehabilitated. Turning to Hearing Impairment, the success ratio is 8.21. Only Benign or Unspecified Neoplasm has a higher rate of success (11.22). Within the Hearing Impairment category, impairments less than deafness do best (10.82), while those who are deaf and unable to talk do worst (4.60). The latter rate, however, is higher than the average for all disabilities, and exceeds five other disabilities in successful rehabilitation. A deaf VR client is a comparatively good risk.

Table V.11 also enables a comparison between the number of deaf and the number of blind persons served. In 1970, 5,915 deaf and 7,364 blind clients were rehabilitated—a rate of 124 blind to 100 deaf clients. But blindness occurs less than one third as often as deafness. The prevalence rate for blindness is 225 per 100,000 (Hatfield, 1973) while deafness, without regard to age at onset, has a prevalence rate of 873 per 100,000. There are 388 deaf persons to every 100 blind persons in the population. Obviously, the rehabilitation budget is not distributed in proportion to the size of the population to be served.[2] If it were, in keeping with the 7,364 blind clients, the number of deaf clients would have been 28,572!

To elicit deaf persons' views of VR, several questions were asked in the NCDP. To the question concerning knowledge of VR, almost 2 out of 3 respondents said they knew about VR (Table V.12). The recognition is almost exactly as frequent for males as females, whites as nonwhites. More than half of the same respondents answered that they had sought assistance from VR (Table V.13). Half of the requests were for education or training. Next most frequent request was for assistance in obtaining employment. About 1 out of 6 applicants sought hearing aids.

Proportionally more nonwhites than whites sought VR assistance, and slightly more females than males. All groups requested education and training most frequently, except nonwhite females, who most often came to VR looking for employment. Nonwhite females also applied for hearing aids more than the other three groups.

Of those who sought VR assistance, 74 percent said they did receive help. Nonwhite females and males significantly less often felt that they had received assistance (Table V.14). The NCDP interviewer attempted to distinguish between receiving help and satisfaction with the help received. For those who said they did obtain service, the majority were satisfied (Table V.15). Again, nonwhite females expressed dissatisfac-

---

[2]These remarks should not be construed as a criticism of RSA; nor should the conclusion be drawn that funds now allocated to blind clients be given to those who are deaf. Rather, the number of deaf persons served should be adjusted to meet their needs. The purpose of the comparison is to suggest that not enough effort is being made on behalf of deaf clients, rather than that too much is being done for those who are blind. (See Williams and Sussman, 1971; Schein, 1973B.).

# Table V.10

**Percent Distribution of Principal Occupation of Employed Respondents 16 to 64 Years of Age, by Age at Onset of Deafness: United States, 1972.**

| Principal Occupations | All Ages | Born Deaf | Ages at Onset | | |
| --- | --- | --- | --- | --- | --- |
| | | | 0-3 Years | 3-5 Years | 6-18 Years |
| All occupations | 100.0 | 100.0 | 100.0 | 100.0 | 100.0 |
| Professional and Technical | 8.8 | 10.0 | 5.6 | 9.6 | 12.5 |
| Nonfarm Manager and Administrators | 1.4 | 1.6 | 1.0 | .5 | 2.9 |
| Sales | .5 | .9 | — | — | 1.5 |
| Clerical | 15.0 | 14.3 | 16.7 | 15.5 | 11.7 |
| Craftsmen | 21.3 | 18.4 | 25.5 | 20.9 | 19.8 |
| Operatives Nontransit | 34.7 | 35.9 | 36.3 | 34.2 | 26.4 |
| Operatives Transit | 1.2 | .7 | .7 | 2.1 | 2.9 |
| Laborers Nonfarm | 6.2 | 6.8 | 3.2 | 9.1 | 8.1 |
| Farmer and Farm Managers | .8 | .9 | .7 | 1.1 | — |
| Farm Laborers | .8 | 1.1 | .5 | .5 | .1 |
| Service Workers | 9.2 | 9.0 | 9.8 | 5.9 | 13.5 |
| Private Household Workers | .2 | .2 | — | .5 | — |

tion far more frequently than did the other three groups, and nonwhite males were also less satisfied than either white males or females.

Of those who were dissatisfied with the VR service they received—a very small number—the modal complaints centered about the counselors. Twenty percent said the counselor was either incompetent or uninterested. Another 16 percent did not agree with the advice given to them. Sixty percent of the responses were other highly specific reasons. Of course, these data cannot be interpreted as any measure of the VR counselors' abilities. A counselor who denies a client's request for service because it is infeasible or illegal may be perceived as "unfeeling" or "not knowing his job" by the client. Furthermore, a counselor who is unable to communicate with the deaf client may appear incompetent to the client, who cannot for that reason appreciate the counselor's knowledge and skills. The client is also not necessarily the best judge of the quality of counseling he has been given. He may feel pleased with an outcome which is far less than he could have achieved, simply because it is so much better than he had expected. Nonetheless, the high degree of expressed satisfaction (nearly 85 percent) should be kept in mind; it is reflected in the high rehabilitation ratio for deaf and hearing impaired clients shown in Table V.11.

On the other hand, 45 percent of the adult deaf sample said they had not sought VR assistance, and 26 percent of those who did, said they were not accepted. From these scanty data, the appropriate VR thrusts to increase rehabilitations amongst deaf adults would seem to be best directed toward bringing more of them into the rehabilitation process. Nonwhite deaf persons particularly seem underserved.

### Employer Attitudes

A number of studies have found employers reluctant to hire deaf workers (Rickard, Triandis, and Patterson, 1963; Williams, 1972). Rickard et al. found general prejudice against hiring disabled applicants. Deafness was rated as worse than tuberculosis and wheelchair-bound and better than epilepsy, ex-prison and ex-mental hospital by personnel directors. Similar ratings were given by school administrators, except when the hypothetical applicant sought a position as third-grade teacher. Then the deaf applicant rated worse than all but the epileptic.

Williams (1972) asked 108 Minnesota employers about hiring persons with ten specified disabilities. Only 45 percent said they would hire a deaf person for production job "always" or "usually but not always"; 25 percent responded "sometimes but not usually" and 30 percent "never". Asked about management jobs, the employers were even more negative toward hypothetical deaf prospects, 75 percent saying never or not usually. Fifty-one percent, however, said they would hire a deaf

# Table V.11

## Number and Percent Distribution of State VR Clients, by Selected Major Disabling Conditions and Rehabilitation Status, FY 1970

| Major disabling condition | Closed from applicant status | | Rehabilitated | | Not Rehabilitated | | Rehabilitation |
|---|---|---|---|---|---|---|---|
| | Number | Percent | Number | Percent | Number | Percent | Ratio |
| All disabilities | 132,530 | 100.0 | 256,544 | 100.0 | 72,921 | 100.0 | 3.52 |
| Hearing impairments | 4,074 | 3.1 | 14,334 | 5.6 | 1,745 | 2.4 | 8.21 |
| Deafness | 1,595 | 1.2 | 5,915 | 2.3 | 967 | 1.3 | 6.12 |
| Unable to talk | 665 | 0.5 | 2,123 | 0.8 | 462 | 0.6 | 4.60 |
| Able to talk | 930 | 0.7 | 3,792 | 1.5 | 505 | 0.7 | 7.51 |
| Other hearing impairments | 2,479 | 1.9 | 8,419 | 3.3 | 778 | 1.1 | 10.82 |
| Visual impairments | 11,118 | 8.4 | 22,420 | 8.7 | 3,861 | 5.3 | 5.81 |
| Blindness, both eyes | 2,569 | 1.9 | 7,364 | 2.9 | 1,545 | 2.1 | 4.77 |
| Other visual impairments | 8,549 | 6.5 | 15,056 | 5.9 | 2,316 | 3.2 | 6.50 |
| Orthopedic impairments | 30,194 | 22.8 | 45,688 | 17.8 | 14,156 | 19.4 | 3.23 |
| Absence/amputation of extremities | 2,090 | 1.6 | 9,520 | 3.7 | 1,723 | 2.4 | 5.53 |
| Mental illness | 38,635 | 29.2 | 63,267 | 24.7 | 29,448 | 40.4 | 2.15 |
| Mental retardation | 10,037 | 7.6 | 30,356 | 11.8 | 7,629 | 10.5 | 3.98 |
| Benign/unspecified neoplasms | 410 | 0.3 | 2,447 | 1.0 | 218 | 0.3 | 11.22 |
| Allergies | 2,287 | 1.7 | 2,437 | 1.0 | 573 | 0.8 | 4.25 |
| Endocrine disorders | 2,228 | 1.7 | 4,105 | 1.6 | 860 | 1.2 | 4.77 |
| Epilepsy | 3,012 | 2.3 | 4,267 | 1.7 | 1,487 | 2.0 | 2.87 |

Source: Schein, 1973B

person for a clerical position. These results did not seem to differ by size of company (range 45 to 10,000 employees).

Phillips (1973) elicited a number of employer stereotypes of deaf workers: (a) safety risks, (b) inflexible, (c) difficult to train, etc. Nonetheless, many companies expressed a willingness to hire a deaf person. The majority, however, had no experience with deaf employees.

Having deaf employees appears to favorably alter employer misconceptions. Rosenstein and Lerman (1963) obtained uniformly good ratings from the employers of the deaf females being followed-up after graduation from a school for deaf children—the largest proportion of whom held production jobs. Favorable experiences cannot be expected from every deaf employee and some employers are prone to label all deaf workers unacceptable on the basis of a single bad example (Craig and Silver, 1966; Phillips, 1973). Silver (1970) summarizes his company's relations with its deaf employees in these words:

I am pleased to say, we have had some outstanding deaf employees advance to more challenging and more responsible positions. But for the most part, success in modern industry depends greatly on ability to communicate and, although many deaf people compensate admirably, most are unable to improvise well enough to qualify for supervisory positions. Obviously this limitation affects the deaf person in many ways on the job, but the most discouraging aspect is that it impairs his chances to be even considered for advancement (page 11).

The single largest employer in the United States is the federal government. A study of employment practices in civil service did not reveal any pattern of overt prejudice toward deaf employees (Bowe, Delk, and Schein, 1973). Barriers to employment do occasionally arise for deaf people in civil service, but there is every indication that the Civil Service Commission will take vigorous steps to eliminate these impediments when they are documented. Bowe et al. conclude their investigation of complaints by deaf persons by noting:

We cannot leave this report with the impression that all deaf respondents had complaints of discrimination. We talked with a number of deaf persons in Federal employment who are 'wedded to their jobs.' They have only praise for their treatment at every step, from application, through orientation, to promotion. They consider federal employment second to none, much to be preferred over private or State employment. That so many enjoy civil service is as it should be. Our task, on the other hand, has been to locate deaf persons who do not share these happy views. We conclude our report knowing that some deaf persons have faced and are facing barriers to employment, job satisfaction and promotion (page 15).

## Table V.12

**Percent Distribution of Knowledge of Vocational Rehabilitation
of Respondents 16 to 64 Years of Age, by Sex And Race: United States, 1972**

| Knowledge | Both Sexes | Male | | | Female | | |
|---|---|---|---|---|---|---|---|
| | | Total | White | Nonwhite | Total | White | Nonwhite |
| All Persons | 100.0 | 100.0 | 100.0 | 100.0 | 100.0 | 100.0 | 100.0 |
| No Knowledge Of Voc. Rehab. | 34.4 | 34.0 | 33.6 | 38.0 | 34.7 | 34.4 | 37.7 |
| Knowledge Of Voc. Rehab. | 65.6 | 66.0 | 66.4 | 62.0 | 65.3 | 65.6 | 62.2 |

As a minority group, deaf persons are likely to suffer occasional abuse in the labor market. The literature does not clearly establish that, in practice, deaf individuals are deprived of their right to succeed because of unreasoned prejudice against them. Surely not every instance in which a deaf person is denied entry to employment or discharged or denied promotion is unjustified. Some deaf people are unskilled, uncooperative, poorly motivated. But these few should not stand in the way of the many who are talented, energetic, highly motivated and cooperative.

While the NCDP did not gather data from employers regarding deaf workers, it recognizes the importance in the employment equation of acceptance by industry. As will be noted in the next section, the future will likely face deaf job applicants with the necessity of seeking jobs from employers who have had no previous experience with deafness. Such fine organizations as the President's Committee for the Employment of the Handicapped will need to lend their good offices in making these introductions productive. The deaf workers can be depended upon to do the rest.

## Future Employment Prospects

By 1980, the United States labor force will contain 100 million workers, according to projections by the Bureau of Labor Statistics (Stewart, 1970). That means an estimated growth of 22.0 percent above the 1968 labor force of 82 million. In this rapid rise in number of gainfully employed persons, will those who are deaf be able to increase their proportions in the labor force? Will their rates of employment rise or fall?

The government anticipates a radical shift in industries, with service-producing industries continuing their sharp increase in the proportion of the labor force. In 1980, 68 million workers—almost 1 out of 7 in the labor force—will be employed in service-producing industries. The goods-producing industries will have a small increase in actual numbers employed but a decline in the proportion of the labor force, despite the projected outpouring of goods. Mining and agriculture are expected to lose workers, and manufacturing to grow at a much lower rate in the Seventies than in the Sixties. Only the construction industry has a projected rate of increase among the goods-producers.

Within the service-producing industries, employment in wholesale and retail trade and finance is expected to increase at the same rate as the total labor force, almost 22 percent. Services—personal, business, health, and education—and government employment should increase faster than the overall rate. While they will have increases, transportation, communication and public utilities will add employees at a lesser

# Table V.13

**Percent Distribution of Kind of Assistance Requested from Vocational Rehabilitation by Respondents 16 to 64 Years Of Age, by Sex And Race: United States, 1972**

| Assistance Requested | Both Sexes | Male | | | Female | | |
|---|---|---|---|---|---|---|---|
| | | Total | White | Nonwhite | Total | White | Nonwhite |
| All Assistance | 100.0 | 100.0 | 100.0 | 100.0 | 100.0 | 100.0 | 100.0 |
| None Requested | 44.8 | 46.8 | 48.0 | 34.3 | 42.7 | 43.6 | 34.4 |
| Hearing Aid | 9.3 | 7.4 | 6.9 | 12.0 | 11.3 | 10.5 | 18.0 |
| Job Training | 11.2 | 11.7 | 11.0 | 18.9 | 10.6 | 11.1 | 6.6 |
| Further Education | 15.5 | 15.8 | 15.9 | 15.4 | 15.2 | 15.4 | 13.1 |
| Employment | 14.7 | 12.4 | 12.5 | 12.0 | 17.1 | 16.3 | 23.5 |
| All Others | 4.6 | 5.9 | 5.7 | 7.4 | 3.2 | 3.1 | 4.4 |

94

rate than for all industries. In terms of jobs, then, almost 7 out of every 10 will be in the service-producing group by 1980, as opposed to 6 in 10, in 1968.

What about the occupational breakdown? How will these shifts in patterns of industrial employment affect the distribution of occupations? Demand for professional and technical occupations is expected to increase 50 percent by 1980. Managers and administrators will continue to hold about 10 percent of the positions in the labor force. Clerical and sales employment are also expected to increase nearly 50 percent, while craftsmen's share of the labor force will decline slightly. Jobs for semiskilled workers will rise more slowly than the overall increase in projected employment. The number of nonfarm laborers will remain constant, meaning a decline in share of the labor force. Service workers will increase almost as sharply as professional and technical, clerical and sales occupations. Farm workers are expected to decline in both actual numbers and percent of labor force. Figure V.1 pictures these projected trends from 1947 to 1980 in more general categories of employment.

To keep pace with the changes in occupational and industrial changes, deaf workers will need to alter drastically their established employment patterns. As noted in Table V.6, the major share of deaf employees, nearly half of them, are in manufacturing. By 1980, manufacturing is expected to employ less than one fourth of the labor force. Of the next three other major industrial categories—Services, Trade, Public Administration—deaf people are only reasonably well represented in the latter. In Services and Trade, deaf workers must increase substantially by 1980, in order to maintain a distribution in industry similar to that for the general population.

In terms of occupations, deaf workers are far behind in professional-technical, clerical, sales and service positions—the four fastest growing categories. Deaf workers have higher proportions than they should have in the craftsmen and operator categories, if they are to maintain their present and anticipated share of the labor force. Deaf persons are also grossly underrepresented among the managers, officials and proprietors, and greatly overrepresented among laborers, farm and nonfarm workers combined.

The Bureau of Labor Statistics's (BLS) forecasts, considered in the light of their present employment, predicts serious problems may arise for deaf workers. Recognizing that the present occupational conditions are unfavorable for deaf persons, VR administrators, parents, deaf leaders, and educators should be deeply worried about the future. Both young and old, incoming and ongoing workers face the threat posed by our shifting economy. While numbers of jobs should increase, the ones most often held by deaf persons are more likely to decrease, at least as a

## Table V.14

**Percent Distribution Requested Assistance from Vocational Rehabilitation by Respondents 16 to 64 Years of Age, by Sex And Race: United States, 1972**

| Outcome | Both Sexes | Male | | | Female | | |
|---|---|---|---|---|---|---|---|
| | | Total | White | Nonwhite | Total | White | Nonwhite |
| All Outcomes | 100.0 | 100.0 | 100.0 | 100.0 | 100.0 | 100.0 | 100.0 |
| Did Not Receive | 26.0 | 26.2 | 25.2 | 34.8 | 25.7 | 24.3 | 36.1 |
| Received Help | 74.0 | 73.8 | 74.8 | 65.2 | 74.3 | 75.7 | 63.9 |

## Table V.15

**Percent Distribution of Reported Satisfaction with Vocational Rehabilitation Services for Persons 16 to 64 Years of Age Who Requested and Received Services By Sex and Race: United States, 1972**

| Satisfaction With Assistance | Both Sexes | Male | | | Female | | |
|---|---|---|---|---|---|---|---|
| | | Total | White | Nonwhite | Total | White | Nonwhite |
| All Persons | 100.0 | 100.0 | 100.0 | 100.0 | 100.0 | 100.0 | 100.0 |
| Not Satisfied | 15.4 | 15.8 | 14.9 | 24.0 | 15.0 | 12.8 | 35.5 |
| Satisfied | 84.6 | 84.2 | 85.1 | 76.0 | 85.0 | 87.2 | 64.5 |

# Figure V.1

**Percent of Labor Force by Major Occupational Categories,
for Selected Years: United States, 1947-1980.**[1]

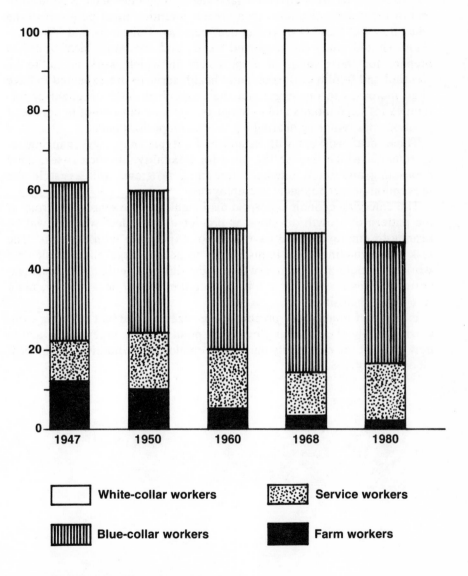

[1]1947-1968 proportions are actual; 1980 projected.
Source: Stewart, 1970.

*97*

share of the total market. This latter statement, of course, means greater competition for many of the positions deaf workers now hold.

Whether the future will prove as inhospitable to deaf workers as current projections suggest will depend upon several factors, not the least of which is the accuracy of the projections. Assuming the economy does develop as BLS envisions (and the agency does have a good prior record for prognostication), then greater attention must be given to the education and training of young deaf persons. Educators and VR counselors should study the projected trends and encourage deaf youth to prepare for those areas of employment in which work is apt to be plentiful and fulfilling. Business and health services are expected to have large increases in openings, and these openings offer excellent opportunities for accountants and cytologists, to name but two of hundreds of positions not requiring hearing for successful performance.

Those deaf workers with established careers may face changing requirements which impose the need for flexibility. In such cases, good counseling and brief, intensive retraining programs will assist in the prevention of technological unemployment.

The emerging economic portrait also highlights the employers' role. If the pattern of growth develops as predicted, then deaf workers will be turning to employers who have no prior experience with deafness. The task of persuading these industrialists to accept large numbers of deaf workers should not be overwhelmingly difficult, judging by past experience. However, effort will be required; employer acceptance is not a foregone conclusion.

Is the deaf community presently organized to conduct a strong campaign? Surely the mounting evidence points to the urgency for action now to avert the potentially dangerous employment situation for the deaf labor force of 1980.

## CHAPTER VI

# Economic Status

THE INFORMATION about employment and occupation does not adequately describe the economic condition of deaf persons. An important additional measure is annual income. Another is quality of housing. Both of these are discussed in this chapter, in an effort to comprehend the economic impact of deafness.

### Family Income

The incomes of families whose heads of household are prevocationally deaf fall below those of families in the general population (Table VI.1). The deaf families median income is 84 percent as much as the United States average. For white deaf heads, the comparison is slightly more favorable—85 percent. But for nonwhite and female deaf heads of households the figures are worse. Nonwhite deaf males head households whose median income is 74 percent of that for nonwhite male heads in general. Similarly, white deaf female heads have median family incomes that are 74 percent of those for white female heads in general, and for nonwhite deaf female heads the comparison yields a rate of 73 percent for those who are deaf.

It should be noted that within the general population, there is a progressive decline in median family income from white males, to nonwhite males, to white females, to nonwhite females. The actual dollar range for the median annual income is from $11,143 to $3,645. Since in each case families with deaf heads of household are from 16 to 27 percent below the corresponding averages for the general population, the deaf family's median incomes range from $9,450 to $2,662. Over half of the families headed by a nonwhite deaf female had an annual income below $3,000, while 21 percent headed by nonwhite deaf males were in the same low bracket.

# Table VI.1

**Percent Distribution of Family Income for Deaf Heads of Households Compared to General Population Households, by Race and Sex: United States, 1971.**

| Respondents' Sex and Race | Total | Annual Income | | | | | | Median | |
|---|---|---|---|---|---|---|---|---|---|
| | | Under $3000 | $3000-4999 | $5000-6999 | $7000-9999 | $10,000-14,999 | $15,000 And Over | Deaf | General[a] |
| All Groups | 100.0 | 10.8 | 9.8 | 14.3 | 27.2 | 26.3 | 11.6 | 8662 | 10,285 |
| Male | 100.0 | 6.4 | 7.2 | 14.1 | 29.7 | 30.1 | 12.7 | 9263 | 10,930 |
| White | 100.0 | 5.3 | 6.2 | 13.6 | 30.4 | 31.0 | 13.4 | 9450 | 11,143 |
| Nonwhites | 100.0 | 20.8 | 19.2 | 20.0 | 20.0 | 17.5 | 2.5 | 6000 | 8,067 |
| Female | 100.0 | 35.9 | 24.7 | 15.8 | 12.8 | 4.9 | 5.9 | 4146 | 5,114 |
| Whites | 100.0 | 31.3 | 27.7 | 14.5 | 13.3 | 6.0 | 7.2 | 4347 | 5,842 |
| Nonwhites | 100.0 | 56.4 | 10.9 | 21.8 | 10.9 | — | — | 2662 | 3,645 |

[a]Source: U.S. Bureau of the Census, 1973.

**Personal Income**

Family income may confound the relationship between earnings and deafness, since other contributors to family income may not be deaf (see Chapter III). For that reason, individual income provides a clearer assessment of economic status of deaf persons. Note that the data in Tables VI.2 to VI.5 are for the incomes of *employed* deaf persons. As will be seen, this fact is critical in making comparisons with the general population.

The deaf individuals' median incomes are from 62 to 76 percent of their general population peers. Overall, deaf earnings are 72 percent of those for individuals at large. White deaf females do best, earning 76 percent as much as white females. The remaining contrasts with their general counterparts show nonwhite deaf males 62 percent, white deaf males 74 percent, and nonwhite deaf females 62 percent of corresponding earnings.

With the exception of white deaf males, the income distributions exhibit a marked positive skew. Almost 40 percent of nonwhite deaf males and nearly 50 percent of nonwhite deaf females earned less than $3,000 in 1971. A little more than one fourth of white deaf females also earned less than $3,000. At the other end of the distributions, less than 8 percent of nonwhite deaf males, 4 percent of white deaf females, and 3 percent of nonwhite deaf females earned $10,000 or more. Twenty percent of white deaf males earned $10,000 or more and 14 percent earned less than $3,000—a somewhat less skewed distribution of income than for the other three groups.

**Other Deaf Samples.** Unlike the NCDP, some surveys of other deaf samples have found their earnings to be higher than the general population. For example, Lunde and Bigman (1959) reported, "While the median income for the deaf group is $3,465, that for the general population in 1956 was only $2,818" (page 26). The general population average, however, is for all persons having some income from wages or salaries. Another comparison would be with the median income for all employed persons, a group resembling the deaf sample which consisted only of employed persons. In that comparison, the deaf sample is below the general population: $3,465 to $4,041. The deaf workers earn 86 percent as much as general population workers, a rate higher than that found for the same comparison in the NCDP. The Lunde-Bigman sample, it should be noted, had fewer females and far fewer nonwhites, both groups tending to have lower earnings than white males.

Schein (1968) also compared the median income of employed deaf persons in Washington, D.C. to the general population averages. Substituting the correct comparison does not alter the finding that white deaf males' median earnings ($6,473) exceeded that for employed white males

## Table VI.2

**Percent Distribution of Personal Income from Wages and Salary by Sex and Race of Respondents 16 to 64 Years of Age: United States, 1971.**

| Respondent's Sex and Race | Total | Income | | | | | | Median Deaf | Median General[a,b] |
|---|---|---|---|---|---|---|---|---|---|
| | | Less than $3000 | $3000-4999 | $5000-6999 | $7000-9999 | $10,000-14,999 | $15,000 & Over | | |
| All Groups | 100.0 | 20.1 | 20.2 | 21.3 | 23.8 | 12.6 | 2.1 | 5915 | 8188 |
| Males | 100.0 | 16.1 | 12.8 | 20.2 | 30.5 | 17.4 | 3.0 | 7084 | 9631 |
| White | 100.0 | 13.8 | 12.2 | 20.4 | 32.0 | 18.3 | 3.3 | 7338 | 9902 |
| Nonwhite | 100.0 | 39.1 | 18.8 | 18.8 | 15.6 | 7.8 | — | 4166 | 6771 |
| Females | 100.0 | 27.7 | 34.1 | 23.3 | 11.1 | 3.5 | .3 | 4306 | 5701 |
| White | 100.0 | 25.8 | 34.4 | 24.3 | 11.6 | 3.6 | .3 | 4405 | 5767 |
| Nonwhite | 100.0 | 47.7 | 30.9 | 12.4 | 6.2 | 3.1 | — | 3166 | 5092 |

[a]Source: U.S. Bureau of the Census, 1973.
[b]Includes persons 14 and 15 years old and 65 and older.

($6,174). The median for white deaf females ($3,542) is 95 percent of that for employed white females ($3,747). The findings for nonwhite deaf males and females remain unchanged: they are far below the median incomes for employed nonwhite males and females. The Washington, D.C. sample at that time deviated from the general pattern of lower individual earnings for deaf workers only with respect to those who were white, and then less in the case of females than males.

In HIS '62 (Gentile et al., 1967), the prevalence of hearing impairment decreased as family income increased. Figure VI.1 illuminates this relationship. There is a small deviation in the overall trend for persons 65 years and over; the rate of impairment rises slightly between the highest two income categories. This may be accounted for by the larger presence of very old people in the $7,000-and-over group, due to the tendencies for longevity to be positively related to income and for the frequency of hearing impairment to increase with age.

**Income and Occupation.** As would be expected, the best-paying jobs for deaf workers are in the Professional and Technical category (Table VI.3). Nonfarm managers and administrators earn only a little less on the average. The medians for both groups are more than half again as great as the median for all employed deaf persons. Nonfarm laborers average more than twice as much as farm laborers and somewhat more than farmers and farm managers. The latter, however, may have small cash income, though their earnings in terms of real income may be far higher.

**Age at Onset of Deafness.** Personal earnings are directly related to age at onset of deafness. Those born deaf have the lowest average, and those who lost their hearing after age 6, the highest. The difference between the medians is $1,208, a substantial sum. Figure VI.2 shows the persistent tendency across the four categories of ages at onset.

**Additional Sources of Income.** About one third of the deaf males interviewed lives in, or heads, a household that received some money from governmental sources in the form of social security, welfare or vocational rehabilitation payments. For households containing white deaf males, about 3 in 10 received some government support, of which Social Security benefits were the major additional source of income for 18 percent of the total. Welfare and VR were less than 4 percent for each. Welfare and social security payments contributed to a little more than 3 percent of deaf families, with various other combinations amounting to less than 2 percent.

Half of the households in which nonwhite deaf males live received income from these government sources. One fourth received welfare payments and one eighth social security. Social security benefits and welfare combined were received by almost 8 percent. Vocational re-

# Figure VI.1

**Number of persons with binaural hearing loss per 1,000 population, by family income.**

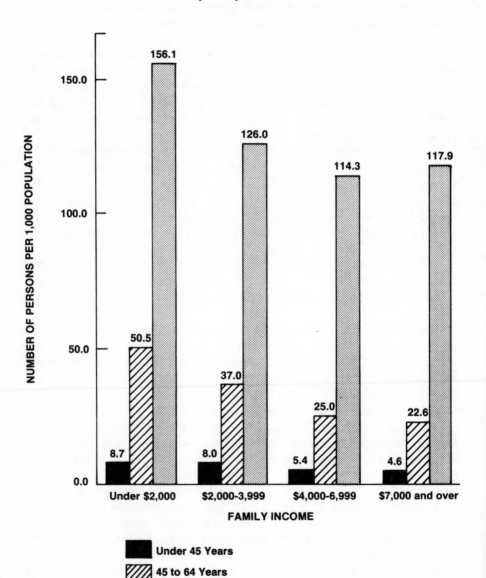

Source: Gentile, et al. 1967.

## Figure VI.2

**Median Personal Income of Employed Deaf Persons 16-64 Years of Age, by Age at Onset of Deafness: United States, 1971.**

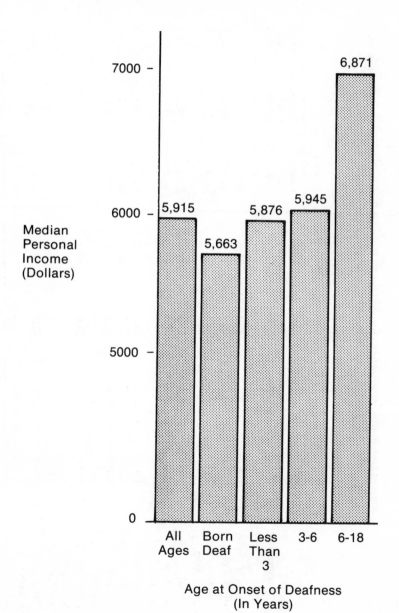

# Table VI.3

**Percent Distribution of Principal Occupations by Personal Income from Wages and Salaries. Respondents 16 to 64 Years of Age: United States, 1971.**

| Principal Occupations[a] | Total | Personal Income from Wages and Salaries | | | | | | Median Income Deaf |
|---|---|---|---|---|---|---|---|---|
| | | Under $3,000 | 3,000 to 4,999 | 5,000 to 6,999 | 7,000 to 9,999 | 10,000 to 14,999 | 15,000 and Over | |
| All Occupations | 100.0 | 19.7 | 20.1 | 21.4 | 24.1 | 12.6 | 2.0 | $5,950 |
| Prof. & Tech. | 100.0 | 12.8 | 5.3 | 11.7 | 28.7 | 30.9 | 10.6 | $9,111 |
| Nonfarm Mgr. & Adm. | 100.0 | 14.3 | 14.3 | 7.1 | 21.4 | 28.6 | 14.3 | $8,999 |
| Clerical | 100.0 | 13.4 | 25.0 | 29.3 | 22.0 | 9.1 | 1.2 | $5,791 |
| Craftsmen | 100.0 | 8.5 | 11.5 | 19.2 | 36.3 | 21.8 | 2.6 | $7,882 |
| Operatives (Nontrans.) | 100.0 | 23.2 | 25.6 | 23.2 | 19.9 | 7.8 | .3 | $5,104 |
| Operatives (Trans.) | 100.0 | 7.7 | 7.7 | 38.5 | 38.5 | 7.7 | — | $6,799 |
| Laborers Nonfarm | 100.0 | 34.4 | 16.4 | 18.0 | 26.2 | 4.9 | — | $4,899 |
| Farmers & Farm Mgrs. | 100.0 | 40.0 | 20.0 | 20.0 | — | 20.0 | — | $3,999 |
| Farm Laborers | 100.0 | 66.7 | 11.1 | 22.2 | — | 1.0 | — | $2,251 |
| Service Workers | 100.0 | 38.8 | 32.2 | 17.6 | 10.4 | — | — | $3,698 |

[a]Sales and private household workers not included.

# Table VI.4

**Percent Distribution of Personal Income by Age at Onset of Deafness: United States, 1971.**

| Age at Onset of Deafness | Total | Under $3000 | $3,000-4,999 | Personal Income $5000-6999 | $7000-9999 | $10,000-14,999 | $15,000 And Over | Median |
|---|---|---|---|---|---|---|---|---|
| All Ages at Onset | 100.0 | 20.1 | 20.2 | 21.3 | 23.8 | 12.6 | 2.1 | 5,915 |
| Born Deaf | 100.0 | 23.3 | 19.2 | 22.6 | 20.4 | 12.0 | 2.5 | 5,663 |
| Less than Three | 100.1 | 19.4 | 21.6 | 19.9 | 25.1 | 12.3 | 1.4 | 5,876 |
| Between 3-5 | 99.9 | 17.1 | 22.9 | 21.1 | 25.7 | 11.4 | 1.7 | 5,945 |
| Between 6-18 | 100.1 | 15.7 | 14.6 | 28.4 | 28.4 | 17.0 | 3.2 | 6,871 |

habilitation contributed some income to a little over 3 percent, with another 1 percent receiving conjoint income from vocational rehabilitation and social security.

## Housing

The quality of housing is a factor in assessing socioeconomic status. In the NCDP, interviewers rated the character of the neighborhood in which the deaf person resided on a 7-point scale, ranging from "slum" to "most desired" (Table VI.6).

As a group, deaf persons tend to live in average to above-average neighborhoods. Less than one third of the total sample lived in below-average surroundings. The differences by the head of the household's race and sex, however, are substantial.

More than 70 percent of households headed by a white deaf male are located in average or better neighborhoods. By contrast, less than 30 percent of households headed by a nonwhite deaf male are in average or better neighborhoods. White deaf female heads do less well than their male counterparts, but better than either nonwhite group. Nonwhite deaf female heads do a little worse than nonwhite deaf male heads; only 25 percent live in average or better areas and almost half live in semi-slums or slums.

## Table VI.5

**Percent Distribution of Selected Governmental Sources of Income for Households in which a Deaf Male 16 to 64 Years of Age Lives, by Race: United States, 1971.**

|  | Males | | |
|---|---|---|---|
| Source of Income | All | White | Nonwhite |
| All Sources | 100.0 | 100.0 | 100.0 |
| Nongovernmental | 67.5 | 69.4 | 50.4 |
| Social Security | 17.5 | 18.1 | 12.2 |
| Welfare | 6.1 | 3.9 | 25.2 |
| Vocational Rehabilitation | 3.4 | 3.5 | 3.3 |
| Social Security and Welfare | 3.7 | 3.2 | 7.8 |
| Social Security and Vocational Rehabilitation | .9 | .9 | 1.1 |
| Welfare and Vocational Rehabilitation | .1 | .1 | — |
| Social Security, Welfare and Vocational Rehabilitation | .8 | .9 | — |

# Table VI.6

**Percent Distribution of Character of Neighborhood, by Race and Sex of Deaf Heads of Households 16 to 64 Years of Age: United States, 1972.**

| Sex and Race | Total | Character of Neighborhood | | | | | | |
| --- | --- | --- | --- | --- | --- | --- | --- | --- |
| | | Most Desired | Superior | Above Average | Average | Below Average | Semi-Slum | Slum |
| All Groups | 100.0 | 0.7 | 5.6 | 15.8 | 43.8 | 23.4 | 9.0 | 1.7 |
| Male | 100.0 | 0.9 | 6.3 | 16.9 | 44.4 | 21.9 | 8.2 | 1.4 |
| White | 100.0 | 0.9 | 6.6 | 17.9 | 46.0 | 21.5 | 6.4 | 0.6 |
| Nonwhite | 100.0 | — | 2.7 | 2.7 | 21.6 | 27.0 | 33.3 | 12.6 |
| Female | 100.0 | — | 1.8 | 10.0 | 40.1 | 31.0 | 13.4 | 3.6 |
| White | 100.0 | — | 2.2 | 10.0 | 45.6 | 32.2 | 8.9 | 1.1 |
| Nonwhite | 100.0 | — | — | 10.2 | 15.3 | 25.4 | 33.9 | 15.3 |

109

**Type of Dwelling.** The majority of deaf persons reside in one-family houses (Table VI.7). This holds true for 70 percent of white deaf male heads and 54 percent of white deaf female heads. For nonwhite deaf heads of household, 46 percent of males and 33 percent of females have one-family houses. Most nonwhite deaf female heads live in apartments, as do over one third of nonwhite deaf male heads. Ten percent of nonwhite deaf female heads live in dormitories, rooming houses, hotels, and similar quarters.

**Ownership.** More than 6 out of 10 white deaf male heads of household own their homes (Table VI.8). Conversely, less than 1 out of 5 of their nonwhite peers own their homes. Among the deaf females, 40 percent of those who are white and about 28 percent of those who are nonwhite own their homes.

**Density.** Table VI.9 portrays another aspect of housing—density. Few of the deaf households appear overcrowded. Even one-person families have a median number of rooms close to 3, and a small minority of families live in less rooms than they have family members. Using one room per household member as a measure of density, 6.6 percent have fewer than that ratio. But 20 percent of households have nonwhite deaf heads living in fewer rooms than there are persons living in the household. This ratio of rooms to household members is not by itself a measure of overcrowding. The point is that nonwhite deaf persons by this measure again fall short of the white deaf average.

# Table VI.7

Percent Distribution of Dwelling Unit for Deaf Heads of Household, by Sex and Race; United States, 1972.

| Sex and Race | Total | Type of Dwelling Unit | | | | | |
| | | One-Family | Two-Family | Apart-ment | Trailer | Others[a] | N.R. |
|---|---|---|---|---|---|---|---|
| Male | 100.0 | 68.0 | 4.0 | 21.0 | 2.5 | 3.9 | 0.6 |
| White | 100.0 | 69.6 | 3.8 | 19.9 | 2.7 | 3.6 | 0.4 |
| Nonwhite | 100.0 | 46.0 | 7.1 | 35.7 | — | 7.1 | 4.0 |
| Female | 100.0 | 50.1 | 6.2 | 34.7 | 1.8 | 7.1 | — |
| White | 100.0 | 53.8 | 6.5 | 31.2 | 2.2 | 6.5 | — |
| Nonwhite | 100.0 | 32.8 | 5.2 | 51.7 | — | 10.3 | — |

[a]Includes dormitory, rooming house, hotel, etc.

# Table VI.8

**Percent Distribution of Occupancy Status
by Race and Sex of Heads of Households: United States, 1972.**

| Sex and Race | Occupancy Status | | | |
| --- | --- | --- | --- | --- |
| | Total | Own | Rent | Other |
| Male | 100.0 | 60.7 | 38.5 | 0.8 |
|   White | 100.0 | 63.8 | 35.3 | 0.9 |
|   Nonwhite | 100.0 | 18.9 | 81.1 | — |
| Female | 100.0 | 37.8 | 61.3 | 0.9 |
|   White | 100.0 | 40.0 | 58.9 | 1.1 |
|   Nonwhite | 100.0 | 27.6 | 72.4 | — |

# Table VI.9

**Persons per Room for Households Where Deaf Person Is Head:
United States, 1972.**

| Persons in Household | Rooms in Household | | | | | | | Total Households |
| --- | --- | --- | --- | --- | --- | --- | --- | --- |
| | 1 | 2 | 3 | 4 | 5 | 6 | 7+ | |
| 1 | 105 | 45 | 51 | 72 | 69 | 36 | 18 | 396 |
| 2 | 6 | 3 | 86 | 135 | 176 | 66 | 66 | 538 |
| 3 | | 6 | 6 | 72 | 114 | 129 | 66 | 393 |
| 4 | | | 6 | 60 | 108 | 129 | 90 | 393 |
| 5 | | | 3 | 21 | 42 | 54 | 78 | 198 |
| 6 | | | | 3 | 51 | 24 | 24 | 102 |
| 7+ | | | | 9 | 3 | 30 | 24 | 66 |
| Total | 111 | 54 | 152 | 372 | 563 | 468 | 366 | 2086 |

## CHAPTER VII

# Morbidity and Mortality

T O WHAT EXTENT do other physical ailments tend to accompany deafness? Are prevocationally deaf persons more or less healthy than the general population? Does deafness affect longevity? These and related questions are discussed in this chapter in an attempt to shed further light upon the condition of deaf people and to uncover relationships which will be useful in planning services, as well as in explicating the impact of deafness.

## Age at Onset of Deafness

As part of the definition of prevocational deafness, onset prior to 19 years of age is specified. The actual composition of the prevocationally deaf sample by age at onset is positively skewed (Table VII.1). Almost three fourths of the total is prelingually deaf; i.e., lost hearing prior to 3 years of age. Indeed, more than half lost hearing before 1 year of age. By contrast, not quite 12 percent became deaf at or after 6 years of age.

**Sex and Race.** Males and females have similar distributions of age at onset. The nonwhite sample, however, differs sharply from the white (Figure VII.1). The white deaf group tends to have a larger prelingual component than the nonwhite group—about 74 percent of the white versus 62 percent of the nonwhite samples. More than 1 out of 5 nonwhite deaf males lost their hearing between 6 and 18 years of age, a rate many times larger than that for the other three groups. Nonwhite deaf females had more than twice the percentage in the 3-to-5-year category than any of the other three groups. Since age at onset is related to amount of schooling completed, the disproportionate rate for college attendance found for nonwhite deaf males may be largely explained by this related disproportionality (see Chapter IV).

*113*

# Table VII.1

**Percent Distribution of Age at Onset of Deafness, by Sex and Race of Respondents: United States, 1972.**

| Sex and Race | Total | Born Deaf | Less Than One | 1 - 2 | 3 - 5 | 6 - 11 | 12 - 18 |
|---|---|---|---|---|---|---|---|
| All Groups | 100.0 | 41.4 | 12.6 | 19.6 | 14.9 | 7.9 | 3.6 |
| Male | 100.0 | 41.3 | 14.2 | 19.1 | 13.4 | 8.4 | 3.6 |
| White | 100.0 | 42.4 | 13.9 | 19.4 | 13.5 | 7.3 | 3.5 |
| Nonwhite | 100.0 | 31.4 | 17.6 | 16.7 | 12.7 | 17.3 | 4.2 |
| Female | 100.0 | 41.6 | 10.8 | 20.0 | 16.5 | 7.4 | 3.6 |
| White | 100.0 | 42.1 | 11.1 | 20.9 | 14.9 | 7.5 | 3.6 |
| Nonwhite | 100.0 | 38.0 | 8.1 | 13.1 | 29.6 | 7.1 | 4.0 |

**Other Samples.** The critical period for acquiring deafness appears to be prior to age 3 (Table VII.1). Of the NCDP's prevocationally deaf sample, 7 in 10 were deaf before age 3, and almost 9 in 10 by age 5. The Metropolitan Washington, D.C. sample had a later-deafened overall average, yet 6 out of 10 became deaf before 5 years, and 1 out of 4 were born deaf (Schein, 1968). Lunde and Bigman (1959) reported 8 in 10 were deaf before 6 years of age and nearly 3 in 10 were born deaf. About 7 in 10 persons in the New York State sample became deaf before 4 years of age (Rainer et al., 1963).

The present population of deaf and hearing impaired persons under 21 years of age contains even higher proportions of students whose loss occurred prior to 3 years of age (Table VII.2). For successive academic years, 1968-69 through 1970-71, the Annual Survey of Hearing Impaired Children and Youth found more than 90 percent of the students were prelingually impaired. The proportions reporting loss at birth ranged from over 7 in 10 to nearly 8 in 10. Unless severe epidemics in the next few years generate a substantial amount of adventitious deafness, the prevocationally deaf adults in the next decade will mostly be prelingually and congenitally deaf, with the latter predominating.

### Causes of Deafness

Deafness is multiply determined. It is the common result of diverse causes. Thus, in terms of the hearing loss per se, the cause may be

## Table VII.2

**Percent Distribution of Age at Onset of Hearing Impairment for Students in Special Programs Reporting to the Annual Survey of Hearing Impaired Children and Youth: United States, 1968-69, 1969-70, 1970-71.**

| Age at Onset | Academic Year | | |
| --- | --- | --- | --- |
| | 1968-69 | 1969-70 | 1970-71 |
| At birth | 73.6 | 77.6 | 78.0 |
| Under 3 | 17.0 | 15.0 | 15.1 |
| 3 to 6 | 6.8 | 5.6 | 5.3 |
| 7 and over | 2.6 | 1.9 | 1.6 |
| Numbers Providing this Information | 20,759 | 28,489 | 34,218 |

Sources: Rawlings and Gentile, 1970; Rawlings, 1971; Rawlings, 1973.

# Figure VII.1

**Percent of Prevocationally Deaf Population with Various Onsets of Deafness, by Sex and Race: United States, 1972.**

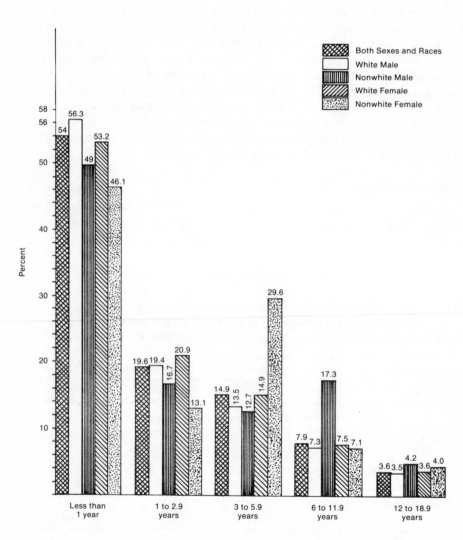

accident, injury, illness, heredity or a combination of these factors. In the fields of education and rehabilitation, the genesis of the loss receives little attention. Understanding the reason for deafness occurring in an individual can be useful, however, in alerting the practitioner to associated characteristics. Furthermore, in the area of prevention generally and genetic counselling particularly, knowledge of the cause of deafness becomes critical.

Gathering information about cause of hearing loss by interview alone or through self-administered questionnaires yields only partially satisfactory data. In many cases of congenital deafness, a specific diagnosis was not made, because the cause was unknown at that time; e.g., maternal rubella was only recently identified as a possible cause of deafness (Murray, 1949). In addition, some adults may never have been told as children the nature of the illness which caused their deafness. Others may have received only a partial or an incorrect explanation. Nonetheless, despite the unreliability in the responses, the overall summarization of factors can be useful to geneticists and epidemiologists. The reader should remember the faulty underpinnings of the tabled responses when studying them.

Illnesses accounted for more than 3 out of 10 cases of deafness (Table VII.3). Spinal meningitis was most frequently listed among the specific illnesses, followed by scarlet fever. The two conditions overlap, since in some instances the organism invading the meninges may be the streptococcus which causes scarlet fever. The same holds true for measles, pertussis, and other acute febrile diseases.

An almost equal portion of respondents said they were born deaf or had become deaf due to illness. About a fourth of those born deaf stated they inherited their hearing loss, and about 1 in 6 implicated maternal rubella. The largest portion — nearly 6 in 10 of those born deaf — could be no more specific than to note that they did not hear at birth.

The latter responses, along with those of the 17 percent who said they did not know why they were deaf, are most likely valid responses. Altogether, more than 1 out of 3 respondents did not specify the cause of their deafness. As noted above, their answers were probably not evasive, they simply did not know the cause of their deafness. The Washington, D.C. survey produced a distribution of causes close to that for the NCDP, including 32.2 percent cause unknown.

**Sex and Race.** The interactions of sex and race with respect to cause of loss appear complex. Nonwhite females and white males reported illnesses less often than white females and nonwhite males. Nonwhite males—more than 1 in 8—gave accidents or injuries as a cause, more than half again as frequently as the other three groups. Nonwhite males also appeared far less often in the category Born Deaf or Heredity.

# Table VII.3

**Percent Distribution of Reported Causes of Deafness, by Race and Sex of Respondents: United States, 1972.**

| Cause | Total | White | | Nonwhite | |
| --- | --- | --- | --- | --- | --- |
| | | Male | Female | Male | Female |
| All Causes | 100.0 | 100.0 | 100.0 | 100.0 | 100.0 |
| Illness | 35.0 | 35.9 | 40.9 | 41.5 | 31.9 |
| Spinal Meningitis | 9.7 | 10.8 | 8.3 | 14.1 | 7.1 |
| Scarlet Fever | 6.2 | 5.7 | 7.5 | 0.5 | 5.1 |
| Measles | 4.3 | 4.2 | 4.5 | 6.9 | 2.0 |
| Whooping Cough | 2.6 | 2.7 | 2.2 | 3.9 | 4.1 |
| Other Illness | 13.2 | 12.5 | 13.4 | 16.1 | 13.6 |
| Accident or Injury | 7.6 | 6.9 | 7.6 | 13.4 | 8.1 |
| Birth Injury | 2.5 | 2.6 | 2.2 | 2.9 | 4.1 |
| Fall | 3.1 | 3.0 | 3.7 | 1.0 | 1.0 |
| Other Injury | 2.0 | 1.3 | 1.7 | 9.4 | 3.0 |
| Born Deaf or Heredity | 31.8 | 33.1 | 32.6 | 19.6 | 27.1 |
| Inherited | 7.6 | 7.9 | 8.2 | 2.9 | 4.0 |
| Mother Had Rubella | 5.2 | 6.0 | 5.0 | 2.6 | 3.4 |
| Born Deaf Other | 19.0 | 19.2 | 19.4 | 14.1 | 19.7 |
| Other Cause | 7.5 | 7.8 | 6.6 | 5.9 | 13.2 |
| Unknown | 17.1 | 16.3 | 17.3 | 19.6 | 19.7 |

Nonwhite females also had a lower frequency in that category, though not as low as nonwhite males. All four groups had about the same proportion of "don't know" responses.

**Student Data.** An analysis of the school records of 41,109 hearing impaired students produced data which strongly implicate epidemics as a cause of loss among those born deaf (Gentile and Rambin, 1973). By plotting the relative number of births for various putative etiologies by birthmonth, a remarkable U-shaped distribution emerged for rubella and a relatively flat distribution for heredity. The seasonal pattern for rubella-deafened births corresponded to the periods of greatest incidence of communicable diseases. Gentile and Rambin promise further analyses to support their contention that other diseases, such as mumps and measles, may also be agents causing prenatal hearing defects. If they are correct, we may see a further reduction in the proportion of unknown causes. This, in turn, should lead to better control over birth defects due to infections of the mother during pregnancy.

## Hearing Aid Use

The majority of the NCDP sample does not use hearing aids (Table VII.4). Less than 3 in 10 state that they presently use a personal hearing aid, while nearly half report they have never used one. Almost one fourth said they have used a hearing aid but do not do so now. For those

## Table VII.4

**Percent Distribution of Hearing Aid Use by Respondents, 1 to 64 Years of Age, by Sex and Race: United States, 1972.**

| | | Hearing Aid Use | | |
| Sex and Race | Total | Never Used | Previously Used | Now Uses |
| --- | --- | --- | --- | --- |
| All Groups | 100.0 | 47.7 | 24.1 | 28.2 |
| Males | 100.0 | 46.4 | 26.1 | 27.5 |
| White | 100.0 | 47.0 | 25.5 | 27.5 |
| Nonwhite | 100.0 | 41.6 | 30.5 | 27.9 |
| Females | 100.0 | 49.1 | 22.0 | 28.9 |
| White | 100.0 | 49.0 | 22.6 | 28.3 |
| Nonwhite | 100.0 | 49.7 | 16.6 | 33.8 |

who do use a hearing aid of their own, its use may be sporadic or full time. It may also be worn as a visible sign of deafness rather than as an amplifier of sounds. Some deaf people find that the aid serves as a cue to the strangers they meet to speak more distinctly and generally alerts others to the wearer's hearing impairment.

The group which formerly used a hearing aid may be expressing dissatisfaction with it. On the other hand, changes in hearing ability or in economic status may have led to abandonment of the aid. HIS '62 found that hearing aid use was directly related to income: as income increased so did the percent of present users (Gentile et al., 1967). Hearing aids are not only expensive to purchase, they are also costly to maintain. Under constant use, batteries must be frequently replaced and repairs made. The hearing aid is an electronic device which demands care in order to continue to function properly.

**Sex and Race.** There are only small differences between white and nonwhite deaf males and females with respect to hearing aid use. The proportion never having used a hearing aid ranges from 41.6 to 49.7 percent. Among present users, nonwhite females have about 20 percent more who currently wear aids than the average for the NCDP sample: 33.8 percent versus 28.2 percent. Conversely, they have proportionally fewer past users than the NCDP sample as a whole: 16.6 percent versus 24.1 percent. The finding by HIS '62 of greater present use of hearing aids among binaurally impaired females does not hold for this prevocationally deaf sample. Lunde and Bigman also noted no sex differences for hearing aid use in their sample.

**Improved Speech Reception.** To estimate the improvement in hearing resulting from use of a hearing aid, the Hearing Scale (see Chapter VIII) was administered twice to NCDP respondents. The first time hearing aid users were asked how they hear without their hearing aid; the second time with their hearing aid. Since the steps on the Hearing Scale form a hierarchy of hearing ability from very poor to excellent, positive responses to higher steps on the scale than previously given indicate improvement in hearing. The results are summarized in Table VII.5.

The majority of hearing aid users—8 in 10—showed by their responses to Hearing Scale II that they heard better with their present aid. One percent expressed a decline and 18.6 percent no improvement. Failure to show a gain in hearing may be due somewhat to the grossness of the Hearing Scale which may have too large increments between steps to reveal subtle increases in auditory performance. Other possibilities are

# Table VII.5

**Percent Distribution of Hearing with Aid, by Race and Sex of Respondents Who Presently Use Aids: United States, 1972.**

| Sex and Race | Total | Hearing Improved With Aid | Hearing Remained the Same | Hearing Got Worse |
|---|---|---|---|---|
| All Groups | 100.0 | 80.4 | 18.6 | 1.0 |
| Whites | 100.0 | 81.4 | 17.7 | .9 |
| Males | 100.0 | 80.3 | 18.0 | 1.7 |
| Females | 100.0 | 82.6 | 17.4 | — |
| Nonwhites | 100.0 | 72.6 | 25.7 | 1.7 |
| Males | 100.0 | 74.7 | 21.7 | 3.6 |
| Females | 100.0 | 70.7 | 29.3 | — |

response error or, of course, that the results are valid in showing no change in speech reception detectable by the individual respondent.

White deaf persons appear to gain more benefit from their hearing aids than nonwhite deaf persons. Eighty-one percent of whites who presently use an aid indicate better hearing with it, compared to 72.6 percent of nonwhite deaf users. In view of their proportionately greater use, nonwhite deaf female responses are paradoxical. Twenty-nine percent showed no improvement in speech reception from use of a hearing aid. Because of their small proportion of prior use and rejection of hearing aids, this finding may result from a large number who are becoming accustomed to their aids.

**Trends.** Three samples of deaf adults at different points in time provide roughly comparable data about hearing aid use. The percents reporting that they never used hearing aids are as follows:

| Sample | Year Interviewed | Percent Never Used Hearing Aid |
|---|---|---|
| Lunde-Bigman | 1957 | 89.9 |
| Washington, D.C. | 1962 | 55.7 |
| NCDP | 1972 | 47.7 |

Contrast these data with the proportion of hearing impaired students in 1969-70 who did not have a personal aid—32.8 percent (Rawlings, 1971).

It seems likely that many of the two thirds who do have their own hearing aids will continue to use them into adulthood. The use of hearing aids by prevocationally deaf adults, then, can be expected to increase.

## Physical and Mental Condition

A deaf person who has an additional disability may rightly be considered severely handicapped. The extra burden of the second disability may be far in excess of what it would be for the single disability because deafness multiples the attendant problems (cf. Schein, 1974). Obtaining medical care for a mild heart condition, for example, may become a problem because communication with physicians and nurses is often difficult. So even those conditions which may, by themselves, be innocuous can become severely disabling when occurring in combination with deafness.

The NCDP sample reported that 1 out of 3 persons had a disability in addition to deafness (Table VII.6). The most frequent additional condition was asthma, which was reported by 8.3 percent of those sampled. Vision was the next most prevalent health problem, accounting for 3 percent of all deaf persons. The remaining conditions—neuropsychiatric disorders, arthritis, heart trouble, mental retardation, cerebral palsy, cleft palate, etc.—had frequencies of less than 3 percent.

**Sex and Race.** Males tended to be somewhat healthier than females. Almost ten percent fewer males reported a health problem than did females. Females claimed far more asthmatics (10 percent versus 5.9 percent for males) and arthritics (2.8 percent versus 1.2 percent for males). Females also reported more visual problems (3.6 percent versus 2.7 percent for males). Though the proportions are tiny, the rates for cerebral palsy are worthy of note, 0.5 percent for females and 1.2 percent for males.

Nonwhites generally have a higher rate of additional disabilities. Asthma is far more prevalent among nonwhite than white males and females. Nonwhite females reported the largest percentages for heart trouble, mental retardation, and visual conditions. Nonwhite males reported the highest percentage of neuropsychiatric conditions.

When all ages up to 64 years are considered, the proportion of deaf persons reporting additional health conditions changes somewhat to 30 percent (Table VII.7). Of these, two thirds have two or more conditions. Bear in mind that these rates are for the noninstitutionalized population. Persons so severely disabled as to require custodial care are not included, nor are the elderly.

# Table VII.6

**Percent Distribution of Health Conditions Reported Other than Deafness by Respondents 1 to 64 Years of Age, by Race and Sex: United States, 1972.**

| Health Conditions | Both Sexes | Male | | | Female | | |
|---|---|---|---|---|---|---|---|
| | | Total | White | Nonwhite | Total | White | Nonwhite |
| All Conditions | 100.0 | 100.0 | 100.0 | 100.0 | 100.0 | 100.0 | 100.0 |
| No Other Condition | 66.6 | 69.9 | 71.3 | 58.0 | 63.2 | 64.3 | 54.4 |
| Asthma | 8.3 | 5.9 | 5.0 | 13.3 | 10.0 | 9.6 | 13.1 |
| Vision | 3.1 | 2.7 | 2.7 | 2.5 | 3.6 | 3.3 | 5.9 |
| Neuropsychiatric Condition | 2.8 | 1.0 | .6 | 4.6 | 1.1 | 1.1 | 1.0 |
| Arthritis | 2.0 | 1.2 | 1.4 | — | 2.8 | 3.1 | — |
| Heart Trouble | 2.0 | 2.0 | 2.1 | 1.8 | 1.9 | 1.5 | 4.9 |
| Mental Retardation | 1.6 | 1.2 | 1.3 | .9 | 1.9 | 1.5 | 4.9 |
| Cerebral Palsy | .9 | 1.2 | 1.2 | .9 | .5 | .5 | 1.0 |
| Cleft Palate | .4 | .4 | .5 | — | .4 | .5 | — |
| Other | 15.1 | 14.4 | 13.9 | 17.9 | 15.9 | 15.7 | 17.7 |

## Table VII.7

**Percent Distribution of Number of Conditions Reported per Respondent: United States, 1972.**

| Number of Conditions Reported | Number | Percent |
|---|---|---|
| Total | 5945 | 100.0 |
| No Condition | 4168 | 70.1 |
| One Condition | 579 | 9.7 |
| Two Conditions | 814 | 13.7 |
| Three or More | 384 | 6.5 |

**Deaf School Children.** In most years, the Annual Survey of Hearing Impaired Children and Youth inquires about physical and mental conditions in addition to auditory disorders which may create an educational problem for the students in the sample. The results for the successive academic years ending 1969, 1970 and 1971 are shown in Table VII.8. The schools responded that 4 out of every 10 students had a condition besides deafness which interfered with their academic progress. This startlingly high rate for multiple disabilities remained fairly stable for the three consecutive samples ranging in size from 21,130 to 34,795 students.

Emotional and behavioral problems accounted for about one fourth and mental retardation about one fifth of the total handicaps. Between 17 and 18 percent of all students had a physical disability. About 7 percent had two additional disabilities.

These sobering statistics apply only to those hearing impaired students who were in school. Those in long-term, custodial care were not included. Apparently, the schools regarded 40 percent of their pupils as severely disabled. Since the data were not confirmed by expert diagnoses, some mislabelling and exaggeration of the conditions may have occurred; but it strains credulity to assume that a very large minority of these students do not have excessive problems besides hearing impairments. Whether they will outgrow and/or overcome some of their extra handicaps must be carefully watched. If they do not, the coming generation of deaf adults will present extremely difficult assignments to Vocational Rehabilitation and others who are concerned with their welfare.

# Table VII.8

Percent Distribution of Additional Educationally Handicapping Conditions
Reported for Deaf Students, by Years and Type of Disability: 1968-71.

| Type of Handicap | Handicaps Reported for Deaf Students, by School Year | | |
|---|---|---|---|
| | 1968-69 (N-21,130) | 1969-70 (N-29,131) | 1970-71 (N-34,795) |
| All Handicaps | 42.0 | 42.0 | 39.3 |
| Behavioral/Emotional Problems | 12.4 | 12.9 | 9.6 |
| Brain Damage | * | .5 | .5 |
| Cerebral Palsy | 3.4 | 3.3 | 3.2 |
| Cleft Lip/Palate | .7 | .7 | .6 |
| Epilepsy | * | .6 | .7 |
| Heart Disorders | .9 | 1.4 | 2.2 |
| Learning Disabilities | * | 3.1 | 2.6 |
| Mental Retardation | 8.0 | 7.2 | 7.0 |
| Orthopedic Disorders | * | .7 | .7 |
| Perceptual-Motor Disorders | 5.5 | 5.5 | 5.4 |
| Severe Visual | 4.2 | 4.5 | 4.9 |
| Other | 6.8 | 1.7 | 1.9 |

*Included under "Other"
Source: Rawlings and Gentile, 1970; Rawlings, 1971; Rawlings, 1973.

**Deaf College Students.** An analysis of the records of 526 entering students at Gallaudet College during the years 1955 to 1959 showed that their physical condition, aside from their auditory disability, was excellent (Schein and Roy, 1961). The records contained a pre-admittance physical examination by the family physician. The information supplied was then checked by the college physician upon admission of the student.

The average age of the males was 19.5 years and of the females 19.1 years. Comparisons of their average heights and weights to the general population 19 years of age showed them to be almost identical to the norms on these two dimensions.

Students and their physicians agreed on their general good health. The family physicians rated the students' physical condition on a 4-point scale, indicating 62 percent excellent, 37 percent good and 1 percent fair.

None rated a student's health as poor. All but 2 out of 526 students answered yes to the question Are you in good physical health? Furthermore, the family physicians recommended to the college that 94 percent of the students required no limitation of physical activity.

Additional disabilities were rare. Less than 3 percent of the students listed a second disability. Of the 12 who did, 6 noted a defect of the extremities, 2 a spinal deformity, and 1 each a problem with mild spasticity, heart condition, or other skeletal deformity.

The splendid impression of excellent health enjoyed by these deaf college students is marred somewhat by the comparison with the number of multiply handicapped children presently in elementary and secondary schools. As described above, the current population in grade-school programs for hearing impaired pupils give evidence of a high proportion of multiple disabilities. The difference between their generally unfortunate condition and the college students' highly favorable one may be due to the two decades separating them. Perhaps a physical and mental decline among deaf children has occurred recently.

However, since only a small proportion of deaf children enter college, another explanation recommends itself. It should be remarked that Gallaudet College has no explicit policy against accepting multiply disabled applicants. Thus it becomes likely that the explanation of the opposite pictures of health exhibited by the two groups of students is simply that those with additional handicaps are less able to attain sufficient academic standing to gain admission to college.

## Insurance

At this time adult deaf males report few problems in obtaining various types of insurance (Table VII.9). To avoid duplication, only responses of males are considered here. Health and life insurance can be purchased by the majority of males in the sample without paying what they believe to be excessive rates. Nonwhite males have twice as many complaints about insurance as whites. Ten percent said they paid extra premiums for life insurance compared to 4 percent of the white males, and 7.5 percent had difficulty with health insurance as against 3 percent of the white males who indicated similar problems.

The availability of coverage from the National Fraternal Society of the Deaf probably contributes a great deal to the relatively small number of complaints about these two forms of insurance compared to those about automobile insurance. As described in the next section of this chapter, the Society does not insure automobiles. Sixteen percent of the deaf respondents feel they either pay too much or find they cannot buy the kind of coverage of automotive risk they want. Of course, some of the remonstrances about high premiums may arise from factors unrelated to

# Table VII.9

**Percent Distribution of Problems in Getting Insurance for Male Respondents 16-64 Years of Age, by Type of Insurance and by Race: United States, 1972.**

| Type of Insurance and Problem | Total | White | Nonwhite |
|---|---|---|---|
| **Automobile** | 100.0 | 100.0 | 100.0 |
| No Problem | 83.9 | 83.8 | 85.0 |
| High Rate | 5.5 | 5.5 | 5.4 |
| High Risk | 7.7 | 8.0 | 5.4 |
| Other | 2.9 | 2.7 | 4.2 |
| **Health Insurance** | 100.0 | 100.0 | 100.0 |
| No Problem | 96.4 | 96.8 | 92.5 |
| High Rate | .9 | 1.0 | — |
| High Risk | 1.9 | 1.4 | 6.4 |
| Other | .8 | .8 | 1.1 |
| **Life Insurance** | 100.0 | 100.0 | 100.0 |
| No Problem | 94.4 | 94.9 | 90.0 |
| High Rate | 2.1 | 1.7 | 5.7 |
| High Risk | 2.7 | 2.5 | 4.3 |
| Other | .8 | .9 | — |
| **Other Insurance** | 100.0 | 100.0 | 100.0 |
| No Problem | 96.6 | 96.8 | 94.6 |
| High Rate | 1.2 | 1.2 | 1.1 |
| High Risk | 1.5 | 1.2 | 4.3 |
| Other | .7 | .8 | — |

deafness. The relatively greater dissatisfaction with this kind of insurance points to the possible need for remedial action like that taken years ago by the deaf community. From all available evidence, deaf drivers are as safe, if not safer than, drivers in general (Schein, 1968). The deaf driver, therefore, should not pay any extra amount for his insurance because he is deaf.

An earlier review of insurance problems encountered by deaf persons drew similar conclusions to those above (Crammatte, 1970). The proportion of companies issuing health and accident policies to deaf clients increased from 61 percent in 1957 to 78 percent in 1969. Though the

NCDP data are generated by the experiences of deaf people, these probably reflect a continuing upward trend in favorable attitudes of insurance companies toward deaf risks. Crammatte further states, "Automobile insurance has been the greatest problem area relative to insurance for deaf persons in recent years" (op. cit., page 25). From the current NCDP data it would appear that efforts by the National Association of the Deaf have succeeded in reducing the severity of the problems associated with automobile insurance. There is, however, a need for continued work to make all insurance available at reasonable cost to deaf consumers.


## Mortality

Do prevocationally deaf persons have the same life expectancy as the population in general? We have been unable to locate any recently published references on this question. Best (1943) makes use of 1910 and 1920 census data to make some tentative observations about longevity. More recent studies based on more reliable data do not appear to have been published, despite the importance of this topic.

The National Fraternal Society of the Deaf (NFSD) headquartered in Oak Park, Illinois, has graciously provided information from their files on death rates. The NFSD, also known as "The Frat," was founded in 1901 to provide life insurance for deaf persons, because most insurance companies either refused to insure them or charged them extra premiums. The NFSD has succeeded in reducing this discrimination over the years, not only with respect to life insurance but also to other types of insurance. Nonetheless, NFSD remains a major insurer of deaf persons, presently having more than 12,000 policies in force.


Another reason for NFSD's success in overcoming prejudice against insuring deaf persons is illustrated in Table VII.10. The Frat's experience has been excellent. The death rates are appreciably lower than would be expected from general population tabulations. The ratios of expected to observed deaths range from 27.74 to 59.17, with a mean of 41.81. Like most insurance companies, NFSD does not insure persons at random. As would be true for most insurance companies, its policyholders tend to be economically better off, healthier, more conscientious, etc., than the uninsured. It is, therefore, of interest to compare the performance of NFSD to other insurers. For the years 1966, 1967, and 1969, the NFSD mortality rates were substantially lower than the average experiences of the 25 largest life insurance companies (Table VII.11).

# Table VII.10

**Ratio of Actual to Expected Deaths of Deaf Persons[a]:**
**National Fraternal Society of the Deaf, 1940-1972.**

| | |
|---|---|
| 1940 - 56.92 | 1956 - 41.96 |
| 1941 - 40.11 | 1957 - 32.89 |
| 1942 - 47.06 | 1958 - 38.75 |
| 1943 - 49.20 | 1959 - 34.56 |
| 1944 - 41.63 | 1960 - 36.60 |
| 1945 - 41.25 | 1961 - 27.74 |
| 1946 - 43.79 | 1962 - 42.19 |
| 1947 - 50.29 | 1963 - 43.17 |
| 1948 - 49.18 | 1964 - 35.30 |
| 1949 - 48.65 | 1965 - 36.93 |
| 1950 - 59.17 | 1966 - 35.15 |
| 1951 - 40.86 | 1967 - 30.12 |
| 1952 - 39.00 | 1968 - 38.26 |
| 1953 - 55.93 | 1969 - 37.44 |
| 1954 - 33.48 | 1970 - 54.31 |
| 1955 - 34.96 | 1971 - 57.77 |
| | 1972 - 43.19 |

Average: 41.81

[a]Based on American Experience 3% and 1958 Commissioner's Standard Ordinary 2.5% Mortality Tables

---

# Table VII.11

**Mortality Rates of the National Fraternal Society of the Deaf**
**Compared to the Average of the 25 Largest**
**Life Insurance Companies: 1966, 1967, 1969.**

| | Mortality Rates[a] | |
|---|---|---|
| Year | NFSD | 25 Companies |
| 1969 | 37.44 | 56.32 |
| 1967 | 30.12 | 54.99 |
| 1966 | 35.15 | 54.37 |

[a]Actual deaths to expected deaths.

The evidence of greater longevity for prevocationally deaf persons may only result from the astuteness of the NFSD's management in its selection of clients. On the other hand, the evidence also indicates that a large portion of the deaf population lives up to and beyond normal life expectancy. A careful investigation of deaths among deaf people certainly needs to be done to determine more precisely the applicable mortality rates. The data provided by NFSD hints that the results of such a study would be very useful to those planning services for the deaf community. In addition, a lower death rate for deaf persons could explain to some extent the sharp rise in prevalence rates for the older age groups.

## CHAPTER VIII

# Design and Execution
# of the Survey

S TUDIES of the prevocationally deaf population are difficult, because early deafness is relatively rare. Even at a prevalence rate of 203 per 100,000 persons, deafness constitutes a "needle in the haystack" problem. Methods have been developed to overcome this difficulty, but they are expensive compared to costs for the usual survey (Hansen et al., 1953; Kish, 1965; Schein, 1968).

A second obstacle arises from the lack of an agreed-upon definition of deafness and of a metric for determining it (Schein, 1964). The U.S. Bureau of the Census (1931) cited methodological problems as its reason for discontinuing its 100-year-old enumeration of the deaf population. Achieving uniformity amongst the census takers in determining whom to count as deaf was one of the principal difficulties. The assumption that most people would agree on the meaning of the word "deaf" received no empirical support.

A nationwide survey of deaf persons also encounters all of the usual problems of questionnaire design and interviewer selection, training and reliability. In each instance, however, these problems are compounded by the difficulties in communication—difficulties which demand accommodation in the structure and conduct of the interview. A census of the deaf population, then, requires special methods and considerable financial resources to do it properly, which may explain, in part, why so little effort has been expended in the past forty years on enumerations of the deaf population of the United States (Schein, 1973).

The National Census of the Deaf Population (NCDP) became feasible because of research which provided economical solutions to these dif-

*131*

ficulties. The description of the methods used to conduct the NCDP reflect many complex decisions, some of which could as well have taken a different tack. For that reason, and because interpretation of the results requires it, a detailed account follows.

The most critical element in the NCDP is discussed first—the definitions of terms used. Then the procedures by which the data were gathered are presented. The NCDP actually involved two studies. The first one established the size of the deaf population, and it made use of the special methodology mentioned above. In the second phase, a sample of the deaf population was drawn to determine the characteristics of deaf adults. The results of both phases have been coordinated with data from other sources to provide a comprehensive portrait of the deaf community. The validity of the picture which emerges can be assessed to some extent by reference to the care taken in gathering the information from which it is constructed. Accordingly, each step is described in as extensive detail as seems warranted by this purpose and by the assistance the detail will provide to interpretation of the results.

## Definition of Deafness

Arguments over definitions can be interminable—and fruitless. A definition is inherently arbitrary, recognizing at some level a theoretical bias or particular interest. Certain aspects of an entity are deemed relevant and all the rest irrelevant to its specification. What is relevant or irrelevant resides in the perspective of the definer and not necessarily in the nature of the defined.

A review of definitions of deafness reveals a bewildering array of variations (Schein, 1964). The most obvious fact emerging from the review is that there is no generally agreed-upon use of the term. In addition to specifying vastly different degrees of impairment, definitions of deafness also may include age at onset, speaking ability, etiology, binaurality, chronicity, etc. The factors considered in a given definition usually reflect the interests of the particular discipline propounding it. Since there is neither statutory penalty nor benefit for being deaf, there is no legal definition of deafness.

### Degree of Impairment

The choice of factors to be included in the definition of deafness presently depends upon the use to be made of it. For the NCDP, a broad specification was sought which would be meaningful in education, rehabilitation, sociology and psychology—a single dimension which would have functional value for those disciplines. Ability to hear and understand speech was selected, both because it is significant to all of the social sciences and because it could be psychologically scaled (vide infra).

**Deafness** then refers to the inability to hear and understand speech.

To describe hearing disorders of less severity than deafness, we shall employ two terms:

**Hearing impairment** to refer to all significant deviations from normal, including deafness.

**Significant bilateral hearing impairment** to encompass losses in both ears, the better ear having some difficulty hearing and understanding speech. Again, this phrase also includes deafness along with the lesser degrees of loss. The relation of these definitions to audiometric values will be discussed after the section on the determination of hearing status by interview.

### Age at Onset of Deafness

Age at onset is a separate consideration from hearing ability. The disability of deafness has variable consequences depending, in part, on the point in the developmental sequence at which it occurs. A person born deaf, for example, will not develop speech without skillful assistance, while persons becoming deaf in adulthood will usually maintain their speaking ability without special help. Rather than having some arbitrary age intruded into its definition, however, the term deafness can be modified by an adjective describing the developmental stage of occurrence. We have elected two terms—many more are possible:

**Prelingual** refers to ages at onset prior to three years of age.

**Prevocational** refers to all ages at onset up to 19 years.

The casual reader may confuse *present age* with *age at onset*. The terms prelingually and prevocationally deaf are used to avoid the complication that would arise from an awkward phrase like "a group presently 25 to 44 years of age for whom the age at onset of deafness was before 19 years of age." Using the proposed nomenclature, the phrase becomes simply "a group of prevocationally deaf persons 25 to 44 years of age." In the latter phrasing, the word age does not appear twice, though it is implied in the term prevocational. Aside from economy of expression, then, this usage should improve readability of the text.

In the NCDP, deafness acquired before or during the educationally formative years (i.e., the first eighteen years of life) received primary

*133*

consideration. It is frequently difficult for an individual to fix a specific date when his hearing loss reached its final ebb, especially when the loss has been progressive over a long period of time. Many congenital losses are probably reported to be of later onset, only because they are undetected at birth. The eighteen-year limit for age at onset is sufficiently broad to ensure reasonably accurate reporting within critical limits. This monograph enables those interested in a lower cut-off point to obtain that information from some of the preceding tables.

The questions used to determine age at onset took advantage of the earlier experience in the National Health Survey (Gentile, Schein, and Haase, 1965), the Washington Survey (Schein, 1965) and the pretests for the National Census of the Deaf Population. The basic question was, "How old were you when you began to have serious trouble hearing or became deaf?" This question was followed up, for those who had difficulty answering it, with alternative responses permitting an approximation. Such freedom of response was especially necessary in the mail survey. In the direct interview, the interviewers dealt directly with the respondent's uncertainty when it arose.

The age at onset of hearing impairment may differ from the age at which it became most severe. Short of obtaining detailed clinical histories of each respondent, however, the generally earlier age appears to be the most feasible compromise for survey purposes. Note also that the age given is usually the age at *awareness* of hearing impairment. This age most likely exceeds the actual onset when it is insidious. For prelingually deaf children, on the other hand, the response "born deaf" is usually based on an untested, through probably valid, assumption, because audiometric testing of neonates rarely occurs (Campanelli and Schein, 1969).

These considerations should have little effect upon the general conclusions drawn from the grouped data based on large samples. The majority of assignments to a particular category are likely to be correct. With small samples, caution should be exercised in imputing relationships to age at onset, unless extra care is used in its determination.

### The Hearing Scales

The process of defining a concept properly culminates in directing its measurement. For the NCDP, a metric was sought which would classify persons questioned by either mail or direct interview.

In preparation for a special survey of hearing in 1962-1963, a series of statements about hearing ability was designed for the National Health Survey (Schein, Gentile, and Haase, 1965). The series formed a psychological scale, in that all responses would be positive to a point beyond which all would be negative. That is, once a person denied being able to hear at one level, he would logically deny being able to hear at all levels requiring greater hearing (see Figure VIII.1). This feature is associated with unidimensionality; i.e., the scale orders hearing ability along a single dimension (Guttman, 1957). Additionally, the scale was found to be robust under several conditions of administration—individual, group and mail—and with several samples of hearing impaired persons (see Table VIII.1). However, Hearing Scale I did not cover a wide range of impairment.

In examining Hearing Scale I, you will note that only 5 of the 9 items enter into the determination of hearing ability. Items d, f, h and i are buffers whose purposes are to contribute to the context and to clarify the critical items, a, b, c, e, and g. The scale begins with the statement least apt to be denied—about the perception of loud noise—and proceeds to the more frequently disrupted ability to hear and understand speech.

## Figure VIII.1

### Hearing Scale I

---

WITHOUT using a hearing aid, what can you hear?

   a. I can hear loud noises.

   b. Most of the time I can tell one kind of noise from another.

   c. If I hear a sound most of the time I can tell if it is a person's voice or not.

*d. I can hear and understand a few words a person says if I can see his face and lips.

   e. I can hear and understand a few words a person says without seeing his face and lips.

*f. I can hear and understand most of the things a person says if I can see his face and lips.

   g. I can hear and understand most of the things a person says without seeing his face and lips.

*h. Most of the time I can hear and understand a discussion between several people without seeing their faces and lips.

*i. I can hear and understand a telephone conversation on an ordinary telephone (that is a telephone without an amplifier).

---

*Buffer items.
Source: Schein, Gentile and Haase, 1965.

# Table VIII.1

**Results of the Use of the Hearing Scale in Five Samples of
Persons with Impaired Hearing**

|  |  | Type of administration | Number of persons in sample | Percent of persons giving scaled responses |
|---|---|---|---|---|
| Sample | I, | Gallaudet students, mail interview | 214 | 91.6 |
| Sample | II, | Gallaudet students, group interview | 171 | 91.8 |
| Sample | III, | Gallaudet students, individual interview | 534 | 90.3 |
| Sample | IV, | Deaf adults from D.C. area, individual interview | 1,132 | 92.6 |
| Sample | V, | Health Interview Hearing Ability Survey respondents | 4,431 | 88.9 |

Source: Schein, Gentile, and Haase, 1965.

A second scale (Figure VIII.2) was designed in 1966 and field tested in 1967 (Schein, Gentile and Haase, 1970). The new scale, Hearing Scale II, differentiated amongst persons with lesser hearing losses. It was found to have satisfactory evidence of unidimensionality, as well as face validity (Table VIII.2). Furthermore, the various scale scores related well to audiometric measures; the average audiometric differences between groups having various scale scores are large and fairly regular, ranging from 14.6 to 20.1 dB. The standard deviations, however, show considerable overlap between scores, cautioning against use of the scale for individual assessments (Table VIII.3).

Hearing Scale II was validated with an ongoing sample 1,637 persons from 10 clinics in various parts of the United States. A sample of 1,132 households in the Philadelphia Standard Metropolitan Statistical Area was drawn for the cross-validation of the scale. The scale appeared as part of a health interview, thus testing it under conditions such as would be met in the Health Interview Survey by the National Health Survey (vide infra). Hearing thresholds for speech were gathered on a subsample of the respondents, in order to confirm the relations between scale scores and audiological measures. The results proved satisfactory.

The reader will find that the version of Hearing Scale II shown in Figure VIII.2 begins with a statement about the most acute level of hearing—a whisper, while Hearing Scale I's initial item refers to the grossest hearing—loud noises. In practice, we have found that Hearing Scale II functions as well when the questions are asked from a to g as from g to a. In the first instance questioning stops with the first yes, in the second with the first no. We use the a-g order when the respondents' anticipated hearing is good, and the g-a order when the respondents' anticipated hearing is poor. This procedure is not only more efficient, it also creates better rapport with respondents.

For survey purposes, then, Hearing Scale II provides adequate differentiation between groups. Indeed, the scale made possible the National Census of the Deaf Population. It provided the means of obtaining uniformity of definition across interviewers. By defining the target population in terms of scale scores, group membership by hearing ability can also be understood with reasonable assurance of consistency in interpretation by the reader.

## Figure VIII.2

### Hearing Scale II

---

**Instructions:** Please answer the next question the way you usually hear with both ears. If you use a hearing aid, please answer the way you hear without a hearing aid.

a.  Can you usually hear and understand what a person says without seeing his face if he whispers to you from across a quiet room?

b.  Can you usually hear and understand what a person says without seeing his face if he talks to you in a normal voice from across a quiet room?

c.  Can you usually hear and understand what a person says without seeing his face if he shouts to you from across a quiet room?

d.  Can you usually hear and understand a person if he speaks loudly into your better ear?

e.  Can you usually tell the sound of speech from other sounds and noises?

f.  Can you usually tell one kind of noise from another?

g.  Can you hear loud noises?

---

## Table VIII.2

**Number and Percent Distribution of Persons, by Scaled and Inconsistent Responses to the Hearing Ability Scale According to Sex and Hearing Aid Use: Clinic Sample**

| Sex and hearing aid use | Total | Scaled | Non-scaled incon-sistent | Total | Scaled | Non-scaled incon-sistent |
|---|---|---|---|---|---|---|
| | Number of persons | | | Percent distribution | | |
| **Both sexes** | | | | | | |
| All persons | 1,634 | 1,307 | 327 | 100.0 | 80.0 | 20.0 |
| Never used aid | 1,201 | 1,006 | 195 | 100.0 | 83.8 | 16.2 |
| Now uses aid | 240 | 148 | 92 | 100.0 | 61.7 | 38.3 |
| Formerly used aid | 193 | 153 | 40 | 100.0 | 79.3 | 20.7 |
| **Male** | | | | | | |
| All persons | 800 | 655 | 145 | 100.0 | 81.9 | 18.1 |
| Never used aid | 591 | 502 | 89 | 100.0 | 84.9 | 15.1 |
| Now uses aid | 107 | 72 | 35 | 100.0 | 67.3 | 32.7 |
| Formerly used aid | 102 | 81 | 21 | 100.0 | 79.4 | 20.6 |
| **Female** | | | | | | |
| All persons | 834 | 652 | 182 | 100.0 | 78.2 | 21.8 |
| Never used aid | 610 | 504 | 106 | 100.0 | 82.6 | 17.4 |
| Now uses aid | 133 | 76 | 57 | 100.0 | 57.1 | 42.9 |
| Formerly used aid | 91 | 72 | 19 | 100.0 | 79.1 | 20.9 |

Source: Schein, Gentile and Haase, 1970.

**Audiometric Equivalence of Scale Scores.** It is tempting to relate hearing levels for speech to each of the scale scores, but in doing so recognition must be given to the meaning of such correlation. The questions about hearing are a different means from audiometry of getting at the same entity—functional hearing ability. Hearing Scale II asks the individual to tell how he hears under particular circumstances. An audiological examination, on the other hand, presents him with pure

*138*

tones at varying degrees of loudness and asks that he indicate when he can perceive them; the resulting establishment of pure-tone thresholds at 500, 1000 and 2000 Hz yields a measure from which hearing for speech can be accurately, but not perfectly, predicted. Thus the Hearing Scale and the audiometer are both means of determining how well the individual can hear speech. They should be highly correlated, but at a level less than unity. For interpretation of the Hearing Scale scores, audiometric measures are helpful. Similarly, the Hearing Scale assists in explicating the functional meaning of a given hearing level for speech.

With these caveats in mind, the reader will note that the most likely better-ear average (BEA) for a person having a particular score on Hearing Scale II appears in Table VIII.3. For example, those having a score of 4 on Hearing Scale II (i.e., a response of No to question 4) will most likely have a BEA of 63.3 dB. These average hearing levels link the descriptions of speech discrimination to pure-tone thresholds.

## Table VIII.3

**Mean Better-Ear Average, in Decibels, and Standard Deviation for Scores on Hearing Scale II**

| Scale Score[a] | Mean Better-Ear Average in Decibels, ISO | Standard Deviation |
|---|---|---|
| 1 | 13.7 | 11.7 |
| 2 | 28.3 | 16.3 |
| 3 | 42.2 | 16.7 |
| 4 | 63.3 | 18.5 |
| 5-8 | 81.8 | 20.5 |

[a]Score refers to highest item in Hearing Scale II to which person responds Yes (see Figure VIII.2). Thus a score of 1 is assigned if a person responds Yes to item 1 (and, therefore, to all subsequent items). A score of 2 means that the respondent answered No to the first item and Yes to all remaining items. A score of 8 is given when all seven answers to the scale are negative.
Source: Schein, Gentile, and Haase, 1970.

**Age of Subjects.** The target population for the NCDP includes all ages. However, it does not follow that estimates for all ages will be uniformly good. As with most chronic impairments, prevalence of hearing loss increases dramatically with age. The lower rates for younger ages, particularly ages below three years, may reflect substantial underreporting due to the difficulty of diagnosing deafness in infants. However, detection of hearing impairment in neonates can be accomplished readily

(Campanelli and Schein, 1969), and such detection is valuable in alerting parents to the necessity for diagnostic follow-up and for early implementation of appropriate treatment. Unfortunately, infant screening for hearing impairment occurs rarely.

Across adults, age probably makes no difference to prevalence of deafness until the seventh decade (Schein, Gentile and Haase, 1965). Determining hearing loss in senile persons, of course, introduces a new set of problems associated with their debilitated condition. Responses to Hearing Scale II were found to be affected by age, in that older respondents had higher BEA's than younger persons with the same scale score, suggesting that responses about hearing ability should be qualified by the implicit phrase "for that age" (Schein, Gentile, and Haase, 1970).

Thus, age is apt to be a factor in the accuracy of estimates of deafness: estimates for the very youngest children and oldest adults will probably be associated with the most substantial errors.

**Hearing Aids.** The NCDP's definition of deafness makes no reference to hearing-aid use. By analogy to the definition of blindness, it may seem that a definition of deafness should include some mention of correction. The analogy, however, does not hold. Unlike eyeglasses, hearing aids are not as widely used by those who could benefit from them. Whereas eyeglasses are relatively inexpensive and carefree, hearing aids are expensive and require costly maintenance. Eyeglasses are prescribed; hearing aids are not. Furthermore, the hearing aid only amplifies sound; so in the case of sensorineural losses it cannot compensate for the damage to central-nervous-system tissue. Lastly, adaptation to eyeglasses is virtually instantaneous, but adaptation to hearing aids takes time and training. For these reasons, the NCDP's definition of deafness is not modified by reference to correction.

## The Survey Model for Determining Prevalence

The NCDP used a variation of the Hansen, Hurwitz and Madow (1953) model for determining the size of a rare population embedded in a larger one. This model consists of three steps:

Step 1: Compile a substantial list of those with the rare characteristic.

Step 2: In a probability sample of the general population, seek those with the rare characteristic.

Step 3: Compare those found in Step 2 with those on the list. For every rare person not on the list multiply by the sampling ratio for the general population and add the product to the list total.

The weighted sum of the elisions provides an approximation of the number of missing persons from the list. Alternatively, Step 1 and 2 provide independent estimates of the population size, and they may be combined to yield a single estimate.

This model was elaborated by Waksberg (1961) to apply specifically to surveying the deaf population. The key consideration concerns clustering; i.e., the possibility of uneven geographic distribution of deaf persons within the general population. Unlike some racial or ethnic minorities, deaf persons do not appear to reside more frequently, in a systematic fashion within particular residential areas. The NCDP, therefore, selected the more general application of the sampling model.

As a procedural matter, an addition was made to the originally prescribed steps. After compiling the list (Step 1), the NCDP verified each entry by mail. This additional step and the justification for it have been presented at length elsewhere (Schein and Delk, 1973) and are summarized below.

*List Building*

The first step was to build a list of the deaf population. Names and addresses of deaf persons were gathered from every part of the United States. To avoid duplication of effort, names of children enrolled in schools and classes for the deaf were not specifically requested, since the Annual Survey of Hearing Impaired Children and Youth (Gentile and Di Francesca, 1969) already had extensive information on this segment of the population and had agreed to make its data available to the NCDP.

The list building involved soliciting names of presumed deaf persons from two different groups: (a) the organized deaf community, such as agencies that serve deaf people and organizations for and of the deaf, and (b) sources outside the organized life of the deaf community.

The NCDP used a variety of techniques to obtain names and addresses of deaf persons. Table VIII.4 summarizes the program. Staff members met with key persons in various organizations to gain cooperation. Face-to-face encounters overcame most resistance that arose. Snowballing (asking known deaf persons for the names and addresses of other deaf persons) proved helpful. The large number of lists from organizations of deaf persons resulted from the cooperation of the deaf community's leaders, who appeared to recognize the NCDP's potential value almost as soon as they became aware of it.

Other activities to build the name list ranged from personal appearances at conventions by NCDP staff members to the distribution of posters. Articles and announcements describing the NCDP appeared in a variety of lay and professional publications. The New York State Tem-

# Table VIII.4

**Sources Contacted for Assistance in Publicizing
the National Census of the Deaf Population**

| Type of Source | Number Contacted |
|---|---|
| Sources Designed to Reach the General Population | |
| Periodical Publications | |
| Newspapers, general circulation | 1,847 |
| Newspapers, black | 27 |
| Magazines, general consumer | 76 |
| Printing trade publications (including union) | 11 |
| Other | 77 |
| Public Utilities | |
| Gas and electric power companies (using mail stuffers) | 237 |
| Gas and electric power company consumer publications | 115 |
| Telephone companies (using mail stuffers) | 28 |
| Sources Designed to Reach Persons Concerned with Hearing Impairment | |
| Clubs of the deaf | 175 |
| "Little Paper Family" (Periodical press of the deaf) | 72 |
| Conventions of organizations of deaf persons | 45 |
| President's and Governor's Committees on Employment of the Handicapped | 100 |
| Hearing aid dealers' trade publications | 3 |
| Others (including professional journals) | 47 |

porary Commission on Deafness adopted a resolution officially endorsing the NCDP, and the Mayor of Hampton, Virginia issued an endorsement of it. Arrangements were made for mention of the NCDP in utility companies' mail stuffers and for radio and television spot announcements in many parts of the country. Other procedures included direct mail contact with leaders of each state affiliate of the National Association of the Deaf to enlist their assistance. The experience of an earlier attempt at list building indicated that these diversified efforts were necessary to gathering a large representative sample of deaf persons (Schein, 1968).

One factor substantially aiding the list building was a memorandum from the commissioner of the Rehabilitation Services Administration to heads of all State vocational rehabilitation (VR) agencies. His assurance that the NCDP would maintain strict confidentiality of information given it and his urging that States cooperate undoubtedly increased the number of participating VR agencies.

**Ethnic Minorities.** Because of the concern that Black and other minority group deaf persons would be overlooked, the NCDP called together leaders of the Black community and persons familiar with Spanish-speaking and low-income deaf persons. The meeting developed a series of recommendations and led to a special effort to identify these group members (Schein and Ries, 1970). Because of the importance of enumerating ethnic and racial-minority deaf persons, the text of that report is reproduced in Appendix B.

**Results of List Building.** The NCDP's list of deaf persons grew to 440,211 by the time it was necessary to halt acceptance of new entries. The preliminary closing date for list building was December 31, 1970. At that time NCDP had a list of 383,967 persons who were presumed to be deaf. In addition, 56,244 names were received by the final closing date of April 30, 1971. A large portion of the additional names came from State VR agencies and the balance from verification questionnaires which were returned late. The results are summarized in Table VIII.5 which shows the sources of the 440,211 names and addresses. A more detailed breakdown will be found in Appendix A.

*Verification*

The verification of the name list was a variation of the Hansen, Hurwitz and Madow model. Four purposes motivated this interpolated step: (a) to remove any remaining duplications in the list after computer matching, (b) to make certain that those on the list met the criteria for inclusion in the NCDP, (c) to determine if the persons were alive as of the survey date, and (d) to affirm the correctness of their addresses or to obtain the right current address for those who had moved. This procedure also yielded basic demographic information about the deaf persons on the list.

**Pretest of Verification Questionnaire and Procedures.** The verification program was pretested in several ways, in order to detect and eliminate any inadequacies in questionnaire design or flaws in the mailing procedures. The principal pretest consisted of a mailing to 1,043 persons, distributed as follows:

1. 500 persons scattered across the nation, of whom 400 were known to be deaf and 100 were drawn at random from telephone directories;

2. 238 deaf persons in the Minneapolis-St. Paul area, a sample of whom were interviewed by the National Center for Health Statistics in pretesting the 1971 Household Interview Survey;

3. 305 persons in the State of Maryland, of whom 205 were deaf and 100 were drawn at random from Maryland telephone directories.

The pretest consisted of an original mailing of a questionnaire to all participants and two successive follow-up mailings to nonrespondents. The results of the three mailings are summarized in Table VIII.6. The original mailing brought a return of 43.7 percent. That figure may be deceptively low, as the Post Office treated some unknown, but large, number of the questionnaires as third-class mail, delaying their delivery past the pretest deadline. On the first follow-up, half the nonrespondents were sent a second questionnaire with a covering letter, half received only the questionnaire. The response rates in these two halves were increased by 29.1 and 24.4 percentage points, respectively. The second follow-up varied two conditions: (a) letter or no letter and (b) original or abbreviated form of the questionnaire. The increased response resulting from the various forms of the second follow-up ranged from 5.8 percentage points (no letter, long form) to 13.3 points (letter, short form).

## Table VIII.5

### Total Number of Names Received, by Source

| Source | Total Names |
| --- | --- |
| All Sources | 440,211 |
| Organizations of the Deaf | 76,558 |
| Schools and Classes | 73,205 |
| Department of Motor Vehicles, Deaf Drivers | 19,326 |
| Hearing and Speech Clinics | 17,518 |
| Agencies Not Classified Elsewhere | 84,333 |
| Department of Vocational Rehabilitation | 7,170 |
| Churches and Religious Organizations | 68,307 |
| Publications | 23,818 |
| Mass Appeal | 26,953 |
| Individuals | 17,892 |
| Students and Parents | 3,181 |
| Black Deaf | 3,182 |
| Snowballing (from Verification Questionnaire) | 11,602 |
| Other | 7,166 |

The response rates for the several variations in mailing procedures ranged from 73.9 to 86.1 percent. There was a statistically significant difference between the responses from deaf persons and those of hearing persons. On the original mailing, the response rate for deaf respondents was 46.4 percent, while for the random sample, ostensibly consisting mostly of hearing persons, the rate was 11.6 percent. Differences by geographic area were not statistically significant.

The pretest checked the questionnaire design as well as the mail procedures. Forty personal interviews were conducted in Silver Spring, Maryland, 65 in eastern Maryland, and 36 in Minneapolis, Minnesota. The interviews attempted to elicit misconceptions of the instructions and questions which would provide clues for redesigning the questionnaire. Some minor details in design were criticized, but the wording appeared to be unambiguous. Of the 14 percent of the interviewees who mentioned some problem in completing the form, over half complained about the type size being too small. Revision of the questionnaire took this and other criticisms into account.

The mail returns were also carefully checked for adequacy of response and internal consistency. As a final measure, the firm of Erdos and Morgan, Inc., mail-survey specialists, were retained to examine the final draft and suggest any modification that their experience suggested might improve the rate or quality of response. It is believed that the great care exercised in the design of the mail questionnaire and mailing procedures were reflected favorably in the final outcome.

Figure VIII.3a-b reproduces the questionnaire. It was printed on postcard stock edged with glue which sealed the margin when folded into an envelope. Once the responses were made, the form was ready for mailing back to the NCDP.


**Elimination of Duplication.** The preliminary closing date for the list building was December 31, 1970. At that time we had amassed 383,967 names and addresses. These data were transferred to a computer tape and processed to eliminate duplicates. The computer program for detecting duplicates performed as follows:

1. The names on the list were sorted by:
    a. zip code
    b. last name
    c. initial letter of first name
    d. sex
    e. first two characters of street address
    f. remainder of first name
    g. identification number

# Table VIII.6

**Pretest of Verification Program**

**Percent of Responses to Mailed Verification Questionnaire for Original Mailing and Two Follow-up Mailings, by Several Combinations of Procedures: National Census of the Deaf Population, 1970**

| Contents of | | | | Response Percentage | | |
|---|---|---|---|---|---|---|
| Original Mailing | First Follow-up | Second Follow-up | | Original Mailing | First Follow-up | Second Follow-up |
| Long Form | Long Form | Long Form | Percentage on this mailing | 43.7 | 24.4 | 5.8 |
| | | | Cumulative percentage | 43.7 | 68.1 | 73.9 |
| Long Form | Long Form | Short Form | Percentage on this mailing | 43.7 | 24.4 | 12.6 |
| | | | Cumulative percentage | 43.7 | 68.1 | 80.7 |
| Long Form | Long Form | Long Form with Letter | Percentage on this mailing | 43.7 | 24.4 | 12.6 |
| | | | Cumulative percentage | 43.7 | 68.1 | 80.7 |
| Long Form | Long Form with Letter | Short Form | Percentage on this mailing | 43.7 | 29.1 | 6.9 |
| | | | Cumulative percentage | 43.7 | 72.8 | 79.7 |
| Long Form | Long Form with Letter | Short Form with Letter | Percentage on this mailing | 43.7 | 29.1 | 13.3 |
| | | | Cumulative percentage | 43.7 | 72.8 | 86.1 |

2. Comparisons were made on the zip code, last name, initial letter of first name of each entry with the preceding entry. If the entries matched on these points, they were tested by the next steps below. If they did not match on these points, they were accepted as independent and entered on the master list.

3. Further comparisons were made for the first two characters of the street address and remainder of the first name. If these differed, the names were considered to be unique. If Steps 2 and 3 produced a match and the sex code was identical to the sex code of the preceding entry, the second name of the matched pair was eliminated from the list.

The computer detected 133,967 duplicates within the list of 383,967. A little over one third of the names were classified as duplicates and removed from the master list. Some duplication certainly remained in the list, nonetheless. Females who marry generally change their surnames, and the computer could not detect these redundancies. Variations in a name — Jack for John, as an example — would be treated as representing separate persons. Conversely, the computer program might incorrectly eliminate some persons; e.g., a child living at home and having the same name as the like-sexed parent. The verification procedure, however, should have rescued such names, because the questionnaire (Figure VIII.3b, item 6) asked for the names of all deaf household members. While the computer program had room for error — some built in, so as to avoid frequent elimination of valid entires — the screening for duplication would have been economically infeasible without it. The computer completed inspection and matching of the 440,369 names and addresses in less than one hour!

**The Mailing.** A master list of the 250,000 names and addresses remaining after computer processing for duplications was used to mail out verification questionnaires. The results of the mailings are shown in Table VIII.7. Of the questionnaires ostensibly delivered to the addressees, the overall response rate was 73 percent — a figure close to the 80 percent anticipated on the basis of the pretest. The "return rate," which includes questionnaires returned by the Post Office as undeliverable, was 77 percent for the three mailings combined. The relatively small proportion of incorrect addresses (39,643 of 250,000, or 16 percent) suggests that the sources of names and addresses provided good, up-to-date information.

In May, 1972, after receiving long-promised additional names (largely from California) and screening them for duplication, a supplementary mailing of 41,248 was made. The return from this mailing totalled 21,500 including 15,212 completed questionnaires and 6,288 undeliverable, making a return rate of 52 percent. Had funds been available for the two

# Figure VIII.3a

## Mail Form Used in Verification Phase

---

**YOUR HELP NEEDED IN FIRST CENSUS**
**OF DEAF PEOPLE IN FORTY YEARS !**

If there is a mistake in your name or address, print your correct name and address here:

FIRST          MIDDLE          LAST

STREET No.          STREET

CITY          STATE          ZIP

### WHAT TO DO IF YOU RECEIVE MORE THAN ONE QUESTIONNAIRE:

1. Fill out **one** questionnaire completely.

2. On the extra questionnaires check this box.

   EXTRA QUESTIONNAIRE ☐

3. Return **all** questionnaires to the Census.

Dear Friend:

This form is an important part of the first census of deaf people in 40 years, and the results will help in the planning of future services. Please help to supply the needed information.

The Census must know the hearing ability of every person to whom a form is addressed. Even if the person to whom this form is addressed is **NOT DEAF,** the form should be completed for him or her.

Some deaf children will be counted at the school or class they attend, some at home. If this form is addressed to the child's home, do not change the address to show the school address.

If you receive more than one questionnaire. **PLEASE READ INSTRUCTIONS AT TOP OF THIS PAGE.**

Those concerned with deafness realize how little is known about deaf persons in the United States. We hope that all citizens will cooperate with the Census.

**NOW PLEASE ANSWER THE QUESTIONS ON THE OTHER SIDE OF THIS FORM.**

**SPECIAL NOTE TO PARENTS OF HEARING IMPAIRED CHILDREN**—If this form is addressed to you. please do not fill it out for your hearing impaired child. The Census needs to know about your hearing ability.

Postage Will be Paid by Addressee

No Postage Stamp Necessary If Mailed in the United States

**B U S I N E S S   R E P L Y   M A I L**
First Class Permit No. 39482—Washington, D.C.

NATIONAL CENSUS OF THE DEAF
P. O. BOX 9041
WASHINGTON, D.C.   20003

# Figure VIII.3b

## Mail Form Used in Verification Phase

---

### NATIONAL CENSUS OF THE DEAF

All information received is kept **confidential.** Names and address will not be published or used for any purpose except for the census. Please print.

---

Please give the following information about the person **to whom this form is addressed:**

A. NAME

`12-19` FIRST          `20-23` MIDDLE (Maiden, if married)          `24` LAST

B. BIRTHDATE
`44-45` Month          `46-47` Day          `48-49` Year

C. `50` SEX

D. SOCIAL SECURITY
`51-59` NUMBER (if any)

E. `60` COLOR OR RACE

`1` ☐ Male     `2` ☐ Female

`1` ☐ White  - ☐ Negro or Black

`3` ☐ Spanish-American (Puerto Rican, Mexican-American)

`4-7` ☐ Other: which?

---

**PLEASE ANSWER QUESTIONS ABOUT HEARING FOR THE WAY YOU HEAR WITHOUT A HEARING AID.**

1. Please tell how well you hear by marking **ONE** of the statements below for **EACH** ear.

   `61` a. **IN LEFT EAR (without hearing aid)**
   `1` ☐ My hearing is good.
   `2` ☐ I have a little trouble hearing.
   `3` ☐ I have a lot of trouble hearing.
   `4` ☐ I am deaf.

   `62` b. **IN RIGHT EAR (without hearing aid)**
   `1` ☐ My hearing is good.
   `2` ☐ I have a little trouble hearing.
   `3` ☐ I have a lot of trouble hearing.
   `4` ☐ I am deaf.

2. Be sure to answer **every** question **either** yes or no. Answer the way you hear **without a hearing aid.**

   `64` a. Can you usually **hear and understand** what a person says without seeing his face if that person whispers to you from across a quiet room?  `1` ☐ Yes   ☐ No

   b. Can you usually **hear and understand** what a person says without seeing his face if that person talks in a normal voice to you from across a quiet room?  `2` ☐ Yes   ☐ No

   c. Can you usually **hear and understand** what a person says without seeing his face if that person shouts to you from across a quiet room?  `3` ☐ Yes   ☐ No

   d. Can you usually **hear and understand** a person if that person speaks loudly into your better ear?  `4` ☐ Yes   ☐ No

   e. Can you usually tell the sound of speech from other sounds and noises?  `5` ☐ Yes   ☐ No

   f. Can you usually tell one kind of noise from another?  `6` ☐ Yes   ☐ No

   g. Can you hear loud noises?  `7` ☐ Yes   `8` ☐ No

3a. How old were you when you began to have serious trouble hearing or became deaf?
`66`
   `1` ☐ At birth
   `2` ☐ Less than 1 year old
   `3` ☐ I was about ............ years of age. `67-68`
   `3` ☐ I'm not sure. (See 3b.)

   b. I'm not sure, but I was:
   `4` ☐ Less than 6 years old
   `5` ☐ Between 6 and 11 years old
   `6` ☐ Between 12 and 18 years old
   `7` ☐ 19 years old or over
   `8` ☐ I don't have serious trouble hearing and I am not deaf.

4. Are you **now** a student at a school or in a class for those with hearing problems, or a school or class for the deaf?
`69`   `1` ☐ Yes     `2` ☐ No (go to question 5)
   If yes, what is the name of the school?............................................................
   In what city and state is it located?............................................................
   CITY          STATE

5a. Are you **now:**
`70`   `1` ☐ Married   `2` ☐ Widowed   `3` ☐ Divorced   `4` ☐ Separated   `5` ☐ Never Married

   b. `71` If you are **now** married, which of the following best describes your husband's (or wife's) hearing **without a hearing aid?**
   `1` ☐ His (or her) hearing is good.
   `2` ☐ He (or she) has a little trouble hearing.
   `3` ☐ He (or she) has a lot of trouble hearing.
   `4` ☐ He (or she) is deaf.

6. If there are any deaf people **living in your home** who have not received a form like this one, please write their full names and ages here.
`72`
   Name........................................................ Age............
   Name........................................................ Age............
   Name........................................................ Age............

It is extremely important that this form be returned immediately.  THANK YOU FOR YOUR COOPERATION
**Fold top third of form down; moisten seal below; firmly attach; no postage required.**

---

# Table VIII.7

## Response Rate for Original and Two Follow-up Mailings: National Census of the Deaf Population, 1971

| | Original Mailing | | First Follow-up | | Second Follow-up | | All Mailings | |
|---|---|---|---|---|---|---|---|---|
| | Number | Percent | Number | Percent | Number | Percent | Number | Percent |
| **Mailout** | 250,000 | 100 | 129,761 | 100 | 76,727 | 100 | — | — |
| **Return** | 120,239 | 48 | 53,034 | 41 | 20,002 | 26 | 193,275 | 77[a] |
| **Response** | 91,097 | 41 | 46,011 | 37 | 16,524 | 23 | 153,632 | 73[b] |

[a]Percent based on original mailing of 250,000
[b]Percent based on original mailing less 39,643 returned by Post Office as undeliverable.

planned follow-up mailings, it is reasonable to estimate that the return would have been increased by about 20 percent, yielding more than 8,000 additional names. Unfortunately, budgetary limitations forced abandonment of plans for the customary follow-ups.

The Post Office returned 45,931 (including the May mailing) as undeliverable because of incorrect addresses or lack of forwarding addresses. To determine whether any significant number of these represented errors by Post Office clerks, a small sample of 125 were remailed. Only four were not returned a second time; presumably they were delivered to the addressee. It was concluded that the likely error rate (3 to 4 percent) was too small to justify the added costs of remailing the entire 45,931.

**The Verified List.** Of the 291,248 questionnaires mailed, 214,775 were returned — 168,844 completed by the addressees (Table VIII.8). About 40 percent of the completed questionnaires were from persons whose responses met the criteria for prevocational deafness. These names were then cross-checked by the Annual Survey of Hearing Impaired Children and Youth, and the unduplicated deaf children from their records added to the verified list. The final compilation came to 98,448. We believe this register to be the largest confirmed list of persons having the same disability so far assembled. Indisputably, the nearly 100,000 entries constitute the biggest roster of deaf persons ever gathered.

## Table VIII.8

**Summary of List Building and Mail Verification:
National Census of the Deaf Population, 1971**

| | |
|---|---|
| Total Names and Addresses Received | 440,211 |
| Duplicates Eliminated by Computer | 148,963 |
| Total Number of Questionnaires Mailed | 291,248 |
| Total Return | 214,775 |
| Questionnaires Returned by Addressee | 168,844 |
| Questionnaires Returned by Post Office as Undeliverable | 45,931 |
| Questionnaires Not Returned | 76,473 |

## Obtaining an Independent Estimate of Deafness

Once the list size has been determined, the next question was What proportion of all deaf persons is on the list? In other words this question asked how complete is the list and, hence, what is the size of the deaf population. Step 2 of the survey design endeavored to answer this question by obtaining an independent estimate of prevocational deafness from a sample of the population.

Essentially, to obtain the estimate would require drawing a national sample of the United States and inquiring about the hearing of each sample person. The cost of such a survey, however, would be extremely high. To keep costs within the NCDP budget and yet to attain a large enough sample of the population to provide a stable estimate, we decided to "piggy back" this survey on an existing one. After lengthly negotiations, the National Center for Health Statistics agreed to expand the 1971 National Health Survey to include the NCDP's questions in the extensive schedule of items about health—an appropriate context for the items on hearing ability.

The National Health Survey was established by Congress to gather information every year about the health of the nation. In the Health Interview Survey, interviews are conducted annually in a carefully drawn national sample of 42,000 households, containing about 134,000 persons. This sample size approximates that of Design 2 in Appendix C.

A more detailed description of the sampling plan for the 1971 Health Interview Survey (HIS '71) appears in Appendix D. The multistage, stratified sample used by the National Health Survey has many advantages, combining precision and economy. For the NCDP, the major advantage pertained to the extensive coverage of the United States afforded by the HIS sample.

**HIS '71 Interview.** During the calendar year 1971, interviewers from the U.S. Bureau of the Census visited about 800 households each week. Among the questions they asked were the screening questions "Does anyone in the family *now* have . . .

"(a) Deafness in one or both ears?
"(b) Any other trouble hearing with one or both ears?
"(c) Tinnitus or ringing in the ears?"

For every household member for whom a yes response was given to any of these screening questions, the interviewer asked the (a) Hearing Scale II, (b) rating for each ear and (c) age at onset of hearing impairment. These questions were identical to those used by the NCDP to determine if a person was prevocationally deaf. The health interview also gathered the usual demographic information—age, sex, race, marital

*152*

status, etc.—plus data about chronic and acute illnesses, physician visits, hospitalization, etc.

**List Comparisons.** To fulfill the third step of the model, the deaf persons found by HIS '71 had to be checked against the NCDP verified list. This critical maneuver required careful data processing by computer. Because the National Health Survey is forbidden by law to release any information about the individuals in its samples, it did the computer processing.[1]

The results of the computer matching appear in Table VIII.9. Of the 253 prevocationally deaf persons in the HIS '71 sample, 53 were matched with persons on the NCDP verified list. The 200 unmatched cases represented the portion of the prevocationally deaf persons not on the verified list. Since every person in HIS '71 represents a portion of the United States population, the number of prevocationally deaf persons in the population can be estimated by multiplying each sample person by the applicable sampling weight. The sample weight derives from the probability of a person being in the sample. In general, the HIS '71 sample contains 1 out of every 1,500 people in the United States—a probability of selection equal to 1/1500. However, a particular household's members may have a greater or lesser probability of selec-

## Table VIII.9

**Results of Matching of Lists of Prevocationally Deaf Persons Found
by the Health Interview Survey 1971 to Those on the Verified List
of the National Census of the Deaf Population**

| List | Number<br>Prevocationally Deaf Persons |
|------|----------------------------------------|
| Health Interview Survey 1971 | 253[a] |
| National Census of the Deaf Population | 98,448 |
| Both lists | 53 |

[a]The HIS '71 list contained 134,000 names of which 253 met the criteria for prevocational deafness.

---

[1]Of course, the NCDP also could not reveal any information about persons in its files. However, being a nongovernmental agency, the NCDP could more easily straddle the administrative hurdles. Only the computer "read" the two complete lists. Following the reading, the computer's memory was cleansed of the data from the NCDP and HIS files. Thus no person other than NCDP employees could learn a name from the list. Only employees of the two organizations had access to the data on a day-to-day basis, and they all swore oaths of confidentiality as a condition of employment (see sample oath in Figure VIII.4).

tion because of the manner in which the sample was selected. Therefore, each individual had a sample weight reflecting the portion of the population he represented.[2]

*Results of Estimation Procedures*

The above procedures each produced figures which, when combined, yielded the estimate of the total prevocationally deaf population—410,522. The components of that estimate are shown in Table VIII.10. To the verified list containing 72,458 persons must be added the unduplicated portion of the Annual Survey's roster, 25,990. This total of 98,448 is then added to the estimate derived from HIS '71 of prevocationally deaf persons not on the combined lists. The result is the total estimate of the prevocationally deaf population.

The numerical outcome of each of the steps in the survey model appear in Table VIII.11. The list-building efforts brought in 440,211 names and addresses of deaf persons. After computer matching, the list was refined to 291,248. Following mail verification, 72,458 prevocationally deaf persons remained. The unduplicated names from the Annual Survey of Hearing Impaired Children and Youth's roster brought the verified total to 98,448. These persons were added to HIS '71's estimate of the prevocationally deaf population *not* on the verified list. The total, then, is made up of an actual count of persons identified by NCDP (98,448) plus an estimated number of additional persons (312,074). This combination of actual and estimated amounts is the essence of the survey model

## Table VIII.10

**Estimated Total Prevocationally Deaf Population by Components of Estimate: National Census of the Deaf Population, 1971**

| Component | Estimate |
|---|---|
| All Components | 410,522 |
| National Health Survey (HIS '71) | 312,074 |
| Annual Survey of Hearing Impaired Children and Youth | 25,990 |
| NCDP Verified List | 72,458 |

[2]For a discussion of weighting, see Hansen, Hurwitz and Madow (1953) or similar statistical text.

*154*

used. As discussed in Chapter II, a smaller standard error attaches itself to the estimate derived in this way than from a survey alone, because the identified portion has no error assignable to it. Thus the standard error of the 410,522 is only 6.3 percent, a relatively small amount of expected sampling variability.

## Survey of Characteristics of Prevocationally Deaf Adults

The second objective of the NCDP was to determine the principal characteristics of the prevocationally deaf population, the first objective being to determine its size. Selecting the general areas of inquiry occupied a number of experts in several conferences. Choosing the specific questions and arranging their wording was the responsibility of the NCDP staff.

**Questionnaire Design.** The questionnaire for the direct interviews consisted of three forms (See Appendix D). Form A contained questions of a general nature concerning the deaf person's household. Each

## Table VIII.11

**Numbers of Prevocationally Deaf Persons in Each Step of the Estimation Process and Total Estimated Population Derived from the Survey Model: National Census of the Deaf Population, 1971.**

| Steps | Numbers of Prevocationally Deaf Persons |
|---|---|
| 1. Compile a list of deaf persons | 440,211 |
| 1a. Eliminate duplications by computer processing | 291,248 |
| 1b. Verify list | 72,458 |
| 1c. Add Annual Survey of Hearing Impaired Children unduplicated portion | 25,990 |
| 1d. Total unduplicated, verified list | 98,448 |
| 2. Derive an independent estimate of deafness—HIS '71 | 312,074 |
| 3. Combine list plus unduplicated portion from HIS '71 to obtain total prevocationally deaf population. | 410,522 |

prevocationally deaf adult household member was then asked the questions in Form B. The categories of information obtained are outlined in Table VIII.12.

Form A established the household members, their age, sex, marital status, race, and relation to the head of the household. Some items relating to the whole family were asked; such as, total income, possession of a phone, home tenure, etc. Questions concerning hearing ability and age at the onset of hearing loss, if any existed, were asked to determine which household members met the criteria established for the study's target population.

In addition to the questions asked of the household members, the neighborhood in which the household was located was rated on a seven-point scale. The interviewer also assessed the communication ability of the deaf respondent.

Form B was administered only to members of the household who met the criteria for deafness. The schedule of questions covers (a) education and training, (b) occupation and recent work history, (c) modes of communication, (d) personal health and disability, (e) needs for various services, (f) experience with vocational rehabilitation.

The interviewers asked the questions on Form C when a child was absent from the household, usually having grown and left home. The responses established the age, sex and hearing status of the offspring —data necessary for the section on fertility and family composition.

Considerable attention was given to the wording of individual questions and to the order of their presentation. To test not only the questionnaire for the interview but also the interviewing procedures in general, several pretests were conducted. Two preliminary pretests were organized, one in Washington, D.C. and the other in New York City. Following these trials and further revision of the questionnaire and its accompanying Interviewer's Manual, a full field test was carried out in Prince George's County, Maryland. In each case interviewers were given intensive training in the use of the questionnaire. The pretests covered a total of 112 deaf persons. Census staff members accompanied and observed the interviewers during one fourth of the interviews in order to identify any problems at first hand.

*Sample Selection for Characteristics Survey*

Of the likely alternatives, direct sampling of the verified list was chosen for the survey of characteristics. The first three digits of the zip code provided a convenient primary sampling unit (PSU). Using geographical region and community size to stratify the PSU's Mr. Reuben Cohen, the NCDP statistician, established 70 groups of regions contain-

# Table VIII.12

**Categories of Information Obtained from Household Interviews with a Sample of Prevocationally Deaf Adults, in 1972.**

---

**For All Household Members**

I.   Housing
    A. Place of Residence
    B. Type of housing
    C. Home tenure
    D. Interviewer evaluation of
        neighborhood

II.   Demographic Characteristics
    A. Relation to head of household
    B. Sex
    C. Age
    D. Marital status
    E. Race

III.   Hearing Ability. If abnormal,
      ask:
    A. Degree
    B. Age at onset
    C. Cause
    D. Use of hearing aid

IV.   Education

V.   Labor Force Status
    A. Major activity
    B. Occupation
    C. Industry in which employed

VI.   Income
    A. Total family income
    B. Income from public assistance

**For Each Target (Deaf) Adult**

VII.   Education and Training
    A. Age at entry to school
    B. Highest grade completed
    C. Types of schools attended

VIII.  Occupation and work experience
    A. Labor force status
    B. How obtained present job
    C. Communication at work
    D. Supervisory relations
    E. Ten-year work history
    F. Labor union relations
    G. Individual Earnings

IX.   Communication
    A. To others and by others
    B. Self and interviewer ratings of
       abilities
    C. Where learned manual
       communication
    D. Telephone/TTY in home

X.   Health
    A. Other illnesses
    B. Other disabilities
    C. Unmet health needs and
       knowledge of community
       resources

XI.   Insurance Problems

XII.  Experience with Departments of
       Vocational Rehabilitation

XIII. Mobility
    A. Geographical
    B. Intergenerational

---

ing known deaf persons (see Table VIII.13). The complete zip code then allowed for additional clustering of target addresses.

There was some concern about whether available budget would be adequate to cover the desired number of interviews. This brought with it the danger that after field interviewing began funds would be exhausted. In such a case, the interviews gathered would likely be unrepresentative. To forestall such a contingency, Mr. Cohen devised a sequential sampling plan to protect the integrity of the sample. The total desired sample was divided into five interviewing phases. The first phase subsample was selected so that when that part of the work was completed it would be a representative national sample. As resources permitted, additional interviews would be made to bring up the total number. These additional interviews, being drawn from subsequent phases, would be entirely comparable to the first subsample in all necessary characteristics.

Sample phases A and B provided a starting base of approximately 1,500 household interviews, plus 150 supplemental households to include a nonwhite subsample. To this was added an oversample to allow for error and noninterviews. The final sample consisted of 1,838 prevocationally deaf adults. In addition to being geographically distributed (by zip code areas), the sample was stratified by age, sex, race, age at onset of deafness, and marital status.

With respect to the target person, the decision was made to restrict the age range from 16 to 65 years. Information about younger and older deaf persons in a household containing a target person would be limited to the first set of items shown in Table VIII.12 and labelled "For All Household Members." Thus, the survey sample was of prevocationally deaf adults, 16 to 65 years of age, with supplementary information only on older and younger deaf persons.

*Interviewers*

Interviewing placed an unusual burden on this study. Interviewers had to be bilingual; that is, able to communicate both orally in English and manually in the American Sign Language. Moreover, they had to understand the language handicaps suffered by many deaf persons.

**Recruiting Interviewers.** In selecting the interviewers, the census staff had to strike a balance among many factors: availability of personnel, training cost, travel costs and supervisory expenses. The qualifications for a census interviewer were:

Able to communicate well in American Sign Language and in spoken English,
Possession of a high school education or higher,
Availability of an automobile for personal use,

# Table VIII.13

**Distribution of Primary Sampling Units for the National Census of the Deaf Population Household Interview and Location of Interviewer Training Centers**

AREA 1.   Training Center:
               **New York City**

| 11 | Boston, Mass. |
| 13 | Willimantic, Conn. |
| 14 | Providence, R. I. |
| 16 | Manhattan & Staten Island, N.Y. |
| 17 | Westchester Co., N. Y. |
| 18 | Brooklyn, N. Y. |
| 19 | Brooklyn, N. Y. |
| 20 | Long Island, N. Y. |
| 23 | Northern New Jersey |

AREA 2.   Training Center:
               **Silver Spring**

| 12 | Sunbury, Penna. |
| 21 | Philadelphia, Penna. |
| 27 | Lakewood, N. J. |
| 51 | Washington, D. C. |
| 52 | Maryland Suburbs of D. C. |
| 53 | Virginia Suburbs of D. C. |
| 54 | Wilmington, Del. |
| 55 | Richmond, Va. |

AREA 3.   Training Center:
               **Atlanta**

| 56 | Bluefield, W. Va. |
| 57 | Asheville, N. C. |
| 58 | Wilmington, N. C. |
| 59 | Tampa, Fla. |
| 60-61 | Atlanta, Ga. |
| 62 | Decatur, Ala. |
| 63 | Montgomery, Ala. |
| 64 | Knoxville, Tenn. |

AREA 4.   Training Center:
               **Dallas**

| 71 | Clinton, Okla. |
| 72 | McAllen, Tex. |
| 73 | Austin, Tex. |
| 74 | Oklahoma City, Okla. |
| 75 | Tulsa, Okla. |
| 76 | Dallas, Tex. |
| 77 | Dallas, Tex. |

AREA 5.   Training Center:
               **Milwaukee**

| 28 | Columbus, Ohio |
| 29 | Chicago, Ill. |
| 30 | Chicago, Ill. |
| 31 | Chicago, Ill. |
| 35 | Milwaukee, Wisc. |
| 37 | Champaign, Ill. |
| 38 | Green Bay, Wisc. |
| 39 | Madison, Wisc. |
| 42 | Indianapolis, Ind. |
| 43 | Indianapolis, Ind. |

AREA 6.   Training Center:
               **San Francisco**

| 81 | Pocatello, Idaho |
| 91 | Los Angeles, Calif. |
| 92 | Los Angeles, Calif. |
| 93 | San Francisco, Calif. |
| 94 | Spokane, Wash. |
| 95 | Portland, Ore. |
| 96 | San Diego, Calif. |

AREA 7.   Training Center:
               **Cleveland**

| 22 | Pittsburgh, Penna. |
| 24 | Buffalo, N. Y. |
| 25 | Rochester, N. Y. |
| 26 | Erie, Penna. |
| 32 | Detroit, Mich. |
| 33 | Detroit, Mich. |
| 34 | Cleveland, Ohio |
| 36 | Iron Mountain, Mich. |
| 40 | Flint, Mich. |
| 41 | Youngstown, Ohio |

AREA 8.   Training Center:
               **Kansas City**

| 44 | Omaha, Neb. |
| 45 | St. Louis, Mo. |
| 46 | Minneapolis-St. Paul, Minn. |
| 47 | Kansas City, Kans. |
| 48 | North Platte, Neb. |
| 49 | St. Cloud, Minn. |
| 50 | Topeka, Kans. |
| 65 | Louisville, Ky. |
| 82 | Colorado Springs, Colo. |
| 83 | Denver, Colo. |

Freedom to be away from home overnight,
Available for interviewing at least 20 hours a week for 3 months.

To identify persons who met the above qualifications, each state chapter of the National Association of the Deaf was asked to recommend potential interviewers. Also the Registry of Interpreters for the Deaf was asked to identify a sizable number of potential interviewers. In selected areas, knowledgable individuals were contacted for supplementary leads.

An ad hoc selection committee was formed to aid in choosing the interviewers. The selection committee prepared guidelines which eased any pressures favoring a particular local candidate, while ensuring highly qualified interviewers for this specialized task.

Each potential interviewer had two interviews with a member of the NCDP staff. The first was an interview by telephone (using voice or teletype attachment) to assure that the person met all of the qualifications and was interested in interviewing. The second was a personal interview to evaluate communication ability and attitudes about the survey and its potential respondents.

**Training.** The training program was relatively intensive since the trainees were not familiar with the requirements of research interviewing. The 70 primary sampling units were clustered into eight geographic areas. One city within each of the areas was designated as the training center (see Table VIII.13).

Eight separate training sessions were held. Each session lasted about four days and included from 7 to 10 trainees. A training manual was prepared so that every training meeting was conducted uniformly over all eight sets of sessions. An interviewer's manual was prepared and its contents were validated in the full field test. The interviewer's manual was divided into four parts: Part 1 discussed how the NCDP was being conducted; part 2 gave general interviewing instructions, and parts 3 and 4 covered in detail the information each question was intended to elicit and the procedure for asking and recording information (see Appendix E).

The trainees were first introduced to the questionnaire and the field procedures in lectures, followed by a less formal question-and-answer period. Following these sessions the trainees practiced by interviewing the trainers. Each trainee then reviewed the sections of the interviewer's manual for the material covered in that session.

The trainees finally conducted an interview with a deaf person observed by an NCDP trainer before being judged qualified for the field. All persons who went through the training session did not become interviewers. Only the trainees who demonstrated in the observed inter-

## Figure VIII.4

**THE NATIONAL CENSUS OF THE DEAF POPULATION**
**CONFIDENTIALITY OATH**

I do solemnly swear that I will not reveal or discuss with anyone outside of this office any details of any individual's responses to questionnaires administered or processed by this office; nor will I discuss or reveal any information about any individual which is made known to me through the research activities of this office. I understand that failure to abide by this oath shall constitute grounds for my immediate dismissal; and I further understand that unlawful disclosure of such information is also punishable by law.

DATE:_____ SIGNED: _____

WITNESSED BY: _____

---

view that they were capable of conducting interviews rapidly and without error became interviewers.

**Oath of Confidentiality.** To emphasize the importance of keeping all information confidential the trainers formally administered the Oath of Confidentiality to all successful candidates at the conclusion of training meetings (see Figure VIII.4). Interviewers signed individual oaths which were placed in their personnel files in the central office.

**Course of the Interview.** Interviewers attempted to conduct the interview with the assigned deaf person. When that was not possible, a household member 16 years of age or older was accepted as informant. The interview was conducted in whatever form of communication was best understood by the respondent—signs, fingerspelling, speech. As a further aid to communication, questions were printed on flash cards. The interviewer displayed these cards at the appropriate point in the interview. The length of time needed to complete an interview varied widely from as little as 20 minutes to over 2 hours, depending on such factors as size of household, age of target person, and personality of respondent. The average interview, not counting travel time, was about one hour. At no time did NCDP emphasize speed in obtaining an interview. The supervisors stressed the importance of obtaining complete, accurate data.

*161*

## Figure VIII.5

**Postal Card Mailed to NCDP Respondents
Following Their Interview**

**B U S I N E S S    R E P L Y    M A I L**
First Class Permit No. 1560 – Silver Spring, MD.

NATIONAL  CENSUS OF THE DEAF

814    THAYER  AVENUE

SILVER SPRING,  MARYLAND 20910

1. About how long did the interview last? _____

2. How many people live with you in your apartment or house?

   _____

3. How would you rate the interviewer who called on you?

   ☐ Very Satisfactory
   ☐ Satisfactory
   ☐ Not Satisfactory

4. Do you have any comments you'd like to make about the
   interview or the interviewer who called on you?

   _____
   _____
   _____
   _____

**Supervision of the Interviewers.** As soon as the first few examples of the interviewer's work were received in the central office, a staff member called on the telephone (voice or TTY) to discuss with the interviewer what problems he may have had, what progress was being made, schedules of work, etc. Whenever there were errors, these were discussed and the interviewer instructed in the correct procedures. The interviewer was also informed about difficulties with the questionnaires which appeared common to many interviewers.

As a further check on the interviews, a follow-up card was sent to respondent after every completed interview. This follow-up card validated the length of the interview and the number of persons in the household. It also asked the respondent to rate the interviewer (see Figure VIII.5).

At every step in the interviewing phase, close contact was maintained with the interviewers. In some few cases, despite the constant assistance, interviewers were unable to complete their assignments satisfactorily and they were replaced. The various checks by the home office helped to overcome the lack of local field supervision. The telephone consultations especially worked smoothly; continuity was maintained by direct discussion between the interviewers and some of the same people who had done the interviewer training.

**Quality of Interviews.** The interviews were conducted by 58 persons selected because of their skills in communicating with deaf persons. Seven of the interviewers were themselves deaf, the remaining 51 had normal hearing.

The ratings by the persons interviewed provided one measure of interviewer quality. A respondent who rates an interview as unsatisfactory is less apt to provide full, candid responses than one who rates the interview as satisfactory or very satisfactory. Table VIII.14 summarizes the respondents' evaluations. Overall, less than one percent of the respondents rated the interviews unsatisfactory. Considering the numbers of interviewers and the variety of respondents, this result accords high praise to the interviewers. Incidentally, in less than 1 in 100 cases was a card returned indicating the interview had not taken place. In each of the 7 such instances it was subsequently learned that the interview was completed but the person completing the card was unaware of it.

Deaf interviewers did as well as hearing interviewers; the small discrepancy of deaf male interviewers from the overall ratings not being statistically significant. Females, however, received more praise than males, regardless of hearing ability. This finding accords with the general finding in interview surveys that females have an easier time gaining access to homes, are less threatening, and establish rapport more easily.

## Table VIII.14

Percent Distribution of Respondents' Evaluations of Interview, by Sex and Hearing Ability of Interviewers: National Census of the Deaf Population, 1972.

| Sex and Hearing Ability | Respondents' Evaluations | | | |
|---|---|---|---|---|
| | Total | Very Satisfactory | Satisfactory | Unsatisfactory |
| All Interviewers | 100.0 | 70 | 29 | 1 |
| Deaf | 100.0 | 68 | 29 | 3 |
| Males | 100.0 | 62 | 33 | 5 |
| Females | 100.0 | 74 | 25 | 1 |
| Normal Hearing | 100.0 | 70 | 29 | 1 |
| Males | 100.0 | 67 | 32 | 1 |
| Females | 100.0 | 72 | 27 | 1 |

The difference in ratings received by males and females, it should be noted, is relatively small.

**Completion Rate.** The interviewers succeeded in completing 1,476 interviews (80.5 percent). Deaf interviewers attained virtually the same completion rate as hearing interviewers (Table VIII.15). Again, however, females had a higher completion rate than males. In a way, this disparity also reflects interviewer quality. The female interviewers may not only have been more persistent, they may also have been able to overcome resistance to being interviewed more readily than were the male interviewers.

Designing a representative sample does not assure that the completed sample will be representative. For a variety of reasons, the interviews cannot all be conducted. Table VIII.16 summarizes the reasons interview assignments were not fulfilled in the NCDP. Of the 368 unconsummated interviews, nearly half involved a target person who had moved. For 119 target persons, no forwarding address could be obtained despite repeated efforts. In such cases, the interviewer at least contacted neighbors in adjacent dwelling units in an attempt to locate the missing person. Seventeen respondents had moved to other PSU's, but they were not contacted because the interviewer in the new area had completed his or her assignments by the time the new assignment could be made. The remaining 37 persons had moved outside the geographical sampling areas.

*164*

The next most common reason for failing to conduct an interview was absence of the target person at the time the interviewer arrived. Interviewers attempted a variety of stratagems: writing or calling for appointments, meeting respondents at convenient locations, calling at different times of the day, etc. In 66 cases, these attempts proved unsuccessful.

Fifty target persons became ineligible after they were drawn for the sample: 12 died and 24 institutionalized. The remaining 14 joined a household—mostly through marriage—containing another target person. Information in these cases was limited to that gathered for other household members.

Refusal to cooperate rarely occurred. Only 33 persons (less than 2 percent of the assignments) would not permit an interview. Forty-six other cases were lost due to a variety of reasons, including 9 judged uneconomical to obtain because they were located too far from the interviewer's home base.

Overall, the completion rate appears large enough to satisfy statistical requirements. The loss of interviews does not appear to be due to factors apt to seriously bias the resulting sample. Table VIII.17 summarizes the results of the interviewing. Of the 1,834 assignments, 1,476 resulted in valid interviews, a completion rate of 80.5 percent. When the base is reduced by the number found to be ineligible, the rate becomes 82.7 percent. Finally, if persons who could not be located are eliminated, the completion rate is 88.6 percent—a satisfactorily high figure for a nationwide survey.

## Table VIII.15

**Number of Interviews Assigned and Completed, and Completion Rates, by Sex and Hearing Ability of Interviewers: National Census of the Deaf Population, 1972.**

| Sex and Hearing Ability | Interviews | | |
| --- | --- | --- | --- |
| | Assigned | Completed | Completion Rate |
| All Interviewers | 1,834 | 1,476 | 80.5 |
| Deaf | 347 | 276 | 79.5 |
| Males | 172 | 131 | 76.2 |
| Females | 175 | 145 | 82.9 |
| Normal Hearing | 1,487 | 1,200 | 80.7 |
| Males | 654 | 503 | 76.9 |
| Females | 833 | 697 | 83.7 |

# Table VIII.16

**Reasons for not Completing Interviews in the Household Survey of Characteristics of Prevocationally Deaf Adults: National Census of the Deaf Population, 1972.**

| Reason for Noninterview | | Frequency |
|---|---|---|
| All noninterviews | | 358 |
| Respondent moved: | | 173 |
| unable to locate new address | 119 | |
| to another PSU not reassigned | 17 | |
| to an area outside PSU's | 37 | |
| Unable to contact after three call backs or because known to be gone during interviewing period (e.g., on vacation) | | 66 |
| Respondent ineligible | | 50 |
| became part of another eligible household | 14 | |
| institutionalized | 24 | |
| deceased | 12 | |
| Respondent refused to be interviewed | | 33 |
| Other reasons | | 36 |

**Processing the Questionnaire.** Since the reliability and credibility of the survey will in the final analysis depend on the accuracy of interpretation, as well as the initial accuracy of gathering the interview data, it was necessary to carefully oversee the coding process. In the early stages of code development an ongoing sample check was made of the coded interviews for the purpose of discovering the difficulties and faults of the code categories and their application. Inconsistencies of interpretation by two different coders were analyzed to learn whether the difficulty lay in the actual coding instructions or were simply due to inadequate training or insufficient experience on the part of the coding clerks. When the codes and their usage were agreed upon so that coding proceeded in a consistent fashion, then the checking procedure was employed to a different end.

When the final revision of the coding instructions had been written, a complete check (as opposed to the sample check) was made of the coding of each and every questionnaire before code sheets were sent for keypunching. This time the checking was for the purpose of quality control, and was done by having the checker duplicate the steps involved in coding the particular interview. In this procedure all interviews were gone over as if they were being coded for the first time. In no instance were coders assigned the checking of their own coded material. The review was always supposed to be done by a different coder. The coding staff varied in size from time to time, but the group of six persons who were on hand during most of the coding stage provided sufficient flexibility so that these differentiated responsibilities were possible.

The staff for the editing, coding and checking operations had to be chosen with care. Some of the tasks involved especially the final checking, could be at the same time repetitious and demanding, sometimes to the point of boredom and frustration with the consequences of indifference and carelessness. A statistical clerk who had the ability to be thoroughly conscientious on routine work might not have had the

## Table VIII.17

**Rates of Interviews and Noninterviews and Completion Rates in the Household Survey of Characteristics of Prevocationally Deaf Adults: National Census of the Deaf Population, 1972.**

| | |
|---|---|
| Number of persons in sample | 1,834 |
| Number of completed interviews | 1,476 |
| Gross completion rate | 80.5% |
| Number of persons in sample after adjustment for those who became part of another eligible household, died or were institutionalized | 1,784 |
| Completion rate adjusted for respondent ineligibility | 82.7% |
| Number of persons who could not be located because present address incorrect and interviewer unable to obtain forwarding address | 1,665 |
| Completion rate adjusted for respondent ineligible and inaccessible | 88.6% |

imagination to challenge any but the most obvious inconsistencies in the logic of the coding instructions. On the other hand, an individual with sufficient interest and ability to undertake the analytical kind of task imposed by the coding of what is in fact a very complicated sort of interview schedule would not perhaps be effective in the repetitious, sometimes monotonous routine required to get through nearly 3,000 questionnaires. In addition, the coding phase occupied only a few months in the life of the project.

The employment of college students during their summer vacation seemed to be a reasonable way to achieve the sometimes contradictory needs of the project. Such persons are highly capable of the challenge of the difficult coding procedure and, at least for a short time, are willing to persevere with the routine aspects of the job. Their being available on a flexible basis rather than needing full-time employment fitted in very well with the temporary nature of the coding jobs.

Once coded, the data on the questionnaires were punched on cards for computer processing. All keypunching was verified, and checks were run on the computer to eliminate any gross errors that may have filtered through. The data from the survey occupied over 13,300 IBM cards upon completion—or 1,066,080 columns of entries.

# APPENDIX A

# Appendix A

### List of Organizations and Individuals
### Contributing Names to the National
### Census of the Deaf Population,
### Arranged by State.

The building of the list of deaf persons depended upon the voluntary cooperation of a vast number of organizations and individuals. By way of acknowledging their invaluable contributions, we publish their names in the pages which follow. Opposite each entry is the number of deaf persons on the list submitted, some containing thousands of entries and some but one. We appreciated every list, regardless of its size.

To each organization and individual we say Thank You.

## NATIONAL

| | |
|---|---:|
| National Deaf Skiers Association | 181 |
| National Fraternal Society of the Deaf | 5,140 |
| National Deaf Bowling Association | 383 |
| National Congress of Jewish Deaf | 1,052 |
| Registry of Interpreters for the Deaf | 110 |
| American Professional Society of the Deaf | 25 |
| Committee for Deaf Skiers | 96 |
| Alexander Graham Bell Association for the Deaf | 575 |
| Department of the Deaf, Bill Rice Ranch | 15,207 |
| Cultural Directors of NAD | 60 |
| Ancient Order of Delta Masons | 107 |
| International Catholic Deaf Association | 9,711 |
| Ephphatha for the Deaf & Blind | 414 |
| Junior Branch of the International Catholic Deaf Association | 220 |
| Gallaudet College | 5,500 |
| Vibralarm Service | 4,092 |
| The Silent Ambassador Publication of the Assemblies of God | 220 |
| The Endeavor | 1,744 |
| Mrs. Marcellus Kleberg | 191 |
| Anonymous | 1,900 |

## REGIONAL

| | |
|---|---:|
| New England Gallaudet Association of the Deaf | 310 |
| National Literary Society of the Deaf | 83 |
| Eastern Temporal Bone Banks Center | 90 |
| Midwestern Temporal Bone Banks Center | 305 |

## ARIZONA

| | |
|---|---:|
| Arizona State Association of the Deaf | 154 |
| Tucson Chapter | 15 |
| Phoenix Association of the Deaf, Inc. | 156 |
| First Assembly of God Church for the Deaf, Yuma | 63 |
| First Assemblies of God, Phoenix | 459 |
| North Phoenix Baptist Church | 18 |
| The Arizona Cactus, Arizona Public Residential School | 660 |
| Arizona State School for the Deaf and Blind | 689 |
| Phoenix Day School for the Deaf | 19 |
| Gompers Rehabilitation Center | 107 |
| Department of Vocational Rehabilitation | 515 |
| Mrs. Y. Harrison, Scottsdale | 127 |
| Rev. George Almo | 4 |

## ARKANSAS

| | |
|---|---:|
| Arkansas Association of the Deaf | 248 |
| Holcombe Heights Film Club | 12 |
| Christ Church, Ephphatha Class | 26 |
| First Assembly of God, Russellville | 3 |
| First Baptist Church, Lake City | 53 |
| Central Church of Christ, Little Rock | 28 |
| First Baptist Church, Fayetteville | 24 |
| Second Baptist Church, El Dorado | 6 |
| Bluff Avenue Baptist Church | 14 |
| Central Baptist Church | 9 |
| First Baptist Church, Little Rock | 96 |
| First Baptist Church, Mena | 12 |
| East Side Baptist Church, Paragould | 50 |
| Antioch Silent Baptist Church | 70 |
| Arkansas School for the Deaf | 47 |
| Goodwill Industries of Arkansas, Inc. | 4 |
| Arkansas Rehabilitation Research & Training Center | 115 |
| Arkansas Children's Hearing and Speech Center | 54 |
| Easter Seal Rehabilitation Center | 1 |
| Department of Educational Rehabilitation Services | 1,000 |

## CALIFORNIA

| | |
|---|---:|
| California Association for the Deaf | 605 |
| Santa Clara Valley Chapter | 31 |
| Orange County Club for the Deaf | 492 |
| East Bay Club of the Deaf, Inc. | 450 |
| Riverside Club of the Deaf | 25 |

| | |
|---|---:|
| Golden West Club of the Deaf | 1,036 |
| Hollywood Silent Recreation Club | 30 |
| San Francisco Club for the Deaf | 75 |
| Sacramento Club of the Deaf | 73 |
| Stockton Club for the Deaf | 60 |
| Hearing and Deaf Association of Redwood Empire | 15 |
| Southland Mall Group | 8 |
| Freedom Club | 22 |
| Glendale Social Club for the Deaf | 42 |
| Wis-Cal Cinema Club | 20 |
| Orinda Reelers | 4 |
| Sun Valley Movie Club | 15 |
| Arlington Deaf Club | 12 |
| Smothermon Club for the Deaf | 13 |
| Jurupa Hills Movie Club | 80 |
| San Fernando Club of the Deaf | 33 |
| San Gabriel Valley Workshop Association | 2 |
| Southwest Oral Deaf Adults Section | 13 |
| Victoria Club | 14 |
| Chi Club | 19 |
| The Norton Club | 5 |
| California Association of Parents of Deaf & Hard of Hearing | 158 |
| Movie Society for the Deaf | 25 |
| L.E.R.C. Sportsman Club | 11 |
| Sonoma Deaf Social Group | 4 |
| Lafayette Movie Club | 10 |
| Carheljo | 4 |
| El Monte Bowling Club of the Deaf | 20 |
| Ygnacio Valley Society | 5 |
| Montclair Cinema Club | 284 |
| Southern California Women's Club of the Deaf | 146 |
| Inglewood Cinema Group | 26 |
| Joint Organization for the Deaf | 87 |
| Deaf Adults | 51 |
| Shazam Club | 10 |
| Mt. Diablo Social Club | 14 |
| Sierra Literary Society | 53 |
| Sacramento Hearing Society, Inc. | 111 |
| Los Angeles Society for the Hard of Hearing | 2 |
| San Francisco Hearing Society | 251 |
| Oxnard Social Group for the Deaf | 11 |
| La Fista Club | 155 |
| Language and Education Association for the Deaf | 20 |
| Rod and Gun Club of the Deaf | 62 |

| | |
|---|---:|
| Orange County Movie Club | 38 |
| Bowling, Santa Ana | 70 |
| Oralingua Foundation | 48 |
| Lynwood Seventh Day Adventist Church | 102 |
| Bethel Silent Temple | 151 |
| First Assembly of God, Norwalk | 63 |
| First Assembly of God, Corona | 12 |
| Seventh Day Adventist, Santa Cruz | 27 |
| St. Columban's Church | 3 |
| St. Benedict Center | 97 |
| St. Joseph's Center for the Deaf and Hard of Hearing | 261 |
| Seventh Day Adventist Church, Oakland | 18 |
| Temple Beth Solomon of the Deaf | 90 |
| Memorial Lutheran Chapel for the Deaf | 683 |
| Pilgrim Lutheran Church for the Deaf | 404 |
| First Southern Baptist Church, Bakersfield | 2 |
| Temple Baptist Church | 11 |
| Cypress Avenue Baptist Church | 1 |
| Mission Way Baptist Church | 6 |
| First Southern Baptist Church of Fullerton | 1 |
| First Southern Baptist Church, La Habra | 91 |
| First Baptist Church of Rancho Cordova | 3 |
| Magnolia Avenue Baptist Church, Sacramento | 1 |
| Silent Congregation of the First Missionary Baptist Church | 10 |
| Mission of the Holy Spirit St. Mark's Church | 49 |
| First Baptist Church of Van Nuys | 1,225 |
| Church of Christ | 2 |
| Grand Avenue Seventh Day Adventist Church for the Deaf | 16 |
| The Church of Jesus Christ of Latter Day Saints, Torrance | 162 |
| Trinity Episcopal Mission for the Deaf | 194 |
| CCWD-Episcopal, Rev. Robert W. Kley, Huntington Beach | 70 |
| Hebrew Association of the Deaf, Los Angeles | 44 |
| California School for the Deaf | 776 |
| Marlton Junior High School | 17 |
| St. Joseph's School of Religion | 186 |
| Los Alamitos High School | 27 |
| Charlotte Anthony School | 26 |
| Fairford School & Jersey Avenue School, Santa Fe Springs | 169 |
| Marlton Avenue Elementary School | 13 |
| Southern California Hearing Council | 9 |
| White Memorial Medical Center, Speech & Hearing Clinic | 3 |
| Sacramento Hearing Society, Inc. | 44 |
| Fresno State College, Hearing & Speech Clinic | 6 |

*175*

| | |
|---|---:|
| Marianne Frostig Center of Educational Therapy | 2 |
| San Diego State College, Speech & Hearing Clinic | 12 |
| Providence Speech & Hearing Clinic, Orange | 84 |
| University of Redlands Speech and Hearing Clinic | 5 |
| Cedar Sinai Medical Center | 51 |
| University of the Pacific Speech and Hearing Center | 10 |
| Leadership Training Program in the Area of the Deaf | 809 |
| Department of Special Services for the Handicapped | 610 |
| Services to Deaf Persons, Department of Rehabilitations, Sacramento | 4,200 |
| California Association of Parents of Deaf & Hard of Hearing Children | 1,700 |
| El Portal Del Sol School | 1,888 |
| Golden West College, Huntington Beach | 37 |
| Antique Workshop, Sausalito | 1 |
| Fairmount Hospital, Department of Speech Pathology & Audiology | 55 |
| Pacific Union College, Speech & Hearing Clinic | 7 |
| Memorial Hospital of Long Beach, Speech & Hearing Services | 27 |
| V.A. Hospital, Aphasia Unit, Neurology Section | 5 |
| Pepperdine College, Speech Clinic | 1 |
| Society for the Hard of Hearing, Long Beach | 53 |
| Beverly-Hollywood Hearing Society | 41 |
| Children's Hospital | 30 |
| Loma Linda University, Speech Pathology & Audiology Department | 13 |
| California Home for the Aged Deaf | 72 |
| Mr. Masaneri Ebisuzaki, Sobrante | 7 |
| Mr. Abe Miller, San Jose | 86 |
| Victoria Cotter, Oakland | 225 |
| Mrs. Ronald Cooper, Chico | 13 |
| Merrill E. Herson, Los Angeles | 66 |
| Mr. Robert L. Miller | 33 |
| Mrs. Helen Hammons, Alameda | 58 |
| Mr. Donald Ingraham, Mt. View | 368 |
| Mrs. Gary L. Stein, San Diego | 96 |
| Mr. Pat Zavada, Arlington | 62 |
| Holmes Family | 3 |
| Barlow's Family | 91 |
| Schmidt Family | 94 |
| Anonymous | 532 |

## COLORADO

| | |
|---|---:|
| Colorado State Association of the Deaf | 789 |
| Silent Athletic Club of the Deaf | 123 |

| | |
|---|---|
| All Souls Mission of the Deaf | 45 |
| Colorado Springs Silent Club | 38 |
| Family Movie Club, Colorado Springs | 6 |
| The Family Way Club, Denver | 2 |
| Friends Deaf Club, Denver | 31 |
| The Arkansas Valley Deaf Club Inc., Pueblo | 148 |
| Club 108, Colorado Springs | 5 |
| Denver Ski Club for the Deaf | 66 |
| Belmont Baptist Church, Pueblo | 7 |
| First Assembly of God, Pueblo | 14 |
| Denver Temple Baptist Church (Silent Crusaders) | 35 |
| St. Mark's Church, Denver | 48 |
| Bethel Deaf Lutheran Church | 199 |
| First Southern Baptist Church, Colorado Springs | 25 |
| Rockvale Assembly of God | 9 |
| All Souls Mission of the Deaf | 52 |
| Public Residential School | 553 |
| Colorado School for the Deaf and Blind | 86 |
| Denver Public School 5 | 21 |
| University of Denver, Speech & Hearing Clinic | 155 |
| Craig Rehabilitation Hospital, Denver | 1 |
| Pueblo Therapy Center, Inc. | 27 |
| Rocky Mountain Rehabilitation Center | 5 |
| Sewall Easter Seal Rehabilitation Center | 6 |
| Division of Rehabilitation, Denver | 365 |
| University of Colorado Medical Center | 396 |
| District Court City and County of Denver | 369 |

## CONNECTICUT

| | |
|---|---|
| Connecticut Association of the Deaf | 1,600 |
| Hartford Club of the Deaf | 197 |
| Bridgeport Athletic Association of the Deaf | 102 |
| Deaf Skiers Club, Norwalk | 45 |
| Waterbury Silent Club | 66 |
| Meriden Club of the Deaf | 196 |
| Granby Copper Club for the Deaf | 14 |
| National Fraternal Society of the Deaf #25, New Haven | 156 |
| National Fraternal Society of the Deaf #149, Hartford | 18 |
| Connecticut Chapter, Gallaudet College Alumni Association | 303 |
| St. Francis DeSales Deaf Club I.C.D.A., Chapter #50 | 142 |
| International Catholic Deaf Association Chapter #34 | 57 |
| St. Francis Deaf Club, Hartford | 1,031 |
| St. George's Mission for the Deaf of Greater New London | 137 |

*177*

| | |
|---|---|
| Lutheran Church of the Deaf, West Hartford | 648 |
| Ascension Mission of the Deaf | 112 |
| New London Episcopal Mission | 11 |
| American School for the Deaf | 2,087 |
| Mystic Oral School | 117 |
| Public Residential Schools | 39 |
| New Haven Hearing and Speech Center | 338 |
| Easter Seal-Goodwill Industries Rehabilitation Center | 21 |
| Division of Vocational Rehabilitation | 865 |
| Mrs. Doreen K. Elia, Madison | 162 |
| Helen Morgan, Windsor | 11 |

## DELAWARE

| | |
|---|---|
| Wilmington Club of the Deaf Inc. | 66 |
| The Mancus Foundation | 7 |
| Delaware Valley Coordinating Service, Chalfont | 17 |
| Margaret D. Sterck School | 199 |
| Vocational Rehabilitation Service, Wilmington | 89 |
| Mrs. Lillian Wynn, Wilmington | 51 |

## DISTRICT OF COLUMBIA

| | |
|---|---|
| The Frederick H. Hughes Memorial Theater | 62 |
| Sigdeaf | 50 |
| The Metropolitian Baptist Church | 15 |
| Calvary Baptist Church | 397 |
| Mission Helpers of the Sacred Heart, Baltimore, Md. | 4 |
| International Catholic Deaf Association, Chapter #29 Vienna, Virginia | 155 |
| Shiloh Baptist Church | 82 |
| Gallaudet College | 7,212 |
| Public Residential School | 500 |
| Kendall School for the Deaf | 424 |
| Childrens Hospital of D.C., Hearing & Speech Center | 30 |
| The Catholic University of America, Speech & Hearing Clinic | 19 |
| District of Columbia Society for Crippled Children | 5 |
| District of Columbia, Division of Vocational Rehabilitation | 140 |
| District of Columbia Club of the Deaf | 930 |
| Miss Minnie Bache | 1,126 |
| Mrs. Barbara Stevens | 90 |
| Mr. Hubert Anderson | 37 |

*178*

Rev. Otto B. Berg 133
Anonymous 728


## FLORIDA

| | |
|---|---|
| Florida State Association for the Deaf | 802 |
| Palms Club of the Deaf | 144 |
| The Browdad Club | 24 |
| St. Petersburg Silent Club | 188 |
| Tampa Silent Club | 108 |
| Haverhill Baptist Church | 59 |
| Church of Christ | 61 |
| Riverside Baptist Church | 28 |
| First Baptist Church of Inwood | 59 |
| Trinity Baptist Church | 98 |
| Delaney Street Baptist Church | 47 |
| Missionary to the Deaf | 62 |
| Ancient City Baptist Church | 9 |
| First Baptist Church, Jacksonville | 10 |
| Immanuel Baptist Church | 2 |
| First Baptist Church, Pensacola | 11 |
| First Baptist Church, Sanford | 2 |
| First Baptist Church, Tallahassee | 71 |
| First Baptist Church, Tampa | 8 |
| Central Baptist Church | 2 |
| First Baptist Church Silent Class | 1 |
| Deaf Zion Lutheran Church | 437 |
| Public Residential School | 896 |
| Tampa Oral School | 162 |
| Palmetto School | 63 |
| Florida State School for the Deaf and Blind | 64 |
| Division of Vocational Rehabilitation | 2,400 |
| Division of Vocational Rehabilitation, Tampa | 166 |
| Division of Vocational Rehabilitation, Fort Myers | 333 |
| Speech and Hearing Center Inc. | 179 |
| University of South Florida Speech & Hearing Clinic | 6 |
| Hospital Speech Center | 5 |
| Regional Rehabilitation Center, Florida State University | 283 |
| Health Maintenance Program | 51 |
| Sunland Training Center | 27 |
| West Hileah Baptist Church | 2 |
| Sister Kateri, S.S.J. | 126 |
| Mrs. Ruth P. Loveless | 4 |
| Mr. and Mrs. Dan Long | 32 |

Mr. Paul Adams, Florida School for the Deaf 79
Anonymous 1


## GEORGIA

| | |
|---|---|
| Georgia Association of the Deaf | 637 |
| Crussele Freeman Church of the Deaf | 600 |
| Byne Memorial Baptist Church | 14 |
| South Broad Baptist Church | 21 |
| First Baptist Church, LaGrange | 15 |
| Cave Spring Baptist Church | 13 |
| First Baptist Church, Atlanta | 17 |
| First Baptist Church of Chattahoochee | 14 |
| West End Baptist Church | 53 |
| Wheat Street Baptist Church | 23 |
| Curtis Baptist Church | 22 |
| First Baptist Church, Canton | 10 |
| Mable White Memorial Baptist Church | 40 |
| First Baptist Church, Marietta | 29 |
| First Baptist Church, Newman | 13 |
| Morningside Baptist Church | 19 |
| Central Baptist Church | 22 |
| Public Residential School | 349 |
| Georgia School for the Deaf | 1,806 |
| Cobb County Schools | 9 |
| Moultrie Speech and Hearing Center | 8 |
| Northwest Georgia Speech and Hearing Center | 64 |
| Glynn Speech and Hearing Center | 12 |
| Cerebral Palsy Center of Atlanta Inc. | 1 |
| Valdosta Speech and Hearing Center | 25 |
| Office of Rehabilitation Services, Atlanta | 600 |
| Evaluation Center for the Deaf, Cave Spring | 671 |
| Cave Spring Rehabilitation Center for the Deaf | 31 |
| Rev. James T. Scherer (Catholic Center) | 11 |
| Mr. Eugene Perdue | 870 |
| Anonymous | 63 |


## HAWAII

| | |
|---|---|
| Hawaii Club for the Deaf | 180 |
| First Assemblies of God | 24 |
| McKinley High School | 19 |
| Kahala Elementary School | 33 |
| Pearl Harbor Kai Elementary School | 24 |

*180*

| | |
|---|---|
| Mrs. Roy Morikawa, Honolulu | 304 |
| Anonymous | 1 |

## IDAHO

| | |
|---|---|
| Sphinx Club of Boise | 21 |
| Idaho Athletic Club of the Deaf | 40 |
| Panhandle Chapter of Idaho Association of the Deaf | 10 |
| Magic Valley Chapter of Idaho Association of the Deaf | 81 |
| Southwest Club for the Deaf, Idaho Falls | 52 |
| Idaho State School for the Deaf | 338 |
| Idaho School for the Deaf and the Blind | 392 |
| Boise Easter Seal Center | 5 |
| Telex Hearing Aid Service | 102 |

## ILLINOIS

| | |
|---|---|
| Cahokia Chapter, Illinois Association of the Deaf | 126 |
| Jacksonville Chapter, Illinois Association of the Deaf | 40 |
| Springfield Chapter, Illinois Association of the Deaf | 89 |
| Fox Valley Chapter, Illinois Association of the Deaf | 41 |
| Rockford Chapter, Illinois Association of the Deaf | 56 |
| Quincy Chapter, Illinois Association of the Deaf | 80 |
| Chicago Crusaders Association of the Deaf | 52 |
| Northwestern Illinois Regional Association | 242 |
| Aurora Club of the Deaf | 168 |
| Chicagò Club of the Deaf | 258 |
| Chicagoland Lipreaders | 249 |
| Southtown Club of the Deaf, Chicago | 264 |
| Midwest Deaf Golf Association | 280 |
| Bloomington-Normal Deaf Club | 167 |
| Rockford Silent Club | 260 |
| Couples Club, Arlington Heights | 10 |
| Chicago Silent Dramatic Club | 93 |
| Chicago Bel-Bowl Deaf Girls League | 31 |
| Chicago Deaf Bowling League | 39 |
| Gateway Arch Athletic Club of the Deaf | 31 |
| Bowling Association of Illinois | 47 |
| Normal Assemblies for the Deaf | 500 |
| The Assemblies of God | 1 |
| West Fair Baptist Church | 26 |
| First Baptist Church, Marion | 96 |
| Apostolate of the Deaf | 2,806 |
| Holy Trinity Convent | 12 |
| St. Mary's Church | 43 |

| | |
|---|---:|
| Hebrew Association of the Deaf of Chicago | 61 |
| Christ Lutheran Church | 285 |
| Maplewood Park Baptist Church | 83 |
| Lantana Southern Baptist Church | 2 |
| Sterling Baptist Church, Collinsville | 30 |
| Northwest Missionary Baptist Church | 24 |
| First Baptist Church, West Chicago | 4 |
| Larkin Avenue Baptist Church | 4 |
| Suburban Baptist Church | 20 |
| First Baptist Church, Harrisburg | 28 |
| First Baptist Church, Metropolis | 18 |
| First Baptist Church, Salem | 33 |
| First Baptist Church, Springfield | 2 |
| Sterling Baptist Church, East St. Louis | 30 |
| Pennsylvania Avenue Baptist Church | 24 |
| Stony Island Church of Christ | 27 |
| First Baptist Church Deaf Sunday School, Springfield | 2 |
| Decatur Catholic Deaf Society | 32 |
| Our Savior Lutheran Church for the Deaf | 166 |
| All Angels Church for the Deaf | 45 |
| Chicago Catholic Archdiocese | 78 |
| Our Redeemer Lutheran Church | 1 |
| Public Residential School | 1,492 |
| Illinois School for the Deaf | 256 |
| Elim Christian School for the Exceptional Child | 44 |
| Evanston High School | 158 |
| Quincy Public Schools | 47 |
| Aurora Public Schools | 86 |
| Illinois Division of Vocational Rehabilitation | 116 |
| Chicago Police Department, Traffic Division | 1,139 |
| Speech & Hearing Clinic, Northern Illinois University | 35 |
| Chicago-Read Mental Health Center, Audiology Dept. | 13 |
| Elmhurst College Speech Clinic | 17 |
| College of St. Francis, Speech Clinic | 1 |
| Easter Seal Society of Will County | 2 |
| Tinley Park Mental Health Center | 2 |
| Schwab Rehabilitation Hospital | 3 |
| Childrens Memorial Hospital Clinic | 255 |
| Counselor of Hearing Impaired, Goodwill Industries | 27 |
| Augustana College, Speech and Hearing Center | 31 |
| Western Illinois University Speech and Hearing Center | 41 |
| St. Joseph Hospital, Speech and Hearing Clinic | 742 |
| Speech & Hearing Service, Xavier College | 6 |
| Little Company of Mary Hospital, Speech & Hearing Service | 1 |

*182*

| | |
|---|---:|
| Bradley University, Speech and Hearing | 4 |
| Speech Clinic, Hines V.A. Hospital | 3 |
| University of Illinois, Speech and Hearing Service | 30 |
| Illinois Association of the Deaf | 5,000 |
| Radar, Catholic Publication, Chicago | 312 |
| Apostolate of the Deaf | 1,200 |
| Leo and Velda Sons | 12 |
| Miss Genevieve Pogorzelski, Berwyn | 186 |
| Mr. & Mrs. August Bartok, E. St. Louis | 72 |
| Mrs. Vera Langford, Chicago | 460 |
| Mary Ruth Whitman, Audiologist, Project Action | 59 |
| Rev. William Klitz, Chicago | 173 |
| Anonymous | 209 |

## INDIANA

| | |
|---|---:|
| The East Way Club | 14 |
| Angola Club | 39 |
| The Sphinx Club | 20 |
| Devonshire Group | 5 |
| Garden Acre | 8 |
| The Williams Club | 21 |
| The Greater Lafayette Club | 16 |
| Columbus Club for the Deaf | 65 |
| Rork Cinema Club | 39 |
| Bippis Cinema Club | 11 |
| Arrowhead | 4 |
| Indianapolis Chapter, Oral Deaf Adults Section | 1 |
| The Jines Social Club | 93 |
| I.R. 100 Club East | 19 |
| Saturday Night Movie Club | 2 |
| Vincennes Deaf Club | 6 |
| The Norton Club | 9 |
| Richmond Deaf Club | 51 |
| Popcorn Night | 7 |
| Bowling, Indiana | 52 |
| N.E. 465 Clover Club | 14 |
| First Assembly Church | 231 |
| Lighthouse Tabernacle | 16 |
| First Southern Baptist Church | 126 |
| St. Rita Rectory | 32 |
| Franklin Road Church of Christ | 7 |
| Grace Baptist Church | 21 |
| Parkway Baptist Church, Indianapolis | 10 |
| Indian Hills Baptist Church | 15 |

*183*

| | |
|---|---:|
| First Baptist Church, Knightstown | 2 |
| Graceland Baptist Church | 27 |
| Parkway Baptist Church, New Albany | 5 |
| Gary Diocesan Catholic Deaf | 18 |
| Grace Lutheran Church for the Deaf | 59 |
| Temple Baptist Deaf Class | 34 |
| Indiana School for the Deaf, Indianapolis | 1,881 |
| Mater Dei High School | 19 |
| The Communicator, Indiana School for the Deaf | 50 |
| Public Residential School | 127 |
| Wabash Valley Goodwill Industries | 3 |
| Tri-State Hearing and Speech Association | 25 |
| Ball State University, Speech & Hearing Clinic | 108 |
| Indiana University, Speech and Hearing Center | 13 |
| Indianapolis Speech and Hearing Center, Inc. | 17 |
| Purdue University, Department of Audiology & Speech Sciences | 12 |
| State Hospital and Training Center | 10 |
| Indiana Agency for the Blind | 14 |
| Vocational Rehabilitation Division | 4,600 |
| The Silent Hoosier, Indiana Association of the Deaf | 376 |
| The Halls | 6 |
| The Thixton Family | 3 |
| Nathaniel Horwitz and Family, Indianapolis | 4 |
| The Lunds, Indianapolis | 55 |
| The Nicolais, Indianapolis | 5 |
| The Slinkard Family Group | 14 |
| Jeanette Berry, Danville | 425 |
| Rev. Larry Goodman, Evansville | 110 |
| Mrs. Edward M. Mark, South Bend | 96 |
| Mrs. Mary Wagner, Goshen | 30 |
| Albert Rhodes, Jr., Indianapolis | 19 |
| Anonymous | 554 |

## IOWA

| | |
|---|---:|
| Iowa Association of the Deaf | 489 |
| Sioux City Silent Club, Inc. | 60 |
| Des Moines Silent Club | 2 |
| Cedar Rapids Club | 111 |
| Council Bluffs Silent Club | 147 |
| Cedarloo Club of the Deaf | 94 |
| Friends of the Deaf | 6 |
| Jaycees, Ankeny | 15 |
| Mascia Club | 30 |

| | |
|---|---|
| Ottumwa Silent Club | 17 |
| Home Missionary Serving the Deaf | 254 |
| St. Joseph's Church | 26 |
| Faith Lutheran Church | 43 |
| Calvary Lutheran Church | 301 |
| Lutheran Church for the Deaf | 254 |
| Iowa School for the Deaf | 381 |
| Hope Haven for the Handicapped | 26 |
| Polk County Society for Crippled Children & Adults | 41 |
| U.C.P. Center For Greater Cedar Rapids | 19 |
| Grinnell College Speech Clinic | 5 |
| Department of Vocational Rehabilitation | 3,390 |
| The Sign Language, Iowa Association of the Deaf | 361 |
| Davenport Oral Deaf Association | 74 |
| Siouxland Courier, Publication, Sioux City | 560 |
| Rev. Robert Alfers, Underwood | 113 |
| Rev. Ralph Ten Clay, Rock Valley | 4 |
| Francis E. Leander, Ottumwa | 39 |
| Mr. La Vern Mass, Cedar Rapids | 39 |
| Anonymous | 34 |

## KANSAS

| | |
|---|---|
| Kansas Association of the Deaf | 3,680 |
| Kansas City Deaf Center | 57 |
| Wichita Association of the Deaf, Inc. | 136 |
| Hutchinson Club for the Deaf | 18 |
| Olathe Club of the Deaf | 112 |
| Kansas City Kansas Club for the Deaf | 59 |
| Metropolitan Baptist Church | 22 |
| Assembly of God | 69 |
| First Assembly of God | 34 |
| First Southern Baptist Church, Kansas City | 37 |
| St. Paul's Rectory | 44 |
| Riverside Christian Church | 47 |
| Cleveland Avenue Church of Christ | 3 |
| First Southern Baptist Church, Topeka | 11 |
| Kansas School for the Deaf | 962 |
| Institute of Logopedics | 78 |
| Motor Vehicle Department | 1,300 |
| Fort Hays Kansas State College Speech & Hearing Services | 10 |
| Kansas State University Speech and Hearing Clinic | 10 |
| Kansas State Parent's Association for Hearing Handicapped Children | 32 |

*185*

| | |
|---|---|
| Deaf and Hard of Hearing Counseling Service | 260 |
| Division of Vocational Rehabilitation, Topeka | 1,600 |
| Mr. & Mrs. James Connacher, Heington | 2 |
| Mr. William J. Doonan, Wichita | 142 |
| Sister Joyce Seivert, Shawnee Mission | 21 |
| Anonymous | 3 |

**KENTUCKY**

| | |
|---|---|
| Kentucky Association of the Deaf, Danville | 358 |
| Louisville Association of the Deaf | 300 |
| Lexington Deaf Society | 43 |
| First Baptist Church, Frankfort | 16 |
| Porter Memorial Baptist Church | 10 |
| Fourth Avenue Baptist Church | 49 |
| St. Peter and Paul Church | 24 |
| St. Pius X Church | 183 |
| Forest Park Baptist Church | 6 |
| First Baptist Church, Danville | 12 |
| Faith Baptist Church, Georgetown | 7 |
| Bethlehem Baptist Church | 4 |
| Erlanger Baptist Church | 92 |
| Church of Christ for the Deaf | 542 |
| Danville Bible Class for the Deaf | 31 |
| Kentucky School for the Deaf | 2,325 |
| Public Residential School | 920 |
| Lexington Deaf Oral School | 77 |
| Louisville Deaf Oral School | 78 |
| Kentucky Easter Seal, Hearing and Speech Center | 299 |
| Commission for Handicapped Children | 444 |
| University of Kentucky, Speech Pathology & Audiology Clinic | 134 |
| Regional Hearing Conservation Center | 315 |
| West Kentucky Easter Seal Center for Crippled Children & Adults | 19 |
| Brescia College, Speech & Hearing Service | 10 |
| Council of Deaf Children of Northern Kentucky | 146 |
| Bureau of Rehabilitation Services, Danville | 186 |
| Kentucky Association of the Deaf Bulletin | 358 |
| Mrs. Maxine Browne, Erlanger | 81 |
| Mrs. Pat Dye, R.N., Florence | 8 |
| Mr. Phil Lovan, Owensboro | 21 |
| Mr. Daniel Middleton, Danville | 139 |
| Sister Barbara Ann, Louisville | 16 |

## LOUISIANA

| | |
|---|---:|
| Louisiana Association of the Deaf | 800 |
| Baton Rouge Club of the Deaf | 192 |
| The Berke Circle | 261 |
| The Deaf Printer's Club | 38 |
| Shreveport Club of the Deaf | 68 |
| Clerc Cultural Club | 7 |
| First Assembly of God | 35 |
| Assemblies of God | 629 |
| Emmanuel Baptist Church | 9 |
| First Baptist Church, Amite | 27 |
| Catholic Deaf Center | 29 |
| St. Cabrini Rectory | 12 |
| Catholic Deaf Association | 128 |
| First Baptist Church, Ruston | 8 |
| First Baptist Church, West Monroe | 5 |
| Worldwide Missionary & Educational Foundation | 5 |
| First Baptist Church, New Orleans | 176 |
| Louisiana State School for the Deaf | 651 |
| Delgado College, Rehabilitation Services Division | 58 |
| Speech and Hearing Clinic, Hammond | 6 |
| Alexander Speech Center, Shreveport | 2 |
| Grambling College, Speech and Hearing Service | 2 |
| Vocational Rehabilitation, Baton Rouge | 5,728 |
| Deaf & Hard of Hearing, Vocational Rehabilitation, New Orleans | 53 |
| Rev. Marshall R. Larriviere, Abbeville | 236 |
| Charlotte Crowell, Baton Rouge | 21 |
| Miss Angele Carroll, Opelousas | 1 |
| Anonymous | 1 |

## MAINE

| | |
|---|---:|
| Maine Mission for the Deaf | 169 |
| Eastern Maine Parents of Hearing Impaired Children | 17 |
| Penobscott County Club of the Deaf | 26 |
| Lewiston-Auburn Deaf Club | 17 |
| Cumberland County Club of the Deaf | 38 |
| The Assemblies of God Church, Pownal | 355 |
| The Assemblies of God Church, Lewiston | 28 |
| Bangor-Brewer Catholic Club of the Deaf | 13 |
| Faith School Theology | 1 |
| Governor Baxter State School for the Deaf | 474 |
| University of Maine, Speech & Hearing Center | 32 |

*187*

Vocational Rehabilitation Division, Augusta          19
Miss Marjorie Harrison, Lewiston                     29

## MARYLAND

Suburban Maryland Association of the Deaf            597
Montgomery County Association for
   Language Handicapped Children     264
Silent Oriole Club, Inc.                            200
Frederick Scott Key Club                             42
The Landsdowne Club                                   1
The Dankon Club                                       5
Friends Club                                          4
Sonnens, Wheaton                                      4
Meadowbrook Social Set                                3
Silent Clover Society                                47
Bowling, Maryland                                    15
Trinity Assembly of God                             355
First Baptist Church, Frederick                       1
Moderator of Catholic Deaf of Baltimore             567
St. Mary's Church                                     5
Grace Church                                        133
United Church for the Deaf                           38
Forrestville Baptist Church                          75
Oak Grove Baptist Church                             14
Jewish Deaf Society of Baltimore                     81
Second Baptist Church                                38
Maryland School for the Deaf                        581
Public Residential School                           650
Easter Seal Treatment Center, Montgomery County      47
Towson State College, Speech & Hearing Clinic        11
Mount St. Agnes College, Speech and Hearing Center    1
Division of Vocational Rehabilitation, Baltimore    534
The Rosens, College Park                            101
Dr. Wilson H. Graybill, Clinton                     189
Mrs. Eugene Worley, Mt. Rainier                      20
Mrs. Elsie Farris, Cumberland                        14
Mr. Earl Schomber, Frederick                         78
Mr. Harold Bible, Hagerstown                         71
Mrs. Marcellus Kleberg, Kensington                  496
Anonymous                                             6

## MASSACHUSETTS

Boston Deaf Club                                     281
Worchester Deaf Club, Inc.                           49

| | |
|---|---:|
| Boston Guild for the Hard of Hearing | 272 |
| Mohawk Oral Club | 45 |
| Quincy Deaf Club, Inc. | 369 |
| Lynne League for the Hard of Hearing | 19 |
| The Four Seasons Club | 83 |
| Deaf Skiers of Massachusetts | 78 |
| North Shore Club for the Deaf | 25 |
| Boston Oral Club | 66 |
| Deaf Women's Club of Springfield Y.W.C.A. | 16 |
| Essex Theater, Beverly | 107 |
| Worcester Catholic Deaf Center, Holy Cross College | 118 |
| Catholic Guild for the Deaf | 849 |
| Boston Hebrew Association of the Deaf | 46 |
| Beverly School for the Deaf | 229 |
| Boston School for the Deaf | 1,175 |
| Clark School for the Deaf | 898 |
| The Clarke School Parents Conference | 358 |
| Horace Mann School for the Deaf | 759 |
| Public School System of Duxbury | 45 |
| Registry of Motor Vehicles, Boston | 134 |
| Speech and Hearing Foundation, Arlington | 312 |
| Berkshire Rehabilitation Center, Pittsfield | 182 |
| Boston School for the Deaf, Speech & Hearing Service | 531 |
| Holy Ghost Hospital, Cardinal Cushing Rehabilitation Center | 7 |
| Daniels Speech & Hearing Clinic, University Hospital, Boston University Medical Center | 153 |
| University of Massachusetts Communication Disorders | 54 |
| Northeastern University Speech and Hearing Center | 43 |
| The Rehabilitation Center, Fall River | 5 |
| New England Home for the Aged Deaf | 19 |
| Willie Ross School for the Deaf, Longmeadow | 60 |
| Mrs. Meldren Kreps, Williamsburg | 1 |

## MICHIGAN

| | |
|---|---:|
| Michigan Association of the Deaf | 1,952 |
| Oakland Silent Club | 155 |
| Motor City Association of the Deaf, Detroit | 325 |
| Flint Association of the Deaf, Inc. | 214 |
| Rolling Acre Farm, Marcellus | 7 |
| The Mott Program, Flint | 298 |
| Tri-County Center, Inc. Bay City | 9 |
| Flint Hearing Society, Flint | 15 |
| Lansing Chapter of the Michigan Association of the Deaf | 82 |

| | |
|---|---:|
| Grand Rapids Chapter of the Michigan Association of the Deaf | 122 |
| Tri-County Community Council, Detroit | 1,347 |
| Wolverine Deaf Golfers | 58 |
| Michigan State Deaf Bowling Association | 140 |
| Blue Water Hearing League, Port Huron | 53 |
| Riverside Silent Assembly, Flint | 58 |
| First Assembly of God, Pontiac | 205 |
| Wealthy Street Baptist Church for the Deaf | 230 |
| Christian Mission for Deaf Africans, Detroit | 4 |
| Immaculate Conception, Traverse City | 6 |
| Our Savior's Lutheran Church for the Deaf | 321 |
| St. Andrews Episcopal Church, Livonia | 27 |
| Silent Bible Study Class for the Deaf | 40 |
| Reformed Church in America, Hesperia | 396 |
| First Baptist Church of Springfield | 3 |
| Central Baptist Church, Flint | 18 |
| First Baptist Church, Portage | 2 |
| North Prospect Baptist Church | 7 |
| The Assemblies of God Church, New Boston | 46 |
| Deaf Class of Bethany Tabernacle | 32 |
| Niles Church of Christ | 9 |
| Baptist Deaf Mission Work, East Lansing | 370 |
| CCWD-Episcopal, Flint | 52 |
| Green Ridge Christ Reformed Church | 4 |
| Jamestown Reformed Church | 6 |
| Christian Reformed Church, Grand Rapids | 11 |
| Second Christian Reformed, Allendale | 1 |
| Christian Reformed Church, Grand Haven | 3 |
| Oakdale Park Reformed Church, Grand Rapids | 1 |
| Eighth Reformed Church, Grand Rapids | 1 |
| Fifth Reformed Church, Grand Rapids | 2 |
| Madison Square Christian Reformed Church | 1 |
| Christian Reformed Church, Grand Rapids | 4 |
| Zion Lutheran Church, Holland | 2 |
| Park Christian Reformed Church | 2 |
| Messiah Christian Reformed Church | 3 |
| Christian Reformed Church, Kalamazoo | 2 |
| Third Christian Reformed Church, Kalamazoo | 5 |
| East Christ Reformed Church | 15 |
| St. John's VCC, Muskegon | 13 |
| Lakeside Assembly of God | 13 |
| First Reformed Church of Spring Lake | 2 |
| Beverly Christian Reformed Church, Wyoming | 3 |
| Faith Reformed Church, Wyoming | 1 |

*190*

| | |
|---|---:|
| N. St. Christian Reformed Church, Zeeland | 3 |
| Michigan School for the Deaf | 1,113 |
| Lutheran School for the Deaf | 290 |
| Detroit Day School for the Deaf | 9 |
| Saginaw Intermediate School District | 94 |
| Saginaw Public Schools, Handley School | 93 |
| Port Huron School | 35 |
| University of Michigan Speech & Hearing-Camp Shady Trails | 25 |
| Marygrove College Speech & Hearing Clinic | 2 |
| Detroit Orthopedic Clinic Speech & Language Dept. | 9 |
| Northern Michigan University Speech & Hearing Clinic | 295 |
| Eastern Michigan University Speech & Hearing Clinic | 231 |
| Kalamazoo Society for Better Hearing | 20 |
| Department of Labor, Detroit | 2,000 |
| Rev. Dayton Garau, Detroit | 873 |
| Rev. S. J. Commengo, Drenthe | 1 |
| Rev. Frank B. Thompson, Holland | 1 |
| Rev. Peter Vander Weide, Jenison | 3 |
| Rev. William Huyser, Kalamazoo | 3 |
| Rev. J. C. Holt, Kalamazoo | 3 |
| Rev. Albert Potts, Muskegon | 5 |
| Harley K. Cox, St. Joseph | 28 |
| Anonymous | 111 |

## MINNESOTA

| | |
|---|---:|
| Minnesota Association of the Deaf | 1,597 |
| Minnepaul Athletic Club | 113 |
| Thunberbird Club | 6 |
| Fairbault Movie Club | 4 |
| St. Paul Hearing Society | 85 |
| Minneapolis Hearing Society | 1,628 |
| Southern Minnesota Club for the Deaf | 61 |
| Northern Minnesota Club for the Deaf | 55 |
| Worthington Club of the Deaf | 31 |
| Prince of Peace Lutheran Church | 233 |
| Gospel Tabernacle | 2 |
| Summit Assembly of God | 8 |
| Sacred Heart Church | 216 |
| Ephphatha Center for the Deaf and Blind | 46 |
| Bread of Life Lutheran Church for the Deaf | 163 |
| Minnesota School for the Deaf | 2,052 |
| Public Residential School | 744 |
| St. Paul Area Technical Vocational Institute | 119 |
| Division of Vocational Rehabilitation, St. Paul | 2,499 |

*191*

Kenny Rehabilitation Institute, Minneapolis 67
Curative Workshop, Minneapolis 6
N.W. Association of Hard of Hearing 115
Mankato Rehabilitation Center, Inc. 16
Mr. Perl L. Dunn, St. Paul 146
Mrs. Tom Torgerson, Detroit 29
Anonymous 3

## MISSISSIPPI

Mississippi Association of the Deaf 378
Gulf Coast Silent Club 126
Gulf Coast Club of the Deaf 63
Woodland Hills Baptist Church 52
First Baptist Church, Amory 76
Calvary Baptist Church 25
First Baptist Church, Corinth 90
First Baptist Church, Natchez 3
First Baptist Church, Pascagoula 22
Center Ridge Baptist Church, Yazoo City 4
Mississippi School for the Deaf 705
Regional Rehabilitation Center, Speech & Hearing Dept. 25
Division of Vocational Rehabilitation, Jackson 634
Rev. Jerry St. John, Jackson 320

## MISSOURI

Missouri Association of the Deaf 685
St. Louis Bell Club 77
The Silent Berean Fellowship 40
Bowling, N. Kansas City 47
Missouri and Kansas Association of the Deaf, Kansas City 1,285
Kansas City Club for the Deaf Inc. 85
Southern Baptist, Kansas City 500
First Assembly of God, Sedalia 14
Central Bible College, Springfield 17
Englewood Assembly of God, St. Louis 43
St. Joseph Hospital, Kansas City 79
First Baptist Church, Springfield 60
The Community Center for the Deaf 900
Memorial Baptist Church, Columbia 14
East Sedalia Baptist Church 14
Mt. Washington Baptist Church, Independence 6
Second Baptist Church, Liberty 16
Pilgrim Lutheran Church of the Deaf 86

| | |
|---|---:|
| St. Thomas Mission for the Deaf | 105 |
| Wyatt Park Baptist Church | 27 |
| Central Assembly of God, Springfield | 31 |
| Forest Park Baptist Church | 31 |
| First Baptist Church, Marshall | 3 |
| First Baptist Church, Monett | 2 |
| First Baptist Church, North Kansas City | 26 |
| First Baptist Church, Sikeston | 14 |
| Southwest Baptist Church, St. Louis | 50 |
| First Baptist Church, Belton | 7 |
| First Baptist Church of St. John, St. Louis | 12 |
| Armour Heights Baptist Church | 1 |
| Noland Road Baptist Church | 6 |
| Grand Avenue Temple, Kansas City | 27 |
| Missouri School for the Deaf | 917 |
| Public Residential | 360 |
| Central Institute for the Deaf | 1,626 |
| St. Joseph Institute for the Deaf | 597 |
| United Cerebral Palsy of Southwest Mo. Development Center | 4 |
| Fontbonne College Speech Clinic | 1 |
| The Rehabilitation Institute & Physical Therapy Center | 16 |
| Childrens Mercy Hospital Speech & Hearing Clinic | 18 |
| Services for Deaf and Hard of Hearing, Fulton | 270 |
| Lottie L. Riekehof, Springfield | 25 |
| Mr. Raymond Atwood, St. Louis | 16 |
| Mrs. Jerd Sights, Hannibal | 22 |

## MONTANA

| | |
|---|---:|
| Montana Association of the Deaf, Inc. | 175 |
| Montana Association of the Deaf News | 137 |
| Great Falls Club of the Deaf | 40 |
| Livingston Day Club | 5 |
| Missoula Club of the Deaf | 21 |
| Ursline Academy, Great Falls | 29 |
| Carroll College, Catholic | 32 |
| Christ Lutheran Church | 132 |
| Montana School for the Deaf and Blind | 408 |
| Montana Center for Handicapped Children | 66 |

## NEBRASKA

| | |
|---|---:|
| Nebraska Association of the Deaf | 133 |
| Lincoln Silent Club | 132 |

*193*

Omaha Club of the Deaf .......................................... 442
The Family, Omaha .................................................. 6
Merry Mixers Club .................................................. 41
Deaf Family Circle, Omaha .......................................... 7
Lincoln Hearing Society ............................................ 28
The Maple Villagers, Omaha ......................................... 20
Neighborhood Church, Assemblies of God, Gering ...................... 7
Holy Name Catholic Church ......................................... 112
Grace Memorial Church .............................................. 61
Bethlehem Deaf Lutheran Church .................................... 274
Faith Lutheran, Hastings ............................................ 1
Nebraska School for the Deaf ...................................... 364
University of Nebraska ............................................. 149
Division of Rehabilitation Services, Lincoln ...................... 600
The Deaf Nebraskan, Publication ................................... 648
Mr. Gerald Wilson, Mitchell ........................................ 10
Anonymous ........................................................... 4

## NEVADA

South Nevada Association of the Deaf,
Las Vegas Club for the Deaf ....................................... 237
Lake Mead Baptist Association ...................................... 13
State of Nevada Speech and Hearing Clinic ........................... 2
Department of Health, Welfare and Rehabilitation .................. 141
Mr. Richard Muller, Reno ............................................ 1
Anonymous ........................................................... 1

## NEW HAMPSHIRE

Manchester Deaf Club ............................................... 70
Crotched Mountain School for the Deaf ............................. 547
Crotched Mountain Foundation ........................................ 4
Vocational Rehabilitation Division, Concord ....................... 761

## NEW JERSEY

New Jersey Association of the Deaf ................................ 721
Plainfield Hearing Society ......................................... 66
Committee for Deaf Skiers, Camden ................................. 302
Middlesex County Silent Club, Inc. ................................ 641
Lodi Silent Club ................................................... 14
Northern Valley Movie Club ......................................... 13
Delaware Valley Club of the Deaf .................................. 102
Union Social Club for the Deaf and Hard of Hearing ................. 17

The Violet Club of the Deaf, Orange
Inter-County Deaf Association, Hawthorne 14
Columbia Club for the Deaf 11
Bergen Circle 8
Paramus Regional 101
Passaic Silent Club 6
Florence Movie Club 9
The Cinematic Club of Northern New Jersey 8
Northern Regional Club for the Deaf 4
Route 4 of the Deaf, Fairlawn 5
East Paterson Film Club 16
Trenton Silent Club 143
Mercer County Chapter of NJAD 263
South Jersey Hearing Society 63
Calvary Chapel of the Deaf 1,267
Nativity Lutheran Church 20
St. Matthew Lutheran Church for the Deaf 1,260
Hope Lutheran Church of the Deaf, Camden 13
Ephphatha Guild for the Deaf, Atlantic City 55
Hope Lutheran Church for the Deaf, Pennsauken 20
Assemblies of God, Toms River 18
Marie H. Katzenbach School for the Deaf 2,954
Bruce Street School 230
St. Barnabas Medical Center Rehabilitation Department 11
Jersey City State College 17
Hunterdon Medical Center, Speech and Hearing Department 9
Burlington County Memorial Hospital, Speech & Hearing Center 125
The Matheny School, Speech & Hearing Department 15
The Concha, Publication, Plainfield Hearing Society 66
The Catholic Auditor, Publication, Trenton Apostolate of the Deaf 410
Mr. & Mrs. Paul Levenson, Ramsey 78
Edgio Lepre 55
Mrs. George A. Calder, Paterson 11
George B. Bedford, River Edge 117
Miss Betty A. Greene, Westfirld 26
Mr. Arne Olsen, Jersey City 103
Mr. William S. Nordstrom, Fort Lee 4
Anonymous 483


**NEW MEXICO**
First Baptist Church, Dexter 5
First Baptist Church, Clovis 34
Missionary Sisters of Our Lady of Victory 138

| | |
|---|---:|
| Church of Christ | 7 |
| First Baptist Church, Mountainair | 1 |
| New Mexico School for the Deaf | 23 |
| The Rehabilitation Center, Inc., Albuquerque | 2 |
| Vocational Rehabilitation Services, Santa Fe | 535 |
| Mrs. Mary A. Contreras, Santa Fe | 1 |
| Mrs. Esperanza C. Latimer, Santa Fe | 366 |
| Anonymous | 1 |

## NEW YORK

| | |
|---|---:|
| Empire State Association of the Deaf | 12 |
| Union League of the Deaf, Inc. | 600 |
| Rochester Civic Association of the Deaf | 303 |
| Rochester Recreation Club for the Deaf | 64 |
| Syracuse Civic Association of the Deaf | 77 |
| Central New York Recreation Club for the Deaf | 45 |
| Merry-Go-Rounders, New York | 334 |
| New York Society for the Deaf | 3,851 |
| Long Island Club of the Deaf | 144 |
| Mid Hudson Valley Silent Club, Hyde Park | 28 |
| De Sales Youth Club, Inc., Ridgewood | 164 |
| Brooklyn Association of the Deaf, Inc., | 252 |
| Committee for Deaf Skiers, New York City | 218 |
| New York Civic Association of the Deaf | 1,004 |
| Albany Silent Athletic Club | 72 |
| Capital District Civic Association of the Deaf | 289 |
| Flushing Cinema Club | 3 |
| Mutual Friends, Elmont, Long Island | 132 |
| Pittsford Club | 22 |
| Flushing Dactyls | 38 |
| Women's Club of the Deaf | 484 |
| Brighton Cinema Group | 8 |
| Deaf of Ocean Avenue, Brooklyn | 11 |
| New York Catholic Deaf Center | 1,670 |
| Wantagh Group, Long Island | 9 |
| Lefrank Society for the Deaf | 28 |
| Schell Family Circle, Brooklyn | 17 |
| Centereach Group, Long Island | 8 |
| Albany Capitol District Association for the Deaf | 79 |
| The Bronx Silent Club | 36 |
| Rego Park Society for the Deaf | 235 |
| National Theater of the Deaf | 75 |
| Long Island Indians Bowling League | 129 |
| Spoilers Bowling League, New York | 251 |

| | |
|---|---:|
| First Assembly of God, White Plains | 25 |
| Alpha Lutheran Church of the Deaf | 352 |
| The Church Mission to the Deaf, Protestant Episcopal Dioceses of Albany, Central New York, Rochester & Western New York | 696 |
| Syracuse Catholic Deaf Society | 153 |
| Brooklyn Mission & Guild of the Deaf, St. Ann's Church | 215 |
| Church Mission to Deaf Mutes, Synod House | 9 |
| Temple Beth Or of the Deaf | 192 |
| St. Matthew Lutheran Church for the Deaf | 652 |
| El-Bethel Assembly of God | 5 |
| Highland Avenue Baptist Church | 46 |
| Manhattan Baptist Church | 1 |
| Triple Cities Catholic Deaf, Binghamton | 84 |
| Deaf Bible Study, Hollis | 29 |
| Puerto Rican Society for the Catholic Deaf | 45 |
| Buffalo Catholic Deaf Society | 153 |
| Brooklyn Hebrew Society of the Deaf | 133 |
| Assemblies of God, Rome, N.Y. | 3 |
| Assemblies of God, New York | 25 |
| New York School for the Deaf | 1,109 |
| Fanwood Journal N.Y. Public Residential School | 703 |
| New York State School for the Deaf | 1,187 |
| Rochester School for the Deaf | 1,063 |
| Mill Neck Manor Lutheran School for the Deaf | 304 |
| St. Mary's School for the Deaf | 1,105 |
| Cleary School for Deaf Children | 142 |
| St. Joseph's School for the Deaf | 769 |
| St. Francis de Sales School for the Deaf | 139 |
| School for the Deaf, Jr. H.S. 47-M | 80 |
| Sienna College, Loudonville | 133 |
| Long Island College Hospital, Speech Pathology Service | 2 |
| Hofstra University Speech and Hearing Center | 2 |
| The Burke Rehabilitation Center | 97 |
| St. Agnes Hospital, Childrens Unit, Speech Therapy Department | 3 |
| House of the Good Samaritan, Hospital Rehabilitation Department | 3 |
| Albert Einstein College of Medicine | 271 |
| Empire State News | 360 |
| The Silent Press, New York | 2,500 |
| Older American Volunteers Committee | 66 |
| Speech Pathology Audiology Clinic | 536 |
| Queens Speech & Hearing Center, Queens College, University of N.Y. | 52 |
| St. John's University, Speech and Hearing Center | 2 |
| Mount View Hospital, Speech and Hearing Unit | 27 |

*197*

| | |
|---|---|
| Northeastern New York Speech Center, Inc. | 4 |
| State University of N.Y., College Speech Clinic | 3 |
| Montefiore Speech & Hearing Center, Department of Rehabilitation Medicine, Montefiore Hospital | 10 |
| Mount Sinai Hospital Speech and Hearing Center | 26 |
| Suffork State School, BOCES #3 Speech & Hearing Services | 138 |
| N. Shore Hospital, Speech and Hearing Center | 39 |
| Children's Hospital & Rehabilitation Hearing and Speech Center | 19 |
| Special Children's Center, Inc., Ithaca | 5 |
| Rev. Robert Dwyer, Rome | 59 |
| Rev. Eugene Dyer, Westbury | 686 |
| Rev. Don Panburn, Brooklyn | 1 |
| Mrs. Philip J. Knauff, Huntington | 73 |
| Mr. & Mrs. Jonnie C. Johnson, Glen Cove | 1 |
| Mr. Henry L. Buzzard, Peekskill | 64 |
| V. Giaime, Wyandanch | 6 |
| Mr. Walter Eimold, Huntington | 4 |
| Morton Storn, Melville | 1 |
| Sister Mary Marlene, CSSF, Rome | 59 |
| Vincent C. Iannucci, Bronx | 180 |
| Mr. & Mrs. K. Rothchild, Poughkeepsie | 2 |
| Mr. Raymond St. Fort, Brooklyn | 2 |
| Mr. Richard H. Myers, New York | 1,682 |
| Walter M. Schulman, New York | 259 |
| Mr. Edigio Al Lepre, Brooklyn | 1,060 |
| John Schroedel, New York | 64 |
| Anonymous | 211 |

**NORTH CAROLINA**

| | |
|---|---|
| North Carolina Association of the Deaf | 426 |
| Wilson Chapter, Association of the Deaf | 23 |
| Winston-Salem Chapter, Association of the Deaf | 34 |
| Burlington Chapter, Association of the Deaf | 40 |
| Raleigh-Durham Chapter, Association of the Deaf | 76 |
| Kannapolis-Salisbury Chapter, Association of the Deaf | 57 |
| Fayetteville Chapter, Association of the Deaf | 42 |
| Ashville Chapter, Association of the Deaf | 33 |
| Eastern Golf Tournament for the Deaf | 10 |
| Grace Lutheran Church for the Deaf | 63 |
| West Memorial Baptist Church | 9 |
| Holloway Street Baptist Church, Durham | 10 |
| Temple Baptist Church, Wilmington | 14 |
| First Baptist Church, Whiteville | 21 |

| | |
|---|---:|
| Kinnett Memorial Baptist Church | 37 |
| First Baptist Church, Morganton | 77 |
| Oak Grove Baptist Church | 31 |
| Baptist State Convention of N.C. | 39 |
| First Baptist Church, Raleigh | 67 |
| First Baptist Church, Charlotte | 31 |
| First Baptist Church, Kinston | 14 |
| McGill Street Baptist Church, Concord | 7 |
| First Baptist Church, Ellerbe | 1 |
| First Baptist Church, Fayetteville | 30 |
| Flint Grove Baptist Church, Gastonia | 13 |
| First Baptist Church, Greensboro | 29 |
| First Baptist Church, Hamlet | 14 |
| First Baptist Church, Kannapolis | 26 |
| Calvary Baptist Church, Morganton | 12 |
| El Bethel Baptist Church, Morganton | 9 |
| Fellowship Baptist Church, Mt. Airy | 12 |
| Rosemary Baptist Church | 13 |
| First Baptist Church, Rocky Mount | |
| Liberty Grove Baptist Church, North Wilkesboro | 19 |
| First Baptist Church, Salisbury | 13 |
| First Baptist Church, Sanford | 7 |
| First Baptist Church, Thomasville | 21 |
| Woodland Baptist Church, Winston-Salem | 102 |
| First Baptist Church, Shelby | 45 |
| Adamsville Baptist Church, Goldsboro | 26 |
| North Carolina Sunday School Association of the Deaf | 209 |
| North Carolina School for the Deaf | 624 |
| Governor Morehead School | 378 |
| Eastern North Carolina School for the Deaf | 726 |
| Division of Vocational Rehabilitation, Raleigh | 1,946 |
| Western Carolina University Speech & Hearing Center | 9 |
| The Bugler, Publication, North Carolina Association of the Deaf | 610 |
| Miss Elizabeth Larcombe, High Point | 24 |
| Miss Marie Butkus, Morganton | 26 |
| Anonymous | 2 |

**NORTH DAKOTA**

| | |
|---|---:|
| North Dakota Association of the Deaf | 274 |
| St. James Church, Minnewaukan | 19 |
| North Dakota School for the Deaf | 212 |
| North Dakota Banner, Publication North Dakota Residential School | 685 |

*200*

| | |
|---|---:|
| Lewisburg Baptist Church | 20 |
| Riverview Baptist Church | 235 |
| First Baptist Church of Oak Harbor | 2 |
| Heights Baptist Church | 5 |
| Westwood Baptist Church | 5 |
| CCWD-Episcopal, East Sparta | 72 |
| CCWD-Episcopal, Canton | 11 |
| CCWD-Episcopal, Columbus | 13 |
| CCWD-Episcopal, Toledo | 38 |
| Cleveland Hebrew Association of the Deaf | 75 |
| First Baptist Church of Mt. Repose | 1 |
| Ridgewood Baptist Church | 2 |
| Ohio School for the Deaf | 347 |
| St. Rita School for the Deaf | 841 |
| St. John School, Lorain | 115 |
| Lorain County Area Parents Section of Alexander Graham Bell Association | 44 |
| Alexander Graham Bell School | 8 |
| Delaware City County Speech and Hearing Center | 11 |
| Ohio State University Physical Medicine and Rehabilitation Center | 3 |
| Toledo Hearing and Speech Center | 52 |
| United Cerebral Palsy of Columbus and Franklin Co. | 1 |
| Betty Jane Memorial Rehabilitation Center | 16 |
| Clark County Hearing and Speech Center | 13 |
| Columbus State Institute | 73 |
| United Services for the Handicapped | 58 |
| Rehabilitation Services Commission, Columbus | 2,194 |
| Bureau of Vocational Rehabilitation, Columbus | 140 |
| Ohio Home for the Aged and Infirm Deaf | 185 |
| Sister Mary Arthur, Toledo | 30 |
| Sister Mary Ann Logan, CSJ, Cleveland | 18 |
| Rev. John Edwards, Canton | 13 |
| Mrs. Daniel Johnson, Findlay | 143 |
| Dorothy Jackson, Akron | 30 |
| William C. Hillard, Cincinnati | 329 |
| Irene Tunanidas, Youngstown | 90 |
| Ernest Hairston, Ohio | 182 |
| Charles Williams, E. Cleveland | 111 |
| Anonymous | 32 |

## OKLAHOMA

| | |
|---|---:|
| Oklahoma State Association of the Deaf | 448 |
| Central Assembly of God, Muskogee | 35 |

First Assembly of God Deaf Church 40
Central Assembly of God, Tulsa 26
First Baptist Church, Oklahoma City 48
Lonestar Baptist Church 3
First Baptist Church, Shawnee 6
First Baptist Church, Tulsa 29
Ministry with the Deaf, The United Methodist Church 729
Oklahoma School for the Deaf 649
Jane Brooks Foundation 302
Community Speech and Hearing Center, Enid 18
University of Oklahoma Speech and Hearing Clinic 2
Social and Rehabilitation Services, Oklahoma City 1,225
The Okie Visitor 193
The Lamplighter, Publication 554
Mrs. William B. Cox, Tulsa 570
Rev. Joseph Thompson, Sulphur 5


## OREGON

Oregon State Association of the Deaf 204
Portland Association of the Deaf 1,196
Let's Get Together Club, Beaverton 30
Emerald Valley Club of the Deaf 192
Seventh Day Adventist Church, Battle Ground 240
Assembly of God, Lebanon 7
First Assembly of God, Medford 18
First Assembly of God Deaf Church, Portland 378
Oregon State School for the Deaf 362
The Oregon Outlook, Oregon, Public Residential School 666
Hosford School for the Deaf in Portland 176
Eugene Hearing and Speech Center 16
Portland State University Speech and Hearing Clinic 27
Portland Center for Hearing and Speech 148
Vocational Research Project, Salem 1,097
Department of Vocational Rehabilitation, Salem 239
Oregon Association of the Deaf Newsletter 604
Mrs. H.R. Corless, Beaver Creek 4
Mr. & Mrs. Robert Lidfors, Beaverton 63
Clarence Supalla, Beaverton 215


## PENNSYLVANIA

Pennsylvania Society for the Advancement of the Deaf 2,000
Pittsburgh Chapter, Society for the Advancement of the Deaf 534
Lancaster Chapter, PSAD 26

| | |
|---|---:|
| Wyoming Valley Crippled Childrens Association | 12 |
| Home of the Merciful Savior for Crippled Children, Philadelphia | 8 |
| Thomas Jefferson University, Hearing and Speech Center | 43 |
| Pennsylvania School for the Deaf, Speech and Hearing Service | 1,050 |
| California State College Speech & Hearing Clinic, California, Pennsylvania | 16 |
| Indiana University of Pennsylvania | 15 |
| St. Vincent Rehabilitation Center | 24 |
| Blair County Society for Crippled Children & Adults, Speech & Hearing Service | 3 |
| York County Easter Seal Society for Crippled Children & Adults | 5 |
| The Hearing Conservation Center of Lancaster County | 183 |
| Lancaster Cleft Palate Clinic | 1 |
| Lycoming County Crippled Childrens Society, Inc., Speech and Hearing Clinic | 6 |
| Counseling & Community Service Center for the Deaf | 748 |
| University of Pittsburg, School of Education, Program for the Deaf | 75 |
| Pittsburgh Counseling and Community Service | 140 |
| Pennsylvania Rehabilitation Center | 50 |
| Pennsylvania Society for the Advancement of the Deaf | 200 |
| Children's Bus Club | 113 |
| Geneva College Speech Clinic | 2 |
| Ebensburg State School & Hospital, Speech & Hearing Clinic | 1 |
| Clarion State College, Speech and Hearing Clinic | 24 |
| Center for Learning & Communication Disorders, Bloomsburg State College | 2 |
| The Easter Seal Society for Crippled Children & Adults, Speech and Hearing Service | 8 |
| Nelson-Egnatovitch Family, Berwyn | 19 |
| Mr. Hugh Cusack, Philadelphia | 215 |
| Mrs. A. Rivera, Philadelphia | 379 |
| Anonymous | 316 |

**RHODE ISLAND**

| | |
|---|---:|
| Providence Club of the Deaf | 97 |
| Rhode Island Girls Club for the Deaf | 434 |
| Mid-Camp Cinema, Cranston | 9 |
| St. Francis Chapel | 427 |

**SOUTH CAROLINA**

| | |
|---|---:|
| South Carolina Association of the Deaf | 229 |
| Carolina Athletic Association of the Deaf | 13 |
| Mon-Aetna Baptist Church, Union | 15 |

| | |
|---|---|
| First Calvary Baptist Church | 22 |
| First Baptist Church, Anderson | 17 |
| Citadel Square Baptist Church | 26 |
| Arial Baptist Church | 9 |
| West End Baptist Church | 9 |
| West Greenville Baptist Church | 2 |
| Cedar Spring Baptist Church | 21 |
| Westminster Baptist Church | 13 |
| Hampton Heights Baptist Church | 3 |
| The Palmetto Leaf-South Carolina, Public Residential School | 199 |
| South Carolina School for the Deaf and Blind | 487 |
| United Speech and Hearing Services, Greenville | 8 |
| Medical College of South Carolina, Hearing & Speech Facility | 371 |
| Spartanburg Speech and Hearing Clinic | 4 |
| Hearing and Speech Center, Columbia | 297 |
| South Carolina State College Speech and Hearing Clinic | 8 |
| Augusta Circle School | 11 |
| Speech & Hearing, Arthur M. LaBreece, Charleston | 15 |
| Estes School | 7 |
| State Department of Education, Columbia | 487 |
| Mrs. Margie Candler, Greenville | 6 |
| Mr. Thomas Kerr, St. Augustine | 250 |
| Mr. Craig Maddox, Greenville | 543 |
| Rev. Robert W. Short, Sr., Spartanburg | 83 |

## SOUTH DAKOTA

| | |
|---|---|
| South Dakota Association of the Deaf | 207 |
| Pasque Club for the Deaf | 18 |
| Trinity Lutheran Church, Sioux Falls | 100 |
| Apostolate for the Deaf, Sioux Falls | 9 |
| South Dakota School for the Deaf | 688 |
| University of South Dakota, Speech & Hearing Center | 8 |
| South Dakota School for the Deaf, Hearing and Speech Center | 46 |
| Division of Vocational Rehabilitation, Pierre | 340 |
| Anonymous | 3 |

## TENNESSEE

| | |
|---|---|
| Tennessee Association of the Deaf | 123 |
| Bowling League, N. Charleston | 5 |
| Nashville League for the Hard of Hearing | 144 |
| First Baptist Church, Memphis | 53 |
| First Baptist Church, Dyersburg | 4 |

| | |
|---|---:|
| First Baptist Church, Bristol | 22 |
| First Baptist Church, Greeneville | 12 |
| East Ridge Baptist Church | 21 |
| Silent Class, Unoka Avenue Baptist Church | 69 |
| First Baptist Church, Knoxville | 176 |
| Central Baptist Church, Oak Ridge | 11 |
| Central Church of Christ, Nashville | 325 |
| St. Mary's Episcopal Cathedral | 4 |
| Grace Lutheran Church for the Deaf | 778 |
| First Baptist Church, Elizabethton | 2 |
| Immanuel Baptist Church | 8 |
| Deaf Fellowship of Chattanooga | 130 |
| First Baptist Church, Nashville | 39 |
| First Baptist Church, Paris | 5 |
| First Baptist Church, Parsons | 8 |
| Memphis Parents' School for the Deaf and Aphasic | 104 |
| Tennessee School for the Deaf | 247 |
| University of Tennessee Hearing and Speech Center | 30 |
| Memphis Speech and Hearing Center | 23 |
| Middle Tennessee State University Speech and Hearing Clinic | 7 |
| Daniel Arthur Rehabilitation Center | 17 |
| Regional Services for the Adult Deaf, Chattanooga | 178 |
| Division of Vocational Rehabilitation, Nashville | 210 |
| Tennessee Association of the Deaf Newsletter | 593 |
| Rev. William L. Ashbridge, Memphis | 22 |
| Mr. and Mrs. Uriel C. Jones, Knoxville | 4 |
| Mr. Harold Perry, Tennessee | 96 |
| William Wosdrick, Tennessee | 111 |

## TEXAS

| | |
|---|---:|
| Texas Association of the Deaf | 2,700 |
| Fort Worth Silent Club | 107 |
| Houston Association of the Deaf | 319 |
| Beaumont Club of the Deaf | 126 |
| San Antonio Association of the Deaf | 21 |
| Texas Society of Interpreters for the Deaf | 48 |
| Amarillo Silent Club | 24 |
| The Lubbock Silent Deaf Club | 34 |
| Deaf Group of Tarrant County | 105 |
| El Paso Association of the Deaf | 39 |
| Coastal Bend Silent Club | 81 |
| Southeast Texas Movie Club of the Deaf | 116 |
| Congress Avenue Baptist Church | 51 |
| Trinity Baptist Church, Lubbock | 16 |

| | |
|---|---:|
| First Baptist Church, Harlingen | 368 |
| First Baptist Church, El Paso | 5 |
| Hampton Place Baptist Church | 33 |
| First Baptist Church, Amarillo | 36 |
| First Baptist Church, Gainesville | 19 |
| Calvary Baptist Church, Cleveland | 9 |
| First Baptist Church, Midland | 34 |
| Memorial Baptist Church, Baytown | 30 |
| Calvary Baptist Church, Pampa | 4 |
| First Baptist Church, San Angelo | 19 |
| Trinity Baptist Church, Corsicana | 20 |
| First Baptist Church, Lake Jackson | 7 |
| First Baptist Church, Hamilton | 1 |
| First Baptist Church, Beaumont | 23 |
| St. John's Missionary Baptist Church | 25 |
| First Baptist Church, Odessa | 5 |
| First Baptist Church, Tyler | 21 |
| Seventh Street Baptist Church | 42 |
| Calvery Baptist Deaf Fellowship | 55 |
| Baptist Temple, Houston | 56 |
| First Baptist Church, Irving | 55 |
| First Baptist Church, Kilgore | 8 |
| First Baptist Church, Abilene | 31 |
| Fredonia Hill Baptist Church | 12 |
| First Baptist Church, Brownwood | 4 |
| North Park Baptist Church, Sherman | 14 |
| Calvary Baptist Church, Borger | 2 |
| Morgan Avenue Baptist Church | 57 |
| First Baptist Church, Texarkana | 84 |
| St. Francis De Sales Deaf Society, Houston-Galveston Dioceses | 266 |
| St. Ignatius Martyr Church, Austin | 32 |
| Church of Christ, Dallas | 47 |
| Lutheran Deaf Mission, Dallas | 138 |
| First Baptist Church, Houston | 102 |
| Golden Triangle Catholic Deaf Society, Beaumont | 25 |
| Memorial Baptist Church, Baytown | 13 |
| Silent Friends Mission, Dallas | 322 |
| Baptist Temple Church, Houston | 27 |
| Highland Baptist Church, Carrollton | 6 |
| Cedar Crest Church of Christ, Garland | 36 |
| Columbus Avenue Church of Christ | 12 |
| Sunday School Special Class, Dallas | 129 |
| Mother Mary Deaf Group, Dallas | 68 |
| Deaf Department, North Fort Worth Baptist Church | 38 |

Baptist Temple Silent Class, Houston 24
Eisenhauer Road Baptist Church 64
St. Ignatius Rectory, Austin 18
CCWD-Episcopal, Fort Worth 7
International Catholic Deaf Association (#97), El Paso 65
First Baptist Church, Groves 72
First Baptist Church, San Antonio 29
Texas School for the Deaf 1,794
Houston School for Deaf Children 149
Sunshine Cottage for the Deaf 114
Pilot School for the Deaf 17
Division of Vocational Rehabilitation, Houston Special Services 49
Permian Basin Rehabilitation Center 91
Texas Rehabilitation Commission, Waco 54
Department of Vocational Rehabilitation 125
Texas Employment Commission, Odessa 53
West Texas Rehabilitation Center, Abilene 121
Texas Christian University, Speech & Hearing Clinic 52
West Texas State University, Speech & Hearing Clinic 8
Easter Seal Society for Crippled Children & Adults
   of Bexar Co., Inc. 6
Lamar Speech and Hearing Center 152
The Bell County Rehabilitation Center 6
Texas Womans University, Speech and Hearing Clinic 2
Tarrant County Easter Seal Center, Speech Department 83
East Texas State University, Speech and Hearing Clinic 3
East Texas Treatment Center 35
Grayson County Crippled Children & Adults Center 6
Bexar County Hearing Society 22
Callier Hearing and Speech Center 732
Southwest Service Center, Internal Revenue Service 22
Hearing Conservation Services, Speech & Hearing 175
The Deaf Texan, Publication 244
Mr. George Joslin, Garland 750
Rev. Nicholas Curtin, Houston 2
Mrs. R. M. Adams, Dallas 43
Bert E. Poss, Austin 332
Polly Walton, Houston 94
Anonymous 3


**UTAH**

Christ the King Convent 36
Church of Jesus Christ of Latter-Day Saints, Ogden 100

Church of Jesus Christ of Latter-Day Saints, Salt Lake City 174
Our Lady of Victory, Chapter #76 9
Institute of Religion, Salt Lake City 11
Public Residential School 33
Utah Schools for the Deaf and Blind 54
University of Utah, Speech and Hearing Clinic 31
Mr. Robert Sanderson, Roy 520
Anonymous 168

## VERMONT

The Austine School for the Deaf 273
Medical Center Hospital of Vermont,
    Center for Disorders of Communication 10
Vermont Association for the Crippled 4

## VIRGINIA

Virginia Association of the Deaf 176
Tidewater Chapter Association of the Deaf 72
Martinsville Club of the Deaf 29
Potomac Silent Club 223
Richmond Club of the Deaf 118
Milk House Free Theatre Group 30
Gallows Movie Club 10
Northern Virginia Deaf Bowling Association 49
Stardust Club 11
Peninsula Deaf Club 23
Riverside Baptist Church 26
Ash Camp Baptist Church 1,870
Starling Avenue Baptist Church, Martinsville 159
Baptist General Association of Virginia 831
St. Paul's Episcopal Church 38
St. Mark's Lutheran Church 46
Christian Deaf Fellowship & United Evangelical Churches 118
Fredericksburg Baptist Church 19
Beth Car Baptist Church 8
Cool Spring Baptist Church 7
Bethlehem Baptist Church 4
Poplar Springs Baptist Church 6
First Baptist Church, Roanoke 6
First Baptist Church, Staunton 89
Gruver-Walden Missionary Circle 19
Virginia School for the Deaf and Blind 6,604
Virginia Public Residential School 685

Virginia School at Hampton 379
Hampton Institute, Speech and Hearing Clinic 137
Madison College Speech and Hearing Center 8
Crippled Childrens Hospital, Speech and Hearing Service 1
St. Paul's Oral School 123
Western State Hospital 37
Department of Vocational Rehabilitation, Richmond 580
The Virginia Association of the Deaf Bulletin, Publication 195
Rev. John W. Stallings, Norfolk 26
Mrs. Bernard W. Moore, Richmond 731
Mr. Warren C. Blackwell, Charlottesville 1,072

## WASHINGTON STATE
Washington State Association of the Deaf 400
Spokane Chapter, Association of the Deaf 101
Puget Sound Association of the Deaf 388
BEDITU WHWO Club, Vancouver 37
The Ranmorsta Club 7
St. James Cathedral 41
International Catholic Deaf Association, Seattle Chapter 96
Mt. St. Michael's Deaf Society, Mt. St. Michael's Seminary 99
Faith Lutheran Church of the Deaf, Spokane 185
United Evangelical Church of the Deaf 41
Catholic Deaf Study of Yakima 6
Ballard Free Methodist Church 62
Washington School for the Deaf 910
Spastic Childrens Clinic and Preschool 4
Walla Walla College, Speech Clinic 3
Washington State University, Speech & Hearing Clinic,
    Department of Speech 49
Eastern Washington State College, Speech & Hearing Clinic 20
Central Washington State College, Speech & Hearing Clinic 14
Western Washington State College, Speech & Hearing Clinic 127
Harper-Papalia Families 4
Rev. Robert Bickford, Spokane 131
Mrs. Margaret L. Pope, Spokane 305
Mr. Clyde Ketchum 997
Miss June Brice, Pt. Angeles 4
Anonymous 83

## WEST VIRGINIA
Charleston Association of the Deaf 31
Church of Christ, Old Hickory, Tenn. 18

West Virginia School for the Deaf and Blind 900
West Virginia University, Speech and Hearing Clinic 11
Services for Deaf & Hearing Impaired,
   Division of Vocational Rehabilitation 1,549
West Virginia School for the Deaf 86


**WISCONSIN**

Wisconsin Association of the Deaf 838
Milwaukee Safety Commission 269
Northeastern Wisconsin Club of the Deaf 139
Rib Mountain Silent Club 150
Green Bay Club of the Deaf 26
Madison Association of the Deaf 313
Oral Deaf Club, North West Side 33
The Rac-Keno Club of the Deaf 36
Sheboygan Silent Club 15
Manitowoc Silent Club 15
Milwaukee Silent Club 137
Bowling League 51
Madison Association for the Education/Deaf 121
Evangel Deaf Church 92
First Assembly of God, Waukesha 3
Calvary Assembly of God, West Allis 64
St. Andrew's Church 71
Silent Lutheran Church 310
Lutheran Deaf Mission Society 117
Emmanuel Lutheran Church for the Deaf, Milwaukee 93
Silent Mission of St. James Episcopal 20
Emmanuel Lutheran Church of the Deaf, Greenfield 95
Lutheran Laymen's League 33
Holy Family Convent 42
The Wisconsin Times, Wisconsin Public Residential School 149
Wisconsin School for the Deaf 149
St. John's School for the Deaf 578
Wisconsin State University, Speech & Hearing Center 115
Wisconsin State University, Speech & Hearing Clinic,
   Stevens Point 45
Marshfield Clinic 12
Wisconsin State University, Speech & Hearing Services,
   River Falls 11
Wisconsin State University, Speech & Hearing Clinic,
   Whitewater 11
Deaf Community of Pope John 1,025

# APPENDIX B

## Appendix B

# Special Meeting
# on the
# Identification of Black Deaf Persons
# for the
# National Census of the Deaf Population

What follows is a condensation of several hours of intensive discussion about a major problem for the National Census of the Deaf Population—the identification of Black deaf persons. The participants in the conference set aside their individual predilections and devoted themselves fully to considering the issues and proposing ways to meet them. It is for that reason that the proceedings of their deliberations do not separately attribute the ideas expressed; the meeting was a group effort, an effort of which all members of the group can be justifiably proud. It should further be noted that these proceedings are greatly condensed and, in the process of summarization, tend to lose some of the richness of the give and take which so enlivened the discussions. However, no printed record can adequately portray the actual event, so the decision was made to shorten the report in favor of broader distribution and greater emphasis on implementation of the many valuable suggestions.

The presentation begins with a brief review of the studies on deafness in the Black population. The current problems of conducting a census of Black deaf persons are then summarized and followed by suggestions for meeting the problems. The meeting, of course, conformed to no such orderly pattern, but for ultimate usefulness of this document it was felt better to ignore the temporal order in which the points arose, so as to bring similar ideas into juxtaposition.

Finally, the burden of any misstatements or errors of omission cannot be placed upon the participants. The undersigned take full responsibility for such mistakes, though they cannot similarly claim credit for the excellence of this report.

Jerome D. Schein
Project Director

Peter W. Ries
Senior Research Associate

30 September 1970

## Background

Ever since 1830, when the U.S. Bureau of the Census[2] first attempted to enumerate deaf persons, the prevalence rate for deafness has been reported to be higher in the white than the black population. This finding appeared consistently in the eleven decennial censuses to 1930, at which time the Bureau ceased collecting information on deafness, as well as on other chronic conditions.

Supporting the idea that there were proportionally fewer black than white deaf persons was the National Health Survey of 1935-36[1]. Similarly, the 1940 survey of deafness in Georgia[3] reported a lower rate for blacks. In 1959, Lunde and Bigman[4] reported a nationwide study of deaf persons and expressed dissatisfaction with the sampling plan which yielded so few black deaf persons that no separate consideration could be given them. They were perhaps the first researchers to question the validity of the rates previously published. Though the Bureau of the Census gave up morbidity studies because it did not feel it could do them properly, it did not specifically doubt the findings in relation to skin color. The Washington, D.C. survey[7], in 1963, did have some evidence of underenumeration of black deaf persons, but the study did not pursue the issue. We have been left, then, with nearly a 140 years' belief that deafness is less prevalent in the black than the white population.

Reasons for this difference have centered on three kinds of explanations: (a) constitutional, (b) socio-economic and (c) methodologic. Post[5] has hypothesized differences in the genetic makeup of blacks and whites, differences enhanced by selective mating, which lead to superior hearing by black persons. Similarly, Rosen et. al.[6] have proposed a physiological explanation. More frequently accepted as the explanation is the great discrepancy in medical care received by the two groups. For example, the white child stricken by meningitis loses his hearing, but lives, while the similarly afflicted black child, receiving poorer treatment, dies. Preferential medical services for the white population lead to proportionately higher survival rates for premature infants, children suffering high febrile disorders, and other physical assaults associated with deafness. It might also be mentioned in connection with the socio-economic explanations that the black deaf person is less apt to marry, because he earns less money. Thus he is not as likely to have genetically deaf offspring.

The methodologic argument is simple: low socio-economic groups, particularly black persons, are more frequently missed by census takers. Underenumeration is likely to be greater for black deaf than hearing persons, because the former more frequently live in depressed housing and are more difficult to interview than the latter. It has been suggested

*216*

that the lower prevalence rate of deafness among black persons may be the resultant of several of the above factors rather than any one.

Insofar as the explanations are economic and methodologic, they may not hold in the current Census; i.e., it is possible that equal or greater prevalence of deafness may be found in the black population. The black person is slowly experiencing improvement in his economic circumstances. Medical care should be better than in earlier times. Ironically, then, the black population's social and economic gains may lead to proportional reduction of good hearing among its members.

The National Census of the Deaf aims at as accurate an estimation as possible: it is a census of *all* deaf persons. Hence the problems of identifying deaf persons who belong to minority groups are of particular interest. The purposes of this meeting are to develop the means of overcoming the previously cited difficulties of locating black deaf persons and to enlist the support necessary to implement the search program.

### The Problem

It was agreed that the difficulty of locating black deaf persons arises from (a) their lack of education and (b) their alienation from society, both black and white. Their generally low socio-economic condition was not discussed at length, but was tacitly accepted as a major contributing factor.

Many black deaf children in the South never attended school or attended for only a brief time. Thus school records do not offer an adequate source for their names. As an example, it was pointed out that the Mississippi School for the Negro Deaf was so overcrowded following World War II that an estimated 110 children were denied admission over a five-year period. Upon the recent completion of additional facilities an effort was made to find these children, but they had "faded into the Delta."

Similar problems were noted in other Southern states. An exception, in Memphis, Tennessee, probably has occurred because of the good working relations, dating back to 1926, between the Education and Health Departments. One half of the Memphis school-age population is black and one half the deaf students in the day-school programs are black, suggesting that black deaf children are attending school as frequently as white deaf children.

Illiteracy can, unfortunately, be present among children who have gone to school as well as among those who did not. Some black deaf persons are so barren of language as to not know their own names. They may communicate solely with "home signs", gestures developed by family members for communication between themselves and the deaf person. These deaf individuals are not even known to other deaf persons, or if they are, often can only be identified by their name sign. Such individuals would be extremely difficult to locate, without cooperation of their hearing relatives.

Taking a census of black persons may arouse the suspicions of both black and white officials. Black persons frequently regard organized efforts to gain information about them as a preliminary step toward exploitation. Reacting to the civil rights movement of the past decade, white persons in the South, particularly, consider attempts to investigate black persons as potentially coercive. These suspicions pose a serious threat to successful enumeration, especially of so disadvantaged a group as the black deaf adults.

The Census has so far failed in getting a story about it printed in the publications aimed at a black audience (e.g., *Ebony, Jet, Negro Traveler*). Nor have the better-known deaf clubs been able to provide many names and addresses of black deaf persons. Until fairly recently, Negroes were not admitted to membership in many of the deaf organizations. The clubs formed by black deaf persons are financially weak, have few members and are not joined to any nationwide or regional network comparable to the National Association of the Deaf. As a source of names for the Census, then, their membership lists are not apt to be representative of any major proportion of black deaf individuals.

Black deaf persons have been found at or near the bottom of the economic ladder. While white deaf adults tend to earn at the median for the general population, black deaf adults have been found to have average incomes below the average for the black population. It was pointed out that in Georgia, 40 percent of the deaf school population is black, but that 55 percent of the adult rehabilitation caseload is black. The economically depressed character of the black deaf population adds to the difficulty of identifying its members and gathering information about them.

The problem of casefinding just cited is not solely applicable to the South nor only to blacks. Many black deaf persons in other parts of the country also suffer from poor education, social alienation and depressed economic circumstances. Furthermore, the great mobility evidenced in this country over the past few decades applies, in some degree, to black deaf persons. Chicago and Detroit, as examples, are thought to have many deaf adults who have moved from the South. As a group, these deaf men and women are illiterate and nearly unemployable except as unskilled laborers. The Puerto Rican deaf persons living in New York City and the deaf Chicanos in the Southwest present the same problems of identification as do black persons. Other groups as well could be mentioned; e.g., the American Indian. In order to identify a large, representative proportion of the deaf population, then, the program to be outlined below must be implemented across the United States.

## Suggestions for an Identification Program

The solutions proposed have a common theme: community involvement must be sought. In direct terms, the value of the Census must be "sold to the black community". The lack of interest is reflected by the unwillingness of the black press to publicize the Census. The kind of news release which has been effective in other campaigns did not attract their favorable attention. Having a black person prepare a story for distribution may help to get it printed.

The program to improve the enumeration of black deaf persons must begin by establishing the importance of the Census to them. This could be achieved, in a small measure, by using television and radio. Such coverage can be obtained gratis (the stations donating the time credit their public service debt under the Federal Communications Commission regulations), but announcements, especially on television, are usually made at off-hours—very late at night or early in the morning. The cost of purchased time is beyond the resources of the Census.

Posters describing the Census can be helpful. Even more effective would be announcements at large gatherings of black deaf persons; e.g., basketball tournaments, picnics and dances.

Most important, however, is the active participation of black leaders of the deaf community. Among the hearing leaders are ministers, interpreters, and teachers. The black deaf and hearing leaders must be enlisted, at the least, to endorse the Census as a worthwhile endeavor.

Gaining the support of the leadership requires a personal effort. This has begun at the meeting in Washington. The community leaders who attended the conference are making the contacts which will lay the basis for success. The people they contact must, in turn, reach others who will spread "the good word". To the extent that support is gained from the leadership, the program can be expected to yield a rich harvest of names and addresses and a high rate of response to the mail questionnaire.

Special attention will be directed at churches which provide services for black deaf persons. The church in Jackson, Mississippi, for example, may be in touch with many of the previously mentioned black persons who were unable to attend school. Even if the deaf person does not himself go to the church, it is not unlikely that a member of his family does. It is hoped that the ministers of black congregations can be convinced to make announcements from the pulpit encouraging participation in the Census, as well as themselves sending the names and addresses of the deaf persons known to them. A prominent black person will be asked to draft a letter to the ministers urging these actions.

The churches will also provide invaluable assistance to those deaf persons who cannot complete the Census forms because of illiteracy. It has been pointed out that all too frequently their family members are also illiterate. Since the enumeration ultimately depends upon the mail verification, the cooperation of the churches will be helpful in getting the forms completed.

Often the isolated deaf person is known to a welfare agency which may direct him to the local Vocational Rehabilitation Agency. DVR counselors are expected to have extensive files of deaf clients. Occasionally they are forbidden by a state law from giving the names, even to a Federally supported project like the Census. The Census, of course, maintains elaborate precautions to ensure confidentiality and will not release names under any circumstances to anyone. The DVR counselor may, therefore, send the Census the names and addresses of the deaf people he knows, his deaf friends. This he may do informally. He may also request cards from the Census which ask the deaf person if he has any objection to having his name given to the Census. These specially prepared cards, which will be sent to any counselor who request them, fulfill most state requirements for voluntary release of information and are similar to forms used for release of medical records. All of the participants recognized the importance of gaining cooperation of the DVR counselors.

A highly effective means of identifying persons is the "snowball". The snowball technique assumes that deaf persons are most likely known to other deaf persons or to those concerned with them. Beginning with any deaf person, the request is made for him to list his deaf friends. These persons are then contacted to list their deaf friends. And so the snowball grows; each person being the potential source of many new cases. To get the snowball rolling, however, requires the support of the leaders; otherwise the old suspicions will intrude and bring it to a halt. A meeting of black deaf leaders could be held informally by interested persons—a DVR counselor, an interpreter, a minister, a deaf club president—and at that meeting, the Census could be explained and the snowball begun. Again, personal contact seems the most likely means of carrying out the program successfully.

## Summary

As a result of this conference, an excellent program was drawn up to identify deaf members of minority groups, especially the black deaf community. The major problems are lack of education, social alienation, and low economic status. Community involvement through personal contacts is the key step proposed to overcome these obstacles. The initial efforts must be made by the leadership, hearing and deaf, in the community. Following up the leaders' efforts will be letters to the clergy, television and radio announcements, and newspaper stories. The leadership drive should produce a snowball which, ultimately, may yield the greatest number of persons.

The report of this conference cannot end without a reiteration of the Census philosophy. No one working on the Census is interested solely in numbers. Simply knowing how many deaf persons there are in the United States will satisfy none of us. Even the detailed information about the deaf population does not conclude our interest. We are concerned about people. The data we gather is gathered to help people, to improve planning, to see that services are delivered to where the people are, to make certain that the services provided are the services desired. The Census is about people, not numbers. The statistics are only worth gathering insofar as they improve conditions for people.

## References

1. Beasley, W.C. Characteristics and Distribution of Impaired Hearing in the Population of the United States. *Journal of the Acoustical Society of America,* 12, 1940, 114-121
2. Bureau of the Census. The Blind and Deaf-Mutes in the United States: 1930. Washington, D. C. U.S. Government Printing Office, 1931, 23.
3. *Georgia's Deaf.* Atlanta, Georgia: Works Project Administration of Georgia (Official Project Number 665-34-3-90), 1942, 19.
4. Lunde, A.S. and Bigman, S.K. *Occupational Conditions Among the Deaf* Washington, D.C.: Gallaudet College, 1959, 66
5. Post, R. H. Hearing Acuity Variation Among Negroes and whites. *Eugenics Quarterly,* 11, 1964, 65-81
6. Rosen, S., Plester, D., El-Mofty, A. and Rosen, H.V. Relation of Hearing Loss to Cardiovascular Disease. *Transactions of the American Academy of Ophthalmology and Otolaryngology,* 68, 1964, 433-444

# Participants in the Special Meeting on Identification of Black Deaf Persons

Mr. Paul Adams
Florida School for the Deaf
St. Augustine, Florida

Mr. Glenn Anderson
Coordinator
Division of Vocational Rehabilitation
Detroit, Michigan

Mr. Hurbert Anderson, Jr.
President
Capitol City Club of the Deaf
Washington, D. C.

Mr. Frank Bowe
Research Assistant
Sensory Study Section
Social and Rehabilitation Service

Miss Katie Brown
Project Staff
Jewish Vocational Services
Chicago, Illinois

Mr. Edward Carney
President
Council of Organizations Serving
 the Deaf
Washington, D. C.

Mr. Albert Couthen
Teacher
American School for the Deaf
West Hartford, Connecticut

Mr. Marcus Delk
Bureau of the Census
Washington, D.C.

Mr. Ernest Hairston
Project Director
Diagnostic, Evaluation, Adjustment
 Facility
Columbus, Ohio

Mr. Egidio Lepre
Secretary
New York Society for the Deaf
Brooklyn, New York

Mr. John Lopez
Counselor
Vocational Rehabilitation
Communications Impaired Section
Washington, D.C.

Mr. Malcolm J. Norwood
Assistant Chief
Media Service and Captioned Films
Office of Education
Washington, D.C.

Mr. Edward Pearson
Director, Title I Projects
Virginia School for the Deaf
Hampton, Virginia

Mr. Eugene Perdue
Principal
Georgia School for the Deaf
Cave Spring, Georgia

Mr. Harold Perry
Director of Special Education
Memphis (Tennessee) Board of Education

Mr. Alfred Sonnenstrahl
Deaf Placement Administrator
Employment Security Commission
Detroit, Michigan

Reverend Paul Soules
Hyattsville, Maryland

Mrs. Polly Walton
Counselor
Department of Vocational Rehabilitation
Houston, Texas

Mr. William Woodrick
Program Director
Rehabilitation Counselor Training
 Program
University of Tennessee
Knoxville, Tennessee

# APPENDIX C

## Appendix C

# Observations on Sample Design
# for the
# National Census of the Deaf Population

### Reuben Cohen

## General Approach to the Problem

Deaf persons are estimated to comprise less than one percent of the total population of the United States. A common characteristic of the sampling problem for surveys of subpopulations with very low frequency of occurrence in the total population is the availability of lists of names and addresses of some members of the subpopulation. But lists that are available, or which can be prepared, are neither complete nor entirely up to date.

It usually turns out that an efficient approach to a survey requirement of this type is to draw from the prepared lists a sample of addresses where deaf persons are presumed to live. At the same time, an area sample is drawn to provide survey coverage of deaf persons who do not live at addresses on the lists.

Major differences in scope have been discussed for a national survey of the deaf:

*Design Number 1*

A survey designed to:

a. estimate the total number of deaf persons in the United States;

b. estimate the proportion of the total number of deaf who are on available lists, including those prepared especially for the survey;

c. obtain information on characteristics of deaf persons on the lists, but *not* characteristics of nonlisted deaf persons (the term *characteristics* is intended to suggest demography, attitudes, or other measurements made during the course of the survey that might lead to descriptive or analytical statements about the deaf).

*Design Number 2*

A survey designed to provide for the objectives of Design 1, and also to provide estimates of differences between characteristics of deaf persons on prepared lists and characteristics of nonlisted deaf persons.

*Design Number 3*

A survey designed to provide for the objectives of Designs 1 and 2, and also to provide for an analysis of the total deaf population which integrates the list population and the nonlist population.

Cost considerations will naturally have a substantial bearing on the choice among the three alternatives. In a general way, at least, data collection costs as well as the information value of the three design alternatives are cumulative. Data collection costs for Design 1 are also the base costs for Designs 2 and 3. Thus the incremental costs of Design 2 can be evaluated against the information gains provided by estimates of differences in characteristics of listed deaf persons and nonlisted deaf persons. Similarly, the incremental costs of Design 3 can be evaluated against the gains to be derived from an integrated analysis of the listed and nonlisted deaf populations.

The purpose of this paper is to present the general outlines of a sampling plan and to comment on considerations related to field work and other aspects of survey design as they relate to sampling. For purposes of this discussion the field procedure is presumed to include the following steps: (1) the sampling unit is the household, (2) some personal contact by an enumerator or interviewer is to be made at each sample household, (3) deaf/nondeaf status is to be obtained for each resident of sample households, and (4) a questionnaire or other data collection instrument is to be completed for selected deaf persons in sample households.

## Structure of the Area Sample

A number of survey research organizations, including commercial research firms and those operated under academic auspices, have established national area probability samples designed for general survey purposes. The national sample operations of the Bureau of the Census, for its Current Population Survey and other survey work, is also well known. Use of an existing national sample structure for the national survey of the deaf offers a number of advantages. Costs of the basic selection of counties or other types of area units would not be supported entirely by this study (although it is probable that some protion of this basic sampling cost would be included in the indirect cost allocation of the survey organization). Necessary census data and mapping materials are also likely to be available in the files of the survey organization. Most important, however, would be the roster of enumerators and interviewers available to the survey organization within its sample areas. Thus, to the extent that a national pool of interviewers with some field experience would be useful to this survey, it would be highly desirable to use an existing national sample for the present study.

Typically, a national area probability sample has a *stratified, multi-stage* structure. Stratification assures correspondence between the sample and the universe on selected characteristics of areas. Census geographic regions and urbanization (city size) are almost universally used as the basis for stratification of national samples of the United States. Economic or growth characteristics are also widely used as stratification features.[1]

The design of the multi-stage structure of the sample is somewhat more critical than the details of stratification to the requirements of a survey of the deaf. The definition of *primary sampling units* (PSU's) is of special importance. PSU's, the first-stage sampling units, are often defined as counties or groups of counties; in some sample structures PSU's are municipalities or even smaller geographic units such as census tracts or census enumeration districts. The larger units — counties or groups of counties — would be desirable for the survey of the deaf. In part, the larger units would be preferred because they would provide greater geographic dispersion to the sample. Reasons related to preparation and use of lists of deaf people are, however, an important consideration. By and large, it appears that the sources of lists are organized along state or county lines, suggesting a preference for large areas as primary sampling units.

In samples that define PSU's as counties or groups of counties, it is generally the case that metropolitan areas (usually defined in Census terms) are kept intact as PSU's. Large metropolitan areas (e.g., those with more than one million population) are automatically included in the sample as "self-representing" areas.

---

[1]In discussions of general-purpose vs. special-purpose samples, I have often been asked whether stratification especially designed to suit the needs of a specific survey would not be preferred to the general-purpose sample design. "After all," the reasoning goes, "aren't (physicians . . . boy scouts . . . businessmen . . . the poverty population . . . etc.) distributed differently from the total population?" My answer is that the general-purpose sample is usually close to the optimum that might be designed with a specific need at hand. The main requirement is that the special population of interest be reasonable well dispersed geographically. In fact, from my present understanding of the types of data available on the deaf population, it is unlikely that the stratification in a special sample design would differ noticeably from that used in general-purpose samples.

The following would be desirable, as a minimum set of specifications, for a national survey of the deaf population:

| PSU's: | Counties, or groups of counties. Large metropolitan areas included with certainty. |
|---|---|
| Stratification (minimum features): | Census region. Degree of urbanization (size of largest city). |
| Number of PSU's in sample (minimum): | 60 |
| number of counties in sample (minimum): | 200 |

## Preparation of Lists of Known Deaf Persons

Two possibilities for preparation of lists have been considered: (1) a complete enumeration (census) for all parts of the United States, or (2) preparation limited to areas in the national sample. The complete enumeration would be useful if it were desired to maintain and periodically update a national roster of deaf persons. For the stated purposes of the NCDP, however, it would clearly be more efficient to contain the effort to prepare and compile lists of deaf persons within the set of PSU areas selected for the national sample. This would be particularly true if, as noted previously, the sources of lists of the known deaf tend to be organized along state, metropolitan area, or county lines.

We should note that definitions of deafness used by various organizations are unlikely to be consistent with with one another, or with the definitions used for the NCDP. Thus, lists prepared for use in selecting the survey sample should be expected to include addresses of persons who would not be counted as part of the "survey deaf," as well as addresses of persons who have moved, or whose addresses cannot be located.

For present planning purposes, it seems most appropriate to expect substantial variation in list preparation from area to area. It is probably safe to assume that sources of lists would be variously organized. Some would be statewide, some county, some local. Sometimes state and local agencies would work independently, sometimes jointly. Procedures that are set up to handle a variety of situations can always be modified to suit a less complex combination.

In any event, lists compiled by state and local organizations will have to be screened for duplication and arranged in some systematic way suitable for sampling purposes.

## Sampling within PSU's: From Lists

A number of types of random procedures may be utilized in sampling from lists of the deaf within sample areas (selected PSU's); the procedures may differ from area to area.

A simple random-sample approach is likely to be the preferred method in many PSU's. In this method each household listing is given an equal and independent chance of being drawn into the study (e.g., by drawing of random numbers). In some PSU's, however, it may be desirable to introduce some features of stratified and/or cluster sampling. In general, these procedures are likely to lead to gains in efficiency when the sampling fraction within a PSU is small.

The utility of stratification is dependent upon the availability of information about individual listings. As a minimum, the address itself would provide the basis for some geographic stratification. Within large metropolitan areas it would therefore be possible to stratify for central city/suburban residence. Such information as age of deaf person, race, or economic characteristics, if available, might serve as a basis for stratification. If lists are obtained from multiple sources, the different sources could also serve as a mode of stratification.

Cluster sampling would be useful as a technique in geographically widespread sample areas for which small sampling fractions were to be used. In these instances, substantial reductions of interviewer travel time and costs could be achieved by geographic clustering of list addresses into interviewer-assignment units. Assignment units, not individual addresses, would then be selected at random. Efficient assignment units are often interviewer workloads of three or four days, including provision for return visits to households where interviews cannot be completed on the first call.

Sampling fractions within PSU's would be inversely proportional to the probability of selection of the PSU and will therefore vary widely among sample areas. For illustrative purposes, we will assume a listed universe of 250,000 addresses of the deaf — that is, if list preparation efforts to be used within PSU's were applied with equal intensity throughout the United States, a list of 250,000 addresses would be produced. We will also assume that a sample of 5,000 addresses is to be selected from lists within PSU's. The overall sampling fraction is

$$5,000/250,000 = 1/50$$

Some typical sampling fractions for different types of PSU's would then be:

| Type of PSU | Typical Probability of Selection of PSU | Probability within PSU |
|---|---|---|
| Large metro area | 1 | 1/50 |
| Small metro area | 1/10 | 1/5 |
| Predominantly rural | 1/50 | 1 |

The probability of selection of PSU's given above are illustrative of those that would apply in the type of national probability sample structure described earlier for (1) a large metropolitan area selected with certainty, (2) a small metropolitan area with, say, 150,000 population selected from a stratum with a total population of 1,500,000, and (3) a predominantly rural PSU of 30,000 population, also selected from a stratum with a total population of 1,500,000.

## Sampling within PSU's: Area Sample

Two main choices are ordinarily available in the development of a sample of the total population in a county or similar unit: (1) a sample organized entirely in terms of area segments, such as census tracts, census enumeration districts, or blocks; or (2) use of such source materials as city directories for street listings, possibly in combination with area segments defined from Census tabulations or map resources.

For the NCDP, use of a Census-type area segment structure is strongly recommended. There are two main reasons for this: First, directory resources will vary considerably among sample areas. While it is necessary to fashion survey procedures around area-to-area variations in lists of the deaf, there is no reason to do so for the area-sample approach. Uniform area-sampling procedures will simplify the preparation of the sample, interviewer instructions, and other processes associated with the field effort. Second, for the present survey requirement, large area segments (or clusters) such as blocks constitute efficient sampling units.

Some geographic stratification of area segments would be planned within PSU's. As as minimum, strata would be created for central city, other urban, and rural areas. Additional modes of stratification within PSU's would possibly include proportion of nonwhite persons, economic characteristics, and presence of persons in group quarters.

Detailed instructions for contacting households would be prepared for interviewers. The first field step in area segments is visualized as a canvass to enumerate residents, and classify them as deaf or nondeaf.

## Matching Procedure for List and Nonlist Samples

A careful procedure must be established for matching lists of addresses of the known deaf against area-sample address listings. While the time sequence of field survey operations may be viewed in a number of ways, it would appear to be most desirable to carry out this matching procedure after the compilation of lists of the known deaf is complete, and after the first stage of enumeration in area segments is carried out as suggested in the preceding paragraph. Duplications in the coverage of the two subpopulations (the list of the known deaf and the area sample listing) must be determined before the population estimates are developed and refined.

## Residents of Institutions

If desired and if resources are available, special provision should be made in the survey procedure for coverage of residents of selected institutions, particularly specialized institutions for the deaf or those which are believed to include significant numbers of deaf persons. These should be established as a separate stratum, with special sampling procedures adapted to this portion of the deaf population.

## Preliminary Consideration of Sample Size

Sample size for survey research projects is most often jointly determined by consideration of budget and requirements for precision. For the NCDP, major variables affecting data collection costs and precision are:

> Amount of effort devoted to preparation of lists of known deaf persons,
> Number of PSU's in sample,
> Enumeration cost per area-sample household and number in sample,
> Interviewing cost per deaf person and number in sample.

In addition to these factors which can be evaluated quantitatively (although not necessarily precisely specified), there are judgments to be made regarding the scope of effort and the incremental value of information about the nonlisted deaf population (i.e., that portion the deaf population to be located in the execution of the area sample). The question implicit in the latter point is the extent to which the study analyst and users of the study results would feel comfortable with an analysis of the deaf based entirely (Design 1) or mostly (Design 2) on that part of the population appearing in lists of known deaf persons.

Pending further discussion of costs, as well as study objectives, it is premature to develop a mathematically optimum approach to determination of sample size. At an intuitive level, however, it is possible to specify rough approximations to sample size that would satisfy the three major design alternatives:

|  | Enumeration of area sample households | Deaf persons in area sample households | Deaf person interviews* |
|---|---|---|---|
| *Design Number 1*<br>Estimate of size of deaf population; characteristics of persons on lists of the known deaf | 5,000 | 30 | 2,500-4,000 |
| *Design Number 2\*\**<br>Differences between listed and nonlisted deaf population | 50,000 | 300 | 2,500-4,000 |
| *Design Number 3\*\**<br>Integrated analysis of listed and nonlisted deaf population | 250,000 | 1,500 | 2,500-4,000 |

*Includes deaf persons located in enumeration of area sample households.

**Designs are cumulative. Design 2 provides all information contained in Design 1, etc.

These approximations to sample size requirements are based on the following assumptions:

| | |
|---|---|
| Number of deaf persons in population | 400,000 |
| Number of deaf persons on lists of known deaf (if procedures used in area sample were carried out with equal intensity throughout the U.S.) | 250,000 |
| Number of deaf persons not on lists of known deaf | 150,000 |
| Variation among sample areas in proportion of deaf persons on lists of known deaf | .50 - .70 |

**Approximate levels of precision**

For the three design alternatives, the coefficient of variation for the estimated number of deaf persons ranges from 20% for Design 1 to 5%

for Design 3. Interpreted in terms of approximate confidence intervals, the estimates are as follows (assuming a "true" total of 400,000):

| | Confidence intervals | |
| --- | --- | --- |
| | 2 out of 3 probability level | 95 out of 100 probability level |
| Design Number 1 | 320,000-480,000 | 240,000-560,000 |
| Design Number 2 | 360,000-440,000 | 320,000-480,000 |
| Design Number 3 | 380,000-420,000 | 360,000-440,000 |

While Design 1 can be expected to produce a satisfactory level of confidence for the estimated number of deaf, it provides little or no information on the differences in characteristics between the listed and nonlisted deaf. To illustrate this point, the expected number of deaf persons in area sample households would be 30, including perhaps three Negroes. Clearly, there would be little statistical basis for judging whether the Negro deaf are more likely to appear in the listed or in the nonlisted deaf population.

Design 2, with some 300 deaf persons expected to turn up in area sample households, would provide, on a reasonably stable statistical basis, the extent of similarity or difference between the listed and nonlisted populations.

Design 3 provides a sample size at close to the minimum level for which the listed and nonlisted deaf populations can be consolidated for purposes of analysis. Even so, the listed population would be oversampled relative to the nonlisted population. Thus, appropriate weights would be required to merge the two parts of the population. The weighting of the nonlisted deaf would be in the approximate range of 2 to 4, corresponding to the range of 2,500 to 4,000 for the total number of interviews with deaf persons.

# APPENDIX D

# Appendix D

# Statistical Design of the Health Interview Survey, National Center for Health Statistics[1]

The population covered by the sample for the Health Interview Survey is the civilian, noninstitutionalized population of the United States living at the time of the interview. The sample does not include members of the Armed Forces or U.S. nationals living in foreign countries. It should also be noted that the estimates shown do not represent a complete measure of any given topic during the specified calendar period since data are not collected in the interview for persons who died during the reference period. For many types of statistics collected in the survey, the reference period covers the 2 weeks prior to the interview week. For such a short period, the contribution by decedents to a total inventory of conditions or services should be very small. However, the contribution by decedents during a long reference period (e.g., 1 year) might be sizable, especially for older persons.

**General plan.** The sampling plan of the survey follows a multistage probability design which permits a continuous sampling of the civilian, noninstitutional population of the United States. The sample is designed in such a way that the sample of households interviewed each week is representative of the target population and that weekly samples are additive over time. This feature of the design permits both continuous measurement of characteristics of samples and more detailed analysis of less common characteristics and smaller categories of health-related items. The continuous collection has administrative and operational advantages as well as technical assets since it permits fieldwork to be handled with an experienced, stable staff.

The overall sample was designed so that tabulations can be provided for each of the four major geographic regions and for urban and rural sectors of the United States.

The first stage of the sample design consists of drawing a sample of 357 primary sampling units (PSU's) from approximately 1,900 geographically defined PSU's. A PSU consists of a county, a small group of contiguous counties, or a standard metropolitan statistical area. The PSU's collectively cover the 50 States and the District of Columbia.

---

[1]This section is adapted from the back matter accompanying data reports of the National Center for Health Statistics in Series 10 of their publication *Vital and Health Statistics*.

With no loss in general understanding, the remaining stages can be combined and treated in this discussion as an ultimate stage. Within PSU's, then, ultimate stage units called segments are defined in such a manner that each segment contains an expected six households. Three general types of segments are used.

Area segments which are defined geographically.

List segments, using 1960 census registers as the frame.

Permit segments, using updated lists of building permits issued in sample PSU's since 1960.

Census address listings were used for all areas of the country where addresses were well defined and could be used to locate housing units. In general the list frame included the larger urban areas of the United States from which about two-thirds of the HIS sample was selected.

The total HIS sample of approximately 8,000 segments yields a probability sample of about 134,000 persons in 42,000 interviewed households in a year.

Descriptive material on data collection, field procedures, and questionnaire development in the HIS has been published[2] as well as a detailed description of the sample design[3] and a report on the estimation procedure and the method used to calculate sampling errors of estimates derived from the survey.[4]

**Collection of data.** Field operations for the survey are performed by the U.S. Bureau of the Census under specifications established by the National Center for Health Statistics. In accordance with these specifications the Bureau of the Census participates in survey planning, selects the sample, and conducts the field interviewing as an agent of NCHS. The data are coded, edited, and tabulated by NCHS.

**Estimating procedures.** Since the design of the HIS is a complex multistage probability sample, it is necessary to use complex procedures in the derivation of estimates. Four basic operations are involved:

1. *Inflation by the reciprocal of the probability of selection.* The probability of selection is the product of the probabilities of selection from each step of selection in the design (PSU, segment, and household).

---

[2]National Center for Health Statistics: Health survey procedure: concepts, questionnaire development, and definitions in the Health Interview Survey, *Vital and Health Statistics.* PHS Pub. No. 1000-Series 1-No. 2. Public Health Service. Washington. U.S. Government Printing Office, May, 1964.

[3]U.S. National Health Survey: The statistical design of the health household interview survey. *Health Statistics.* PHS Pub. No. 584-A2. Public Health Service. Washington, D.C., July, 1958.

[4]National Center for Health Statistics: Estimation and sampling variance in the Health Interview Survey. *Vital and Health Statistics.* PHS Pub. No. 1000-Series 2-No. 38. Public Health Service. Washington. U.S. Government Printing Office, June, 1970.

2. *Nonresponse adjustment.* The estimates are inflated by a multiplication factor which has as its numerator the number of sample households in a given segment and as its denominator the number of households interviewed in that segment.

3. *First-stage ratio adjustment.* Sampling theory indicates that the use of auxiliary information which is highly correlated with the variables being estimated improves the reliability of the estimates. To reduce the variability between PSU's within a region, the estimates are ratio adjusted to 1960 population within six color-residence classes.

4. *Poststratification by age-sex-color.* The estimates are ratio adjusted within each of 60 age-sex-color cells to an independent estimate of the population of each cell for the survey period. These independent estimates are prepared by the Bureau of the Census. Both the first-stage and poststratified ratio adjustment take the form of multiplication factors applied to the weight of each elementary unit (person, household, conditions, and hospitalization).

The effect of the ratio-estimating process is to make the sample more closely representative of the civilian, noninstitutional population by age, sex, color, and residence, which thereby reduces sampling variance.

As noted, each week's sample represents the population living during that week and characteristics of the population. Consolidation of samples over a time period, e.g., a calendar quarter, produces estimates of average characteristics of the U.S. population for the calendar quarter. Similarly, population data for a year are averages of the four quarterly figures.

For prevalence statistics, such as number of persons with speech impairments or number of persons classified by time interval since last physician visit, figures are first calculated for each calendar quarter by averaging estimates for all weeks of interviewing in the quarter. Prevalence data for a year are then obtained by averaging the four quarterly figures.

For other types of statistics—namely those measuring the number of occurrences during a specified time period—such as incidence of acute conditions, number of disability days, or number of visits to a doctor or dentist, a similar computational procedure is used, but the statistics are interpreted differently. For these items, the questionnaire asks for the respondent's experience over the 2 calendar weeks prior to the week of interview. In such instances the estimated quarterly total for the statistics is 6.5 times the average 2-week estimate produced by the 13 successive samples taken during the period. The annual total is the sum of the four quarters. Thus the experience of persons interviewed during a year—experience which actually occurred for each person in a 2-calendar-week interval prior to week of interview—is treated as though it measured the total of such experience during the year. Such interpretation leads to no significant bias.

## General Qualifications

**Nonresponse.** Data were adjusted for nonresponse by a procedure which imputes to persons in a household which was not interviewed the characteristics of persons in households in the same segment which were interviewed. The total noninterview rate was about 5 percent—1 percent was refusal, and the remainder was primarily due to the failure to find an eligible respondent at home after repeated calls.

**The interview process.** The statistics presented in this report are based on replies obtained in interviews with persons in the sample households. For children and for adults not present in the home at the time of the interview, the information was obtained from a related household member such as a spouse or the mother of a child.

There are limitations to the accuracy of diagnostic and other information collected in household interviews. For diagnostic information, the household respondent can usually pass on to the interviewer only the information the physician has given to the family. For conditions not medically attended, diagnostic information is often no more than a description of symptoms. However, other facts, such as the number of disability days caused by the condition, can be obtained more accurately from household members than from any other source since only the persons concerned are in a position to report this information.

**Rounding of numbers.** The original tabulations on which the data in this report are based show all estimates to the nearest whole unit. All consolidations were made from the original tabulations using the estimates to the nearest unit. In the final published tables, the figures are rounded to the nearest thousand, although these are not necessarily accurate to that detail. Devised statistics, such as rates and percent distributions, are computed after the estimates on which these are based have been rounded to the nearest thousand.

**Population figures.** Some of the published tables include population figures for specified categories. Except for certain overall totals by age, sex, and color, which are adjusted to independent estimates, these figures are based on the sample of households in the HIS. These are given primarily to provide denominators for rate computations, and for this purpose are more appropriate for use with the accompanying measures of health characteristics than other population data that may be available. With the exception of the overall totals by age, sex, and color mentioned above, the population figures differ from corresponding figures (which are derived from different sources) published in reports of the Bureau of the Census. (For population data for general use, see the official estimates presented in Bureau of the Census reports in the P-20, P-25, and P-60 series.)

## Terms Relating to Hearing Impairments

**Hearing Aid Use.** All persons for whom a hearing ability supplement was completed and who reported some trouble hearing in one or both ears were asked if they had ever tried a hearing aid. All persons who answered positively to this question were then asked a series of additional questions and their responses were classified as follows:

*Present user.* Includes persons responding positively to the question, "Do you use a hearing aid now?"
*Former user.* Includes persons responding positively to the question, "Have you ever had a hearing aid for your own use?" and negatively to the question, "Do you use a hearing aid now?"
*Present use unknown.* Includes persons responding positively to the question, "Have you ever had a hearing aid for you own use?" but failing to answer the question, "Do you use a hearing aid now?"
*Never had or unknown.* Includes persons who failed to answer or responded negatively to the question, "Have you ever tried a hearing aid?" Also included in this category are those persons who reported having tried a hearing aid but who either failed to answer or responded negatively to the question, "Have you ever had a hearing aid for your own use?"

**Age at Onset of Hearing Loss.** Each person who reported some hearing loss on the hearing ability questionnaire was asked "How old were you when you began to have hearing trouble or grew deaf?" Since, for many types of hearing loss, it would prove quite difficult for the respondent to provide an exact age of onset, the alternative choices on the questionnaire were designed to indicate that an approximation would be acceptable.

**Cause of Hearing Loss.** Each person who reported some hearing loss on the hearing ability questionnaire was asked "What was the cause of your hearing trouble or deafness?" This question was designed to obtain detailed information about the kind of illness or injury causing the hearing loss. However, because of the small number of cases for any specific kind of illness or injury, they were categorized only as being caused by an "illness' or "injury." The other categories included the following: categories included the following:

*241*

*Hereditary or congenital.* This category includes those responses which indicated that the person was born with the hearing impairment or considered it hereditary.

*Presbycusis.* This includes any response that indicated that the hearing impairment was caused by aging.

*Unknown.* This category includes only those persons who indicated that they did not know the cause of their hearing impairment.

*Other and nonresponse.* This category includes all persons who could not be classified in any one of the categories and those who failed to answer the question.

## Demographic Terms

**Age.** The age recorded for each person is his age at last birthday. Age is recorded in single years and combined into groups suitable for the purpose of the table.

**Income of family or of unrelated individuals.** Each member of a family is classified according to the total income of the family of which he is a member. Within the household all persons related to each other by blood, marriage, or adoption constitute a family. Unrelated individuals are classified according to their own income. The income recorded is the total of all income received by members of the family (or by an unrelated individual) in the 12-month period ending with the week of interview. Income from all sources is included, e.g., wages, salaries, rents from property, pensions, help from relatives, and so forth.

**Educational attainment.** The categories of educational status show the highest grade of school completed. Only grades completed in regular schools, where persons are given a formal education, are included. A "regular" school is one which advances a person toward an elementary or high school diploma or a college, university, or professional school degree. Thus, education in vocational, trade, or business schools outside the regular school system is not counted in determining the highest grade of school completed.

**Race.** In this report, the population has been subdivided into two groups according to "white" and "nonwhite." "Nonwhite" includes Negro, American Indian, Chinese, Japanese, and so forth. Mexican persons are included with "white" unless definitely known to be Indian or of another nonwhite race.

**Residence.** The definition of urban-rural areas used in the National Health Survey is the same as that used in the 1960 census. The urban

*242*

population comprises all persons living in (a) places of 2,500 inhabitants or more incorporated as cities, boroughs, villages, and towns (except towns in New England, New York, and Wisconsin); (b) the densely settled urban fringe, whether incorporated or unincorporated, of urbanized areas (see below); (c) towns in New England and townships in New Jersey and Pennsylvania which contain no incorporated municipalities as subdivisions and have either 25,000 inhabitants or more or a population of 2,500 to 25,000 and a density of 1,500 persons or more per square mile; (d) counties in States other than the New England States, New Jersey, and Pennsylvania that have no incorporated municipalities within their boundaries and have a density of 1,500 persons or more per square mile; and (e) unincorporated places of 2,500 inhabitants or more not included in any urban fringe. The remaining population is classified as rural.

**Size of place.** All persons residing in an urbanized area are included in the urban population. An urbanized area, according to the 1960 census definition, contains at least one city which had 50,000 inhabitants or more in 1960, as well as the surrounding closely settled incorporated places and unincorporated areas.

The remaining urban population is classified as living in urban places outside urbanized areas. These urban places are grouped according to size.

**Farm and nonfarm residence.** The rural population is subdivided into the rural-farm population which comprises all rural residents living on farms, and the rural-nonfarm population which comprises the remaining rural population. The farm population includes persons living in rural territory on places of 10 areas or more from which sales of farm products amounted to $50 or more during the previous 12 months or on places of less than 10 acres from which sales of farm products amounted to $250 or more during the preceding 12 months. Other persons living in rural non-SMSA territory were classified as nonfarm if their household paid rent for the house but their rent did not include any land used for farming.

Sales of farm products refer to the gross receipts from the sale of field crops, vegetables, fruits, nuts, livestock and livestock products (milk, wool, etc.), poultry and poultry products, and nursery and forest products produced on the place and sold at any time during the preceding 12 months.

**Region.** For the purpose of classifying the population by geographic area, the States are grouped into four regions. These regions, which correspond to those used by the Bureau of the Census, are as follows:

| Region | States Included |
|--------|-----------------|
| Northeast | Maine, New Hampshire, Vermont, Massachusetts, Rhode Island, Connecticut, New York, New Jersey, Pennsylvania. |
| North Central | Michigan, Ohio, Indiana, Illinois, Wisconsin, Minnesota, Iowa, Missouri, North Dakota, South Dakota, Nebraska, Kansas. |
| South | Delaware, Maryland, District of Columbia, Virginia, West Virginia, North Carolina, South Carolina, Georgia, Florida, Kentucky, Tennessee, Alabama, Mississippi, Arkansas, Louisiana, Oklahoma, Texas. |
| West | Montana, Idaho, Wyoming, Colorado, New Mexico, Arizona, Utah, Nevada, Alaska, Washington, Oregon, California, Hawaii. |

# Appendix E

Appendix E

# Questions Appearing on Interview Forms in the Household Survey

### Form A

1. I'm going to ask some questions about all the people in this household, so I have to find out who lives here. Let's start with the head of the household—what's his or her name? (ENTER NAME UNDER PERSON #1)

2. Now members of the family who live here—what are their names? (ENTER NAMES)

   (BEFORE ASKING FURTHER QUESTIONS, PROBE)

3. Is there anyone else staying here now, such as a friend, a relative, or a roomer?

   Is there anyone else who usually lives here, but who's away from home now?—traveling or on a vacation, or in a hospital, or away at school or any other place?

   Have we missed any babies or small children?

   Is anyone I've listed away in the armed forces? (IF "YES," DRAW LINE THROUGH NAME)
   (BE SURE THAT THE PERSON NAMED IN FACE-SHEET ITEM "B" IS LISTED)

   (IF NECESSARY, ASK)

4. How is each of these people related to (THE HEAD OF THE HOUSE-HOLD)? (ENTER RELATION)

5. Is (NAME) male or female? (CHECK BOX FOR SEX)

   (ONLY FOR HEAD, SPOUSE, AND EACH UNRELATED PERSON. DO NOT ASK RESPONDENT'S RACE)

6. What is (his/her) race? (CHECK BOX)

7. How old was (EACH) on (his/her) last birthday? (ENTER AGE)

   (IF 14 YEARS OR OLDER, ASK)

8. Is (he/she) now married, widowed, divorced, separated, or never married?

   Now I have some questions about the hearing of each person in your family here. First, (PERSON #1):

9. Has (he/she) ever had a hearing aid for (his/her) own use?

10. Does (he/she) use a hearing aid now?

11. Please look at this card and tell me which statement best describes how well he hears with his *left* ear (without his/her hearing aid). (SHOW CARD)

12. And which one of these best describes how well he hears with his *right* ear (without a hearing aid)?

13. a. (Without a hearing aid,) Can ( _____ ) hear loud noises?
    b. Can ( _____ ) usually tell one kind of noise from another?
    c. Can ( _____ ) usually tell the sound of speech from other sounds and noises?
    d. Can ( _____ ) usually hear and understand a person if he speaks loudly into ( _____ 's) better ear?
    e. Can ( _____ ) usually hear and understand what a person says without seeing his face if he shouts to ( _____ ) from across a quiet room?
    f. Can ( _____ ) usually hear and understand what a person says without seeing his face if he talks in a normal voice to ( _____ ) from across a quiet room?
    g. Can ( _____ ) usually hear and understand what a person says without seeing his face if he whispers to ( _____ ) from across a quiet room?

14. DOES PERSON NOW USE HEARING AID?

15. a. *With* his hearing aid, can ( _____ ) hear loud noises?
    b. Can ( _____ ) usually tell one kind of noise from another?
    c. Can ( _____ ) usually tell the sound of speech from other sounds and noises?
    d. Can ( _____ ) usually hear and understand a person if he speaks loudly into ( _____ 's) better ear?
    e. Can ( _____ ) usually hear and understand what a person says without seeing his face if he shouts to ( _____ ) from across a quiet room?
    f. Can ( _____ ) usually hear and understand what a person says without seeing his face if he talks in a normal voice to ( _____ ) from across a quiet room?
    g. Can ( _____ ) usually hear and understand what a person says without seeing his face if he whispers to ( _____ ) from across a quiet room?

16. How old was (he/she) when (he/she) began to have trouble hearing or became deaf?
    (IF NOT SURE, PROBE UNTIL "YES" ANSWER IS GIVEN)
    Was it before he was 3 years old?
    Was it after he was 3, but before he was 6?
    Was it after he was 6, but before he was 12?
    Was it after he was 12, but before he was 18?
    Was it after he was 18 years old?

*248*

17. Sometimes when a child is deaf, the parents don't find out right away that he can't hear. How about (him/her)—when (his/her) parents found out that (he/she) had trouble hearing or were deaf, how old was (he/she)?

18. Did (he/she) become deaf or have trouble hearing from a sickness, or from an accident, or from something else?
(IF "BORN DEAF," PROBE)
Do you know what caused (his/her) hearing trouble or deafness?
(PROBE)
How did the accident make (him/her) have trouble hearing?
(PROBE)
What kind of sickness was that?

Now I have a few questions about how you and your family live here?

19. (IS THIS A:
One-family house
Apartment
Other: What?
IF YOU ARE NOT SURE, ASK)

20. Do you rent or own your own home here?

21. How many rooms do you have?

22. Do you have a telephone here?

23. What is the number?

24. Does your phone have a special amplifier?

25. Do you have a TTY?
(ONLY FOR HEAD, SPOUSE, AND EACH UNRELATED PERSON.)

26. Now we'd like to know how much income you and your (husband/wife) and (ANY OTHER FAMILY MEMBERS) had last year—in 1971—before taxes. That's all income from pay or profits, or from welfare, or from pensions, or any other money. Just tell me the letter on this card for the amount that fits. (SHOW CARD)
Letter_____

27. Does anyone in your family here get any income from:
Welfare or public assistance (from the city or the county or the state)?
Social security (from the Federal Government)?
Payments from Vocational Rehabilitation?

(FOLLOWING QUESTIONS ARE FOR EACH PERSON)

28. (WHAT IS THE LOWEST NUMBER ANSWERED FOR Q11 AND Q12 FOR PERSON?)

29. (WHICH PART OF Q13 IS CHECKED "NO"?)

30. (AGE AT ONSET OF HEARING TROUBLE—SEE Q16)

31. (IS HIS PRESENT AGE . . . ?)

32. Did (he/she) ever go to a school or class for only the deaf or hard of hearing?

33. For how many years altogether did (he/she) go to school? (IF NOT SURE, PROBE:)
How old was (he/she) when (he/she) first started school?
How old was (he/she) when (he/she) stopped school?
Did (he/she) go to school all those years, or was (he/she) out of school part of that time?

34. What was the last grade of school (he/she) finished?

35. The last school (he/she) went to—did (he/she) finish or graduate from it?

36. What was the last grade of school (he/she) went to?

37. Did (he/she) finish that grade?

38. (IS HIS/HER AGE . . . ?)

39. Last week did (he/she) work at a job at all?

40. Does (he/she) have a job or business, from which (he/she) was temporarily away or on layoff last week? (IF "YES," PROBE)
Why was he away form his job?

41. Has (he/she) been looking for work during the last 4 weeks?

42. Was there any particular reason why (he/she) didn't work last week, such as one of these? (SHOW CARD)

43. In what kind of business or industry does (he/she) work?
(PROBE) Is that mainly in manufacturing, in wholesale trade, in retail trade, or in something else?

44. What kind of work does (he/she) do?
(PROBE) What is the name or title of (his/her) job?
(PROBE) What are (his/her) most important duties?

45. (WHO ANSWERED FOR PERSON?)

46. (IS A FORM B REQUIRED?—SEE Q31)

## Form B

### THE NATIONAL CENSUS OF THE DEAF
### CONDUCTED BY THE NATIONAL ASSOCIATION OF THE DEAF

B-1.     Now I'd like to ask you about your education—the schools you've gone to. When you first started school, how old were you?

B-2.     What is person's age?

B-3.     Did Person Become Deaf Before or After Starting School?

B-9.     What was the name of the (first/next) school you went to? . . . after you became deaf?

B-10.     Which kind of school was it?

B-11.     How many years did you go to that school?

B-12.     Did you go to any other school after that?

B-13.     What was the last grade of school you went to?

B-14.     Did you finish the (LAST) grade?

B-15.     Do you go to any school now?

B-16.     The last school you went to—did you finish or graduate from it?

B-17.     What Is Person's Age . . . ?

B-18.     Did you go to a school or class *for only the deaf or hard of hearing* at any time after September, 1970?

B-19.     What is person's age . . . ?

B-20a.     Has person ever attended college?

B-20b.     Do you have a degree from any college or university?

B-21.     From what college(s) or university(-ies)?

B-22.     What degree(s) did you receive?

*The next questions are about work.*

B-23.     Did you work at all in the last seven days (not counting your own housework)?—that's any time from last (SAME DAY OF WEEK AS TODAY) to yesterday.

B-24.     Do you have a job or business from which you were away or on layoff last week? (IF "YES," PROBE)

    Was it for one of these reasons? (SHOW CARD)

B-25.     Have you been looking for work during the last 4 weeks?

B-26.     Was there any special reason why you didn't work last week? (SHOW CARD)

B-27.  In what year did you last work at all (not counting your own house-work), even for a few days?

B-28.  In what kind of business or industry (do you work/did you work in your last job)?

(PROBE) Is that mostly in manufacturing, in wholesale trade, in retail trade, or in something else?

(IF *NOT* GOVERNMENT AGENCY OR SCHOOL)

B-29.  Is that for a private company, business, or person; or in your own business, service or farm; or without pay in a business or farm owned by your family? (SHOW CARD)

B-30.  What kind of work (do/did) you do?

(PROBE) What is the name or title of your job?

(PROBE) What (are/were) the most important things you (do/did) in your job?

B-31.  In 1971 what was the total amount you earned from all jobs you had?

B-32..  (The job you have now/The last job you had)—how did you get it? Did you ask or apply for it, or was it offered to you without your asking?

B-33.  Did you get the job by yourself, or did someone help you?

B-34.  Who helped you? (SHOW CARD)

(PROBE) Anyone else?

B-35.  What did he do to help? (SHOW CARD)

B-36.  In order to get this job, which of these things did you have to do?

Fill out an application

Talk with owner or manager

Talk with a supervisor or foreman

Take a test to show I could do the work

Pass a physical examination

Other: What?

Now I want to ask you about how people at work tell you things, and how you tell them things.

B-37.  When your boss or supervisor wants to tell you something, which ways does he use *most*? (SHOW CARD)

Ask someone to tell me
Speak
Sign
Fingerspell
Gesture or act out

252

Write
Some other way: What?

B-38. When you want to tell your boss something, which ways do you use *most*? (Show card)

Ask someone else to tell him
Speak
Sign
Fingerspell
Gesture or act out
Write
Some other way: What?

B-39. Is your boss hearing or deaf?

B-40. Are there any people you supervise (or boss) or give orders to about their work?·

B-41. When people you supervise want to tell you something, which ways do they use *most*? (SHOW CARD)

Speak
Sign
Fingerspell
Gesture or act out
Write
Some other way: What?

B-42. When you want to tell them something, which ways do you use the *most*? (SHOW CARD)

Speak
Sign
Fingerspell
Gesture or act out
Write
Some other way: What?

B-43. Are any of the people you supervise deaf?

B-44. And *other* people at work—if they want to tell you something, what ways do they use *most*? (SHOW CARD)

Speak
Sign
Fingerspell
Gesture or act out
Write
Some other way: What?

B-45. If you want to tell them something, what ways do you use *most*? (SHOW CARD)

Speak

Sign
Fingerspell
Gesture or act out
Write
Some other way: What?

B-46. Are any of these people deaf?

B-47. Does this person now have a job?

B-48. Have you been (keeping house/going to school/looking for work) since your last job?

B-49. Since what year have you been (keeping house/going to school/looking for work)?

B-50. In your last job, what kind of work did you do?

(PROBE) What were your most important duties?

B-51. What kind of business or industry was that in?

B-52. Why did you leave that job?
(PROBE, IF "QUIT," "FIRED," "LAID OFF," "RETIRED," "TRANSFERRED")
Why was that?

B-53. In what year did that job start?

B-54. In what year did you start in the job you have now?

B-55. Just before that, what were you doing?—
(IF FEMALE) Working, looking for work, keeping house, or something else?
(IF MALE) Working, looking for work, or something else?
(PROBE—IF "SOMETHING ELSE") What was that?

B-56. What kind of work did you do?
(PROBE) What were your most important duties?

B-57. Was that with the same employer or a different one?

B-58. What kind of business or industry was that in?

B-59. Why did you leave that job?
(IF "QUIT," "FIRED," "LAID OFF," "RETIRED," OR "TRANS-FERRED")

B-60. Why was that?

B-61. (IF "WORKING") In what year did that job start?
(IF "LOOKING FOR WORK") In what year did you start looking for work?
(IF "KEEPING HOUSE") In what year did you start keeping house?
(IF "ILLNESS") In what year did that start?
(IF "GOING TO SCHOOL") In what year did that start?

B-62.     In school were you taught any vocational trades or trained for any jobs?

B-63.     What kind of work were you trained for? (PROBE) Any other kind?

B-64.     Have you ever used any of that training on any job you've had?

Now let's talk about after you left school.

B-65.     After leaving school, did you take any courses or training like these? (SHOW CARD)
(PROBE) Which? Any others?

B-66.     In that (COURSE OR TRAINING), what kind of work were you taught or trained for?

B-67.     Did you finish that (COURSE OR TRAINING) or stop going to it before it was over?

(IF "STOPPED BEFORE IT WAS OVER")

B-68.     Why did you stop going to it?

B-69.     Have you ever used any of that training on any job you've had?

B-70.     Are you a member of a labor union?

B-71.     Have you ever applied to join a union and not been accepted?

B-72.     The next questions are about the ways people use to tell you things and about the ways you use. (SHOW CARD)

When you were a little child, which ways did your parents use *most* to tell you things?

Speak
Sign
Fingerspell
Gesture
Write
Other: What?

(IF NOW MARRIED)

B-73.     When you want to tell your (wife/husband) something, which ways do you use *most*?

B-74.     When (she/he) wants to tell you something, which ways does (she/he) use *most*?

(IF HAS CHILDREN)

B-75.     When you want to tell your child(ren) something, which ways do you use *most*?

B-76.     When your child(ren) want(s) to tell you something, which ways (does he/she)/(do they) use *most*?

B-77.     When you go to a store to buy something, which ways do you use *most* to tell the clerk what you want?

B-78. After you left school, did you have any training to help you do any of these things better? (SHOW CARD)

Speaking
Lipreading (Speechreading)
Signing
Fingerspelling

(IF UNDER 16)

B-79. The next questions are about the ways people use to tell things to each other.

When your parents want to tell you something, which ways do they use *most*? (SHOW CARD)

Speak
Sign
Fingerspell
Gesture
Write
Other: What?

B-80. When you want to tell them something, which ways do you use *most*? (SHOW CARD)

Speak
Sign
Fingerspell
Gesture
Write
Other: What?

B-81. Now I want to ask you about how you use each of the different ways of telling things.

First, speaking—how good is your speaking? (SHOW CARD. CHECK ONE ANSWER ON EACH LINE)

Good
Fair
Poor
Not at all

B-82. How good is your lipreading? (SHOW CARD)

B-83. How good is your signing? (SHOW CARD)

B-84. How about reading signs? (SHOW CARD)

B-85. How good is your fingerspelling? (SHOW CARD)

B-86. And how do you read fingerspelling? (SHOW CARD)

B-87. From whom did you *first* learn to sign?
(PROBE) Where was that?

256

From family
At Gallaudet
At school:
    from teacher or staff
    from other children
Other: Who/where?
Doesn't sign

B-88.    Before I asked you about your hearing. Now we want to know about some other problems that you may have.

    Do you have any trouble seeing without eyeglasses?

B-89.    *With* glasses, do you have no trouble seeing, a little trouble seeing, a lot of trouble seeing, or are you blind?

B-90.    Do you know whether you're what is called "legally blind"?

B-91.    Do you have any of these conditions? (SHOW CARD. CHECK "YES" OR "NO" FOR EACH)

Cleft palate, harelip
Cerebral palsy
Mental retardation
Nervous or mental condition

B-92.    Do you have any other health problem or physical disability? (IF "YES," PROBE) What kind of problem is it?

B-93.    (WAS ANY "TROUBLE SEEING" OR BLINDNESS REPORTED IN B-89, OR ANY CONDITION IN B-91 OR B-92?)

B-94.    Does (your eye trouble/your CONDITION) keep you from doing the things other people your age do? . . . like working (or keeping house/or going to school)?

B-95.    Do you need any special treatment or care for that?

B-96.    Are you getting that (treatment or care) now?

B-97.    Where do you get it? (SHOW CARD)

Hospital
Clinic
Private physician
Private nursing care
Special education
Vocational education
Other: What?

B-98.    Now let's talk about some kinds of help that people may need. Do *you* need any of these kinds of help now?

    Do you need an ear examination or a hearing test?

B-99.    Do you need treatment of any trouble with your ears or hearing?

B-100.　Do you need any other kind of examination or treatment by a doctor?

B-101.　Do you need to get a hearing aid?

(ASK FOR EACH "YES")

B-102.　Is there any special reason why you haven't gotten (KIND OF HELP NEEDED)?

B-103.　If you need help to find a doctor to examine or treat you, or if you need a hearing aid, is there any agency or place in (NAME OF STATE) where you can go to get help?

(IF "YES," PROBE) What is its name?

B-104.　Now here are some other things that some people need help with.

Do you need help to get more education?

B-105.　Do you need help to get more job training?

B-106.　Do you need help to decide what kind of work would be best for you?

B-107.　Do you need advice about changing to a new kind of work?

B-108.　Do you need help to find out what kinds of jobs are open right now?

B-109.　Do you need help to find a job now?

(ASK FOR EACH "YES")

B-110.　Is there any special reason why you haven't gotten (KIND OF HELP NEEDED)

B-111.　If you need more education or training, or advice about work, is there any agency or place in (NAME OF STATE) where you can go for help? (IF "YES," PROBE) What is its name?

B-112.　Do you need to get any training to do any of these better? (SHOW CARD)

Speechreading
Speaking
Using language of signs
Using a hearing aid

B-113.　Is there any special reason why you haven't gotten that training?

B-114.　If you ever need training for these things (POINT TO CARD), is there any agency or place in (NAME OF STATE) where you can get help?

(IF "YES," PROBE) What is its name?

B-115.　Some people say it's hard to get insurance. Have *you* had any trouble getting insurance that you wanted?

B-116.　What kind of insurance did you have trouble getting?

B-117.　What kind of trouble did you have getting it?

*258*

B-118.  Now I'd like to ask about something else. Have you heard of the
_____ Vocational Rehabilitation _____
Sometimes it's called "Voc Rehab" or _____.

B-119.  What would you say is the most important thing the
_____ does?

B-120.  Have you ever asked the _____for any kind of help or
service?

B-121.  What kind?

B-122.  About what year was that?

B-123.  Did you get the help you wanted?

B-124.  Why not?

B-125.  Are you satisfied or not satisfied with the help you got from
_____?

B-126.  Why not?

B-127.  The counselor that you talked to at _____—how did he
tell you things? (SHOW CARD)

Speaking
Signing
Fingerspelling
Gestures, or acting his ideas
Writing
Some other way: How?
(PROBE) Any other way?

B-128.  In what country were you born?

B-129.  In what city or town and state were you born?

B-130A. In what year did you come to the United States?

B-130B. Are you now a citizen of the United States?

B-131.  When you were very young, how well could your father hear?—even if
you are not sure. (SHOW CARD)

His hearing was good
He had a little trouble hearing
He had a lot of trouble hearing
He was deaf

B-132.  How about your mother when you were very young?—How well could
she hear? (SHOW CARD)

Her hearing was good
She had a little trouble hearing
She had a lot of trouble hearing
She was deaf

B-133.   When you were a child, did your parents speak any language other than English at home?

B-134.   What was the highest grade of school that your father finished? (SHOW CARD. CHECK LAST GRADE FINISHED)

B-135.   During the years while you were in school, what kind of business or industry did your father work for most of the time?

(PROBE) Was that mostly in manufacturing, wholesale trade, retail trade, or something else?

B-136.   What kind of work did he do?

(PROBE) What was the name or title of his job?

(PROBE) What were his most important duties?

B-137.   (IS PERSON A FEMALE AGED 14 OR OVER?)

B-138.   How many babies have you ever had, not counting stillbirths?

B-139.   How many of them are living with you in this household now?

B-140.   (IS NUMBER EVER BORN LARGER THAN NUMBER IN HOUSEHOLD?)

B-141.   That's my last question. Thank you very much.

B-142.   (WHO ANSWERED FOR PERSON?)

Self entirely
Self partially

B-143.   (PLEASE INDICATE HERE YOUR OPINION OF RESPONDENT'S USE OF EACH COMMUNICATION SKILL)

Speak
Read lips or speech
Sign
Read signs
Fingerspell
Read fingerspelling

**Form C**

THE NATIONAL CENSUS OF THE DEAF
CONDUCTED BY THE NATIONAL ASSOCIATION OF THE DEAF

C-1. What (is his/her name) (are their names)?
(FOR EACH CHILD ASK C-2 THROUGH C-8 IN A BLOCK)

C-2. (IF NECESSARY, ASK) Is (EACH ONE) male or female

C-3. When was (he/she) born—just the month and the year.

C-4. Please look at this card and tell me how well he (hears/heard) with his *left* ear—without a hearing aid. (SHOW CARD)

C-5. Which one of these best describes how well he (hears/heard) with his *right* ear—without a hearing aid? (SHOW CARD)
(IF ANY "TROUBLE HEARING" OR "DEAF" IN ONE OR BOTH EARS, ASK C-6 THROUGH C-8. IF UNDER 1 YEAR, SKIP TO C-7. IF HEARING "GOOD" IN *BOTH* C-4 AND C-5, GO TO C-1 FOR NEXT CHILD.)

C-6. (CHECK ANSWERS C-6 a-g. STOP ASKING THESE QUESTIONS AFTER A "NO" IS GIVEN.)
a. Can/Could ( _____ ) hear loud noises?
b. Can/Could ( _____ ) usually tell one kind of noise from another?
c. Can/Could ( _____ ) usually tell the sound of speech from other sounds and noises?
d. Can/Could ( _____ ) usually hear and understand a person if he speaks/spoke loudly into ( _____ 's) better ear?
e. Can/Could ( _____ ) usually hear and understand what a person says/said seeing his face if he shouts/shouted to ( _____ ) from across a quiet room?
f. Can/Could ( _____ ) usually hear and understand what a person says/said without seeing his face if he talks/talked in a normal voice to ( _____ ) from across a quiet room?
g. Can/Could ( _____ ) usually hear and understand what a person says/said without seeing his face if he whispers/whispered to ( _____ ) from across a quiet room?

C-7. How old was (he/she) when (he/she) began to have trouble hearing or become deaf?
(IF NOT SURE, PROBE UNTIL "YES" ANSWER IS GIVEN)
Was it before he was 3 years old?
Was it after he was 3, but before he was 6?
Was it after he was 6, but before he was 12?
Was it after he was 12, but before he was 18?
Was it after he was 18 years old?
(IS THIS PERSON NOW ALIVE?)
(GO BACK TO FORM B, AND COMPLETE B-141, B-142 AND B-143)

# APPENDIX F

## Appendix F

# Interviewer's Manual
# for the
# National Census of the Deaf Population

## Introduction

You have joined the first nationwide attempt in over forty years to determine the number and characteristics of the deaf population of the United States. The last enumeration of deaf persons was done by the U.S. Bureau of the Census in 1930. With your help everyone concerned about deafness will be able to have up-to-date information with which to plan research projects and develop educational, vocational and welfare programs. Deaf leaders especially need to know about the size of the deaf population, how well deaf people are adjusting socially and vocationally, what their problems and desires are, and much more.

You provide the vital link in the information chain. From the information you and our other interviewers gather, we will build the mosaic which pictures the current effects of deafness. What you learn in your interviews will have vital, long-term implications. The National Census of the Deaf Population must be done well because it will affect the lives of so many people.

In addition to being as accurate and objective as possible, you also bear the responsibility for maintaining strict confidentiality. The law is clear: ALL information obtained by the Census must be protected. NOTHING can be revealed to those not employed by the Census . Even your intention to interview someone cannot be revealed, except insofar as is necessary in order to arrange an appointment. Knowing how important your work is will make keeping this stricture easy.

Objectivity and accuracy are not easily achieved. As you read this manual, you may occasionally wonder about the extensive instructions. Please remember that they are spelled out in such great detail to help you to be objective and accurate. Furthermore, the instructions will be followed by every interviewer in every interview. In that way your interviews can be directly added to those taken by other interviewers. As many situations as possible have been anticipated and procedures written to prepare you for them. By following the instructions closely you not only maintain objectivity and accuracy, but also comparability.

In the years to come you will remember your Census experience with pleasure. You have a right to feel proud, too. For you are now an integral part of the first nationwide study of deafness in this half of the Twentieth Century.

## What This Manual Contains

We have tried to set down in ths Manual most of the things you will need to know to do a first-rate interviewing job. There are four parts to this Manual:

*Part 1* explains the various activities of the National Census of the Deaf (NCD) and how the interviews are related to the other parts of the Census

*Part 2* discusses general interviewing procedures

*Part 3* explains each question in Form A, the household questionnaire —what the question means, why it is asked, what kinds of answers are acceptable

*Part 4* does the same for Form B, the personal interview form, and for Form C, a special supplement

# PART 1

# How The National Census of the Deaf
# Is Being Conducted

## Organizations Responsible for this Survey

The National Census of the Deaf (NCD) is being conducted by the National Association of the Deaf (NAD). Most of the financial support for the NCD comes from the Social and Rehabilitation Service, a part of the U.S. Department of Health, Education, and Welfare. The rest of the funds for the study come from the NAD itself. Thus the study is being done under the control of deaf people.

In addition, the NCD has set up a National Advisory Committee, including representatives of government agencies and educators who work with the deaf or in programs for the deaf. The NCD has also been endorsed by practically every national organization concerned with hearing and deafness, including the national organizations of deaf people. (For a complete list, see the NCD letterhead on the following page.)

## Who is Included in This Survey

The NCD is concerned with persons who:

1. Are totally deaf, or whose hearing is insufficient for the purposes of everyday life. (The degree of hearing loss is defined somewhat more exactly in questions 8-13 in Form A.)
2. Suffered their loss of hearing before the end of their education (for purposes of this survey, before their 19th birthday).
3. Are under the age of 65.

We are also interested to a smaller degree in the persons who live in the same household with deaf persons as defined here.

## Census Activities Before the Interview Survey

For two and a half years the NCD has been carrying on a number of activities leading up to the interview survey of which you will be a part. Two of these activities are directly related to the interviewing.

### Building a List of Names of Deaf People

The major activity of the Census was compiling a list of persons thought to fit the description under "Who Is Included in This Survey." This list was built up through the cooperation of a very large number of sources, with the assurance that all information supplied to the NCD would be kept confidential and used only for Census purposes. Names and addresses were contributed by organizations of the deaf, government agencies dealing with the deaf, individual deaf persons, and innumerable other sources. When nearly half a million names were compiled, a computer was used to eliminate duplicate listings.

*Verifying the Accuracy of the List*

Each person on the remaining list was mailed a short questionnaire to determine whether the name and address on the list were correct and whether he did have the characteristics required for inclusion in the Census. At the same time a limited amount of additional information was gathered.

## The Interview Survey: How The Interviews Are Related to the Rest of the Survey

The interviewing is only one part of the survey though it is a most important part. Before the interviewing could begin, a number of other steps had to be taken. Once the interviews are over, several other parts of the survey will remain to be completed.

*Selecting a Sample of Persons for Interviews*

From those who returned their mailed questionnaires indicating that they met the criteria for inclusion in this study, a computer was used to select a sample for personal interview. Each person selected in this way is the "Key Person" in the household in which he lives. Each Key Person represents about 100 other deaf persons who were not selected. The Key Persons as a group represent all of the deaf people of the United States. As deaf people live in every part of the country, the sample likewise is scattered among many cities, towns and smaller places in states from coast to coast.

*Planning the Interview*

Considerable time was spent in deciding what kinds of information should be gathered and what kinds of questions would be needed. To help make these decisions previous research was examined and analyzed. The National Advisory Committee for the NCD was brought together and asked to consider what it would be most important to learn. Other experts, deaf and hearing, were consulted. A list of rough ideas for questions was prepared for comment by the Advisory Committee and others. The list was revised, rewritten, and improved several times, until we felt ready to test the questions in actual interviews.

*Pre-Testing the Procedures*

The purposes of pre-testing the questions include finding out whether they will be understood in an interview and whether they will provide the information they are intended to get. Pre-testing also indicates how long the interview is likely to last.

For such reasons pre-tests were conducted (in New York and Washington) with several dozen deaf persons selected from our list. Interviewers were trained to use the questionnaire. Some interviews were observed by members of the NCD staff. In addition, all interviewers reported on problems they had had—for example, questions that had not worked well.

After each pre-test some questions were dropped, some new ones added, and many others were changed. The result was a shorter interview with questions

268

that were clearer and easier to ask and answer. At the same time this Manual of Instructions was revised continuously to make it more useful.

## The Next Phase–Interviewing

When the training period is over, interviews will be made according to the instructions in this Manual. The success of the whole study will depend on how well the interviewers do their job. That is why we place so much stress on training. Without proper interviewing all the planning and pre-testing would be wasted, as would the following stages.

## Advance Publicity to Help the Interviewers

The Census has been and will be widely publicized so that respondents will know about the survey. For more than two years information about the Census has been appearing in publications read by the deaf. Such material will continue to appear until the end of the interview period.

In areas where interviews are to be made, state and local organizations of or for the deaf will be reminded that the survey is under way in their localities. They will be asked to help the survey in any way they can; for example, by telling their members or clients about the survey and urging them to cooperate if they are asked.

Local agencies such as police departments will also be told about the survey, so that they may give whatever cooperation may be needed.

Finally, each Key Person will receive a letter from the NCD office in Washington telling him that he has been chosen to be interviewed and that an interviewer will soon be getting in touch with him.

## Checking the Interviewers' Work

Each completed questionnaire sent in by an interviewer will be checked by the NCD office to see that it has been completely and properly filled out. In that way errors will be noted immediately. In some cases they can be corrected; otherwise, the interviewer can be helped to avoid making the same error again.

In addition, some of each interviewer's work will be spot-checked, by telephone or by mail. This is, of course, one way of assuring that instructions are being followed. It is also a way of checking on respondents' reactions to the survey as a whole.

## Turning Answers into Statistical Tables

Most of the questions on the questionnaire are followed by a list of answers, each with a code number. Some questions do not have a list of coded answers; code numbers will have to be given to the answers after the interviews are completed. Coding clerks in the NCD office will then prepare code sheets for interview, in which the answers will be completely replaced by code numbers. From the code sheets, punch cards and computer tapes will be prepared. When any errors in these have been corrected, they will be put into a computer and statistical tables will be produced.

*Keeping Information Confidential*

Through all of these steps, care will be taken so that the answers given by any person will not be found out by anyone except the Census staff. Questionnaires will be kept in locked files. No name or personal identification will be in the punch cards or computer tapes. No organization, agency, or business firm will be permitted to see any respondent's answer—not even the NAD.

It is to insure that no private information will be revealed that you, as an interviewer, are expected to keep to yourself all facts that you learn. This means that you must not discuss the interview with *anyone* other than your supervisor—not with another interviewer, not with a neighbor of the person interviewed, not with your family.

## The Final Phase—Preparing Reports

The statistical tables turned out by the computer will be used to prepare one or more final reports. These reports will indicate:

The purposes of the Census

The way in which it was carried out

The information that was obtained from the interviews and in other ways

What the information means for programs serving the deaf

Copies of the reports will be presented to the organizations sponsoring the Census or represented on the National Advisory Committee. There will also be copies of one or more reports available to the public.

# PART 2

# General Interviewing Instructions

## Interviewing Deaf Respondents

Interviewing in this survey of deaf people requires an unusual combination of skills. You must be acquainted with the general procedures for conducting a research interview and also have the ability to communicate with all kinds of deaf people. Most of this manual is designed to show you how the interviews are to be conducted. Let us begin by considering communication in the interview. The term "respondent" above refers to the person you interview, who answers or responds to your questions.

## Not All Respondents Will Want
## to Communicate in the Same Way

Most of our respondents will probably be accustomed to communicating in part or entirely by manual techniques—fingerspelling, signing, gesturing, or some combination of these means. Others will be accustomed to relying on verbal modes of communication—speech, lipreading, writing. As an interviewer, you are expected to communicate with all kinds of deaf people, finding the most appropriate mode or combination of modes for each respondent. Be prepared to be flexible and to adapt yourself to the respondent's abilities and preferences.

## "Total Communication" in the Interview

In general you should use simultaneous speech and manual techniques (signing, fingerspelling) throughout the interview. In addition, you have been given a series of printed "Flash Cards" to show the respondent. Each card contains a series of alternative answers to a question. This listing of answers to be chosen by the respondent makes it unnecessary to speak and sign them. Thus you add to speech and signing a third mode of communicating questions to the respondent.

However, just as you must determine whether the respondent can read signs and fingerspelling, so you must observe whether he can read the printed words. If he cannot understand manual communication—or does not wish to use it—you will have to rely on other modes. Similarly, you may have to help the occasional respondent who cannot use the Flash Cards by signing their meaning to him.

## Beginning the Interview

*Introduce yourself briefly*

The first step in the interview is to introduce yourself. Your introduction should be brief, not a long explanation. When the respondent comes to the door, begin by speaking and signing simultaneously. Find out as quickly as possible how the respondent wants you to communicate. If he does not wish to use manual techniques, do not use them. If he can neither lipread nor understand signs, discover how he wishes to proceed.

A suggested introduction is:

"Hello. I'm *(YOUR NAME)* from the National Census of the Deaf. Here is my identification. The National Association of the Deaf is making this Census to gather information about deaf people and their needs all over the United States."

Be sure that your introduction includes your name; the names of the National Census of the Deaf and the National Association of the Deaf; and the general purpose of the Census.

In most cases that will be enough of an introduction so that you can verify whether you are at the assigned address and whether the Key Person lives there. If he does and you are not invited in, ask: "May I come in?" Ordinarily the answer will be: "Yes." Do not try to interview at the door.

## Ask the First Question Promptly

Because of the size of the questionnaire, you will want, if possible, to sit at a table for the interview. After seating yourself, begin immediately with the first question. The sooner the respondent begins to participate in the interview, the better. It is unwise to spend a great deal of time describing the kinds of questions you are going to ask. Doing that takes you away from the purpose of the interview, which is to gather information.

## Interview in Privacy

If persons are present who are obviously not immediate family members, suggest to the respondent that he might like to talk to you in a more private place. With an outsider watching or listening, even though a respondent may not refuse an interview, he may be unwilling to give certain information. Thus you would have an inaccurate or incomplete interview.

## Explaining the Survey

Most respondents will accept a brief introduction as a sufficient explanation of the reason for the NCD. A few, however, will want more information before proceeding. A few others may be reluctant to give information or may refuse to be interviewed because they don't want to be bothered or can't see the value of the Census.

You must be prepared to answer questions about the survey and to persuade doubtful or reluctant persons. The following points will help you:

### Purpose of the NCD

If a respondent questions you about the purpose of the survey, use the explanation in your letter of introduction. If an additional explanation is needed, base it on the material at the beginning of this Instruction Manual, using your own words to suit the respondent's level of understanding.

### "Why this household?"

Some respondents will ask why *they* were chosen and suggest that someone else should be interviewed instead. Explain that each person who was chosen to be interviewed represents about 100 deaf persons. Since there are all kinds of deaf persons—young and old, poor and not so poor, men and women, etc.—we chose some of each kind to be interviewed. We need all of the different ones so that when we put together what they will tell us about themselves, we will have a picture of the deaf people in the United States.

*"How long will it take?"*
Do not say "Just a few minutes," or try to give an estimate. Say instead: "That depends on how many people there are in the family and how many are working," or something of that sort.

Avoid asking a question like: "Are you busy now?" which invites a respondent to say: "Yes" and to turn you away. Assume that the respondent will be willing to be interviewed and that he has the time right now. You will usually be right.

*"I don't have the time."*
Occasionally a respondent will insist that he's too busy to spare the time. Suggest that you can return at another time when he will not be too busy. Agree on a definite time with the respondent—i.e., make an appointment with him. Do not just say: "I'll come back some other time." Remember that a return visit costs extra time and money. When you can, obtain an interview on the first visit.

*"Are you selling something?"*
Because some dishonest businesses pretend to conduct a survey as a disguise for selling, a few respondents may suspect you of being a salesman or of gathering information for a business. If this arises, assure the person that you are not selling or advertising anything. Explain again briefly that this National Census of the Deaf is being made by the National Association of the Deaf and that our purpose is to learn more about deaf people and about what kinds of service or help deaf people may want.

*"I don't give out any information."*
Some persons are reluctant to give any information because they fear that other people will learn about their personal affairs. In such a case, assure the person that the answers he gives you will not be given to anybody outside of the Census staff. All information will be kept strictly confidential and will be used only for statistical purposes. (For example: our reports will not say what a particular person told us about his work. They will say: so many deaf people work in factory jobs; so many have office jobs; so many are printers; so many are teachers.) If it seems useful, show the respondent the Notice at the top of Form A.

Note: This issue of confidentiality may come up at the beginning of the interview, or in connection with any particular question. The same procedures may help.

## Your Own Manner

*Friendly but Businesslike*

Your greatest asset in successful interviewing is your own personality as the respondent sees it. Show a friendly interest in the respondent and what he is telling you. Remember, on the other hand, that over-friendliness and a show of great concern for the respondent's personal affairs may interfere with the interview and result in your obtaining less information while taking more time. Your interest must be balanced by a businesslike manner. If the respondent's reply wanders away from the question, try to cut off his remarks tactfully —preferably by asking the next question.

*Objective*

Your own objectivity in asking questions and recording answers is your best assurance that the respondent will feel at ease and willing to give truthful and complete replies. Do not indicate your personal opinion about the answers you receive, either in words or even by your facial expression.

In some cases the respondent may not be sure which answer to choose. He may watch you to see how you feel about the question or to guess what answer you would approve of. Any expression from you of surprise, disapproval or sympathy may make the respondent give an untrue answer or withhold information.

*Normally Courteous*

It will be very helpful to think of the interview as the kind of conversation you might have with anyone you know and respect. What would be bad manners normally is equally inappropriate in an interview. In particular, avoid "talking down" to a respondent when it is necessary to offer explanations. Be as simple and direct as possible.

## How to Ask the Questions

### Ask Questions in the Order Specified

Like the wording of the questions, the order in which they are to be asked has been worked out through pre-testing and several revisions. If you ask questions out of order, both you and the respondent will become confused. This is particularly important because of the instructions in the questionnaire which tell you that if a respondent gives a particular answer you are to skip over certain questions. Parts of the questionnaire contain a fairly complex "skip pattern" —easy to follow if you ask questions in the correct order, but otherwise thoroughly confusing.

### Answers Given Out of Turn

Sometimes a respondent will tell you not only what you asked about but also other things about which you may want to ask later on. You may find it hard to write down all that he tell you in the appropriate places. Do what you would under normal circumstances: Explain politely that he is giving you so much important information that you cannot write fast enough to get it all down. Explain that there's a place elsewhere in the questionnaire where you have to ask about just what he is telling you and that it will be easiest just to write the answer to your *one* question now and get the other information when the questions come up later. This should be done, of course, in a pleasant and coureous manner so that the respondent will not feel scolded or embarrassed.

## Avoid Asking Questions Already Answered

When the respondent has told you the answer to a question before you have asked it, you should not repeat it. The respondent may feel that you don't understand him or that you aren't paying attention to him. He may become confused or resentful and give you less information on following questions.

The questionnaire reminds you of this point once or twice. For example, the first questions ask for the names of all household members. Then you are to ask about the sex, relationship, and marital status of each person in the household, *if necessary*. Sometimes a respondent, in listing the names of residents, may say something like: "Well, there's me, and my husband, John, and my six-year-old daughter, Sarah." You obviously should not ask for the sex, marital status, or relation of any of these persons.

The same principle applies elsewhere. The respondent may have said that he is getting some kind of help from the State Department of Vocational Rehabilitation. When you come to a question that asks whether he has heard of the agency, you cannot ask it without seeming stupid.

If you are *quite sure* of the information, you may mark an answer without asking the question. In general, however, it is wiser to check on yourself by asking some question such as: "I think that you said that you had some help from the Department of Vocational Rehabilitation. Is that right?"

## Ask Questions As they are Worded

It is very important that you ask the questions as they appear in the questionnaire. A great many hours have been spent in trying out various ways of asking these questions. Adding a word, leaving out a word, changing a word—these can change the meaning of the question from what was intended, so that the respondent's answer may be changed as well. In the later section of this Manual, the individual questions are explained to help you understand what kind of information they are designed to get. You will not, however, always know everything that went into the decision to ask a question in a particular way.

When a respondent finds it hard to understand a question, you may have to try asking it again. In the case of "low-verbal" deaf persons this will put a burden on you. Be sure to stick as closely as possible to the wordings in th questionnaire. If you add a question (see the last paragraphs of this section on the use of "probe questions"), be sure to write down the extra questions you ask as well as the answers you receive. If we cannot tell what question you asked, we will not know to what the words you write down are an answer.

## Do not Influence the Respondent's Answer

Experience in conducting interview surveys shows that many people tend to answer questions in the way what they think is wanted or that may help them in some way. This is especially true when a respondent is unsure of his answer to start with. This makes it especially important for you not to "lead" the respondent by letting him think that you prefer a particular answer.

For example, you will ask deaf respondents about the cause of their deafness. Some respondents will not be sure. You may want to "help" the respondent by asking: "Well—was it spinal meningitis?" because you know that is a frequent cause. The respondent, in turn, may want to "help" you, and so may answer eagerly: "Yes, that was it," when in fact he does not know the cause. Now you have put words into his mouth, and you record an answer that you unintentionally invented.

The same result may follow if instead of asking: "Who helped you get this job?" you asked: "Your school helped you find this job, didn't it?" A respondent might think it was impolite to say: "No."

That is what you must *not* do. That is one reason why you are urged not to make your own "improvements" in the questions.

### Pay Attention to the Respondent

Listen to or watch the respondent until he finishes his statement. Otherwise you may get an incorrect or incomplete answer. This may happen in two ways:

If you write down the answer before you are sure that the respondent has finished, you may miss the latter part of the answer.

If you interrupt the respondent before he has finished, you may get a false impression of what he meant to say. This is particularly true if the respondent is hesitant, or trying to recall something to mind, or just trying to make up his mind. Sometimes a person begins by saying: "I don't know—" while he reflects. Be sure not to cut off the respondent's thinking or his reply.

### Avoid Hurrying the Interview

Even under trying circumstances, do not rush the respondent. If he feels that you are in a hurry to complete the interview and get away, he may be resentful or he may try to cooperate with you by omitting important information which it might take time to explain. You should therefore maintain a calm, unhurried manner. Asking the questions in such a manner will do much to produce the relaxed attentive attitude in the respondent that will lead to a successful interview.

### Repeat a Question When Necessary

The respondent may not understand a question, as you may be able to tell from his answer. In such a case, repeat the question using the same phrasing, perhaps emphasizing a key word or phrase that he seemed not to have noticed. If necessary, preface the repetition of a question with a phrase like: "I see," or "Oh, yes."

### Use the Flash Card Booklet

To keep the interview moving smoothly, become familiar with this booklet, the cards it contains, and their use. While you show the booklet to the respondent, use a second one for yourself. In this way you will always be sure what the respondent is looking at, and you will be ready to help him if necessary.

## Ask Additional Questions
## to Get Complete Information

There are several situations in which you may need to "probe," or ask additional questions. For example:

The respondent's answer does not give the kind of information called for by the question, or the answer is incomplete.

You are not sure exactly what the respondent meant, or you think that you may have misunderstood his answer—he has apparently contradicted himself

Sometimes it is helpful to repeat the answer to the respondent and then pause. This may be enough to bring out additional information. Otherwise, in such a case, ask additional questions—as many as are necessary to be sure that you have obtained a complete and accurate answer.

Do not, however, over-probe. If the respondent says, for example, that he does not know the answer to a question, you should probe to help the respondent give some information. If he says again that he does not know, do not insist that he give some answer. This may annoy or irritate him, cause him to choose *any* answer just to satisfy you, and make him doubt whether we are really concerned with getting accurate answers.

## How to Probe

Probe questions should always encourage the respondent to explain his answers without suggesting specific explanations. Frequently the best probe is a very general one that merely asks for more information; for example:

Please explain that a little more
Can you tell me more about that?
Please describe that to me

Another frequently used probe, which has been indicated for a great many questions right on the questionnaire, is some variation of: "What kind of a . . .is it?" On the questionnaire this usually appears when you have offered the respondent a number of answers to choose from. The last alternative is "Other," followed by: "What?" You should reword this according to the question and the initial answer. Here are some examples:

| Question | Answer | Probe |
|----------|--------|-------|
| Which kind of school was it? | Some other kind | What kind of school was that? |
| What did he do (to help you)? | Something else | What did he do? |
| Did you take any courses like these? | Yes | Which kind? Any other kind? |

In some cases when a general question has not obtained the necessary information, you may need to mention the possible alternatives so that the respondent can understand what sort of answer you expect. This is quite acceptable, *provided that you do not give the respondent only a single choice.*

You will find some suggested probes of this kind at some points in the questionnaire. For instance:

Q. How old were you when you became deaf?
A. I don't know.
Q. Were you less than three years old? were you more than 3 but less than 6 years old? (etc.)
A. It was after I was three.
Q. Were you most probably about 4, or 5 or 6?
A. Probably about 4 or 5.

In this way you help the respondent give as precise an answer as he can, without suggesting only one answer.

In similar cases you will have to make up your probe questions. For example in asking about the persons who live in the home in which you are interviewing, you may be told of a man who lives here part of the year and at other periods lives with his sister. To determine whether he is a member of this household, you would ask:

Does he live the greater part of the year here or with his sister?
NOT: Does he live here most of the time?

## Recording Information from the Answers

Recording the answers is just as important as asking the questions. Only you will see and hear the respondent; what you report incorrectly or incompletely is lost.

For most of the questions there is a list of answers on the questionnaire, and all you have to do is mark the answer box, like this:

2 ☒ Yes

1 ☐ No

| 2 | 1 |
| Yes | No |
| ✔ | |

Use a check-mark (✔) or an X, whichever you prefer.

In a few cases, the instructions on the questionnaire ask you to circle the number (or the letter) for the correct answer, like this:

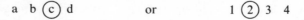

a  b ⓒ d          or          1 ② 3  4

In a number of questions you are asked to write in the answer. Sometimes all you have to fill in is a number, such as someone's age. Because of the amount of space for the answer, you will usually want to use figures (26) rather than write out "twenty-six."

In relatively few cases you will have to write out the respondent's answer. This will be the case where you have marked "Other," since the questionnaire then usually asks: "What?" You also have to write out the person's kind of work or occupation and a few other short answers. You may also want to write a note explaining an answer.

In putting down the answer, whether it is just a check-mark or a sentence or two, follow these rules:

Be sure that you enter an answer for each question you asked.

If the answer is in words, it should be in the respondent's own words, not yours. Of course you may not be able to write down everything he says. You may have to take just the essential part of what he tells you. If he says: "That was before I became sick," you should *not* write: "He said that was before he became sick," or: "That was before he became sick."

Write clearly so that someone who does not know your handwriting can read it. Look at the answer space and try to adjust the size of your writing to it. If you need more space, use the extra space for notes.

Do not use abbreviations. Remember that abbreviations or initials that are familiar to you may not be understood by the office staff.

## Recording "Don't Know" Answers

As indicated earlier, every effort should be made to encourage the respondent to give specific and complete answers to the questions. However, it may happen that the respondent does not have the information requested, and you should not insist on an answer. In such a case, enter "DK" (for "Don't know") in the answer space.

Remember that "DK" means only that the *respondent* does not know the answer. Do not write in "DK" as an answer to a question that you may have overlooked in the interview. If, after an interview, you discover a blank space on the questionnaire for a question that should have been asked, *leave it blank.*

## Family Members Disagree on Answers

Occasionally two members of a family will disagree or give somewhat different answers to the same question. It is wise to provide a moment in which the family members may reconcile their difference of opinion. When possible, ask a neutral probe to bring out the most accurate answer. If they cannot agree:

Accept the answer of the person to whom the question applies, if that person is present

Accept the answer of the head of the household, if the person to whom the question applies is not present. Always accept the answer of the head of the household if the question deals with household or family information (e.g., family income)

Do not, however, indicate by anything you say or by your facial expression that you are giving more weight to the answers of one family member than to those of another.

## After the Interview

### Review Your Work

Be sure to look over the questionnaire— both Form A and Form B—*while you are in the house with the respondent,* so that you can ask any additional questions that may be needed.

You should review all questionnaires again before turning them in to your supervisor. Check to make sure that you have written out any abbreviations that you used during the interview, and similar details.

## Confidential Nature of Interview Answers

All information obtained in your interviews must be held strictly in confidence. It must not be discussed with or disclosed to any person except the research staff of the National Census of the Deaf.

# PART 3

# Form A — Household Interview Form

## Page 1 ("Face Sheet")

### Notice of Confidentiality

You will not usually have reason to read or show this notice to the respondent. The notice is here to be used if the respondent appears to be concerned that what he tells you may be passed on to other people. However, the notice is important because we mean it very seriously.

### Neighborhood Rating Scale

Complete this item *after* the interview. Remember that you are asked to rate the *neighborhood* and not a particular building. If your interview is in the very best neighborhood in the city or metropolitan area, circle "1" even if the house or apartment is unusually small or shabby or dirty. Similarly, if the house in which you interview is very expensive and beautifully kept but stands in an average neighborhood, circle "4."

### Number _____ of _____ Forms A

Complete this item *after* the interview. In most households you will complete one Form A. You will use more than one in these cases:

If there are more than five *related* persons in the household, list the first five on the Form A with the address label on its face sheet. Use an additional Form A for remaining household members.

If there are persons in the household *not related* to other household members (for example, a roomer or a servant who "lives in"), prepare a separate Form A for each.

Copy the 10-digit Identification Number from the address label on to all Forms A for the same household.

When the interview is ended, if you used one Form A, fill out this item to read: "Number *1* of *1* Forms A." If you have used two, fill this item on the first copy to read: "Number *1* of *2* Forms A," and on the second: "Number *2* of *2* Forms A," and similarly for three or more Forms A.

### Number of Forms B

One Form B is completed for each household member who fits the requirements of this Census. Record here *after* the interview the number of Form B questionnaires you made out for persons in this household. If you completed none, enter a zero ("0").

### Interviewer's Name and Number

Sign your name in the space provided *after* you have completed the entire interview for a household or when you are turning in the questionnaire as a final non-interview. (See Items I and J below.)

### Item A. Street Address and Identification Number

These will be entered in advance by the NCD Washington office. Be sure to ask Item A: "Is this (THE ADDRESS ON THE PAGE)?" Make any necessary minor corrections to the address or add a missing ZIP code.

### Item B. Name of "Key Person"

A name will also be entered by the NCD Washington office. We shall refer to the person named here as the Key Person in this household. Verify that this person lives at this address. If he does, ask to go in, and begin the interview with question 1 ("Q1") on page 2. If he does not live here, go on to Item C.

### Items C and D. Present Address of Key Person

Ask Item C to find out whether the Key Person has lived at this address in the last 12 months. Then ask Item D: "Have you his present address?" If "Yes," record that address in Item D. If the address is within your interviewing area, go to it and conduct the interview there. If the address is outside your area, mail the questionnaire with the new address to Washington.

If the Key Person has moved but the present resident does not know his address, mark the "No" box Item D. Make a strong effort to find out whether anyone else can give you his present address. For example, ask neighbors, the building superintendent or near-by storekeepers. If, after trying hard to get a new address for the Key Person, you do not succeed, mail the questionnaire *with an explanation* to Washington.

### Record of Calls (Items E-H)

This is a record for all the visits you make to a household to complete an interview, whether or not you find anyone home. Count as "visits" only attempts *in person* to contact the household, such as ringing the doorbell or knocking at the door. Do *not* include telephone calls.

### Items E and F. Date and Time of Call

For each call enter the date and time in the first blank column; that is, use the first column for the first call, the second column for the second, etc. Fill in this information *before* you knock or ring.

For the date, use an abbreviation (*not* numbers) for the month and numerals for the day (e.g., Mar. 21). For the time, enter the exact time before knocking — not the approximate time. (For example, do not enter 7:27 as "7:30" or "7:25.") Be sure to circle "AM" or "PM."

### Item G. Best Time to Call Back

If nobody (or no responsible adult) is home or if the family is just going out when you call, find out what the best time (date and hour) will be to call again.

This information is for your own use. You may find this out from a child in the household, from a neighboring resident or storekeeper, from a building employee, etc.

If no one can tell you when to return, use your own judgment. If your first call was in the early evening (e.g., around 6 P.M.), make your next call during the day or in the late evening. *Never* make two calls at the same time on the same day of the week; a family that is out on one Thursday at 6 may be out every week at that time. Make up to a total of three calls. If you have not by that time been able to talk to any household member, ask your supervisor for further instructions.

If all members of a household are away (on a trip or vacation, or for other reasons) and are not expected to return in the next four weeks, notify your supervisor and ask for instructions.

### Item H. Result

Show here the result of *this call*. This result might be: "Interview or "No one home or "Only small child home." With the information in Item G this will help you in planning later calls ("call-backs"), and it will leave a record for your supervisor of the calls you have made and their outcome.

### Item I. Interview Completed?

When you finish an interview, mark the "Yes" box here and enter the exact time (to the minute) when you finished. Circle "AM" or "PM." The interval between Item F (the beginning time) and I (the ending time) will show your total time in the house, including any time you had to wait there.

If for any of several reasons you conclude that you cannot complete an interview in the assigned household, mark the "No" box in Item I and complete Item J.

### Item J and K. Reason for
### Non-Interview and for Refusal

Show here the reason for a "final" non-interview — that is, your reason for concluding that you cannot obtain an interview within the rules of this survey. If you have made three unsuccessful calls at the address, your supervisor will indicate whether you are to make further attempts or to return the assignment. In the latter case, you would mark "No appropriate respondent home, repeated calls" or "No one home, repeated calls," as appropriate. The same rule applies to use of the answer: "Away until _____."

Should an assigned person refuse to be interviewed, inform your supervisor. Various measures will be used to persuade reluctant respondents. If you are instructed to return a questionnaire to the office, be sure to complete Item K: "Reason for Refusal."

The other alternative reasons for non-interview are self-explanatory. Remember that "vacant building," when applied to an apartment house or multiple-unit building, means that *all* apartments are vacant, not just that the apartment to which you were sent is unoccupied.

If there is some other reason for a non-interview, mark the "Other" box and *write in* the reason.

## Persons Eligible to be Interview Respondents

This section of your instructions explains who is acceptable to answer the questions in Form- A in various situations. We use the term "respondent" to refer to the person interviewed. We refer to questions as "Q1," "Q2," etc.

## For Q1 Through Q6

These first questions, which ask for the names of household members, how they are related, etc., may be asked of any responsible adult member of the household, whether or not related to the head of the household or the Key Person. For present purposes:

"Responsible" means not mentally incompetent and not too ill to think clearly about the questions and answer them.

"Adult" refers to any person at least 16 years old, or who is or has been married.

Another obvious requirement is that you must be able to communicate with the person; that is, that he must be able to understand the questions and you must be able to understand his answers. For example, if you are a hearing person and the one who answers the door is a low-verbal person, you may not be able to understand one another. Or you may find that the person hears and speaks, but only in a language other than English.

In cases like these, see if there is someone else who can help. Often there is one household member or a neighbor who acts as an interpreter for the household or for its deaf members. Try to find out if there is such a person. If there is and he is not at home, find out when to return.

A child under 16 may be used as an interpreter between you and an older respondent, if necessary, to help you explain some questions; but you must be certain that the child understands your questions and is in fact "translating" correctly both questions and answers.

If you use a proxy respondent for an unrelated person for Q1-6, then when you interview him/her for himself, check Q1-6.

IMPORTANT! Remember that the Key Person is the one with whom we are most concerned. If he is unrelated to other household members — for example, if he is a roomer, a boarder, or one of several unrelated persons living together — you must make your greatest effort to interview the Key Person *first*. For example, if there is no eligible respondent present, ask when the *Key Person* will be home, and arrange an appointment with him. After that, try to get an interview for other household members.

## For the Rest of Form A

The questions in Form A after Q6 may be asked of the Key Person (whose name is on the face sheet) or that person's husband or wife for all persons in the household who are related to them by birth, by marriage or by adoption. This includes both adults and children. However, any related adult who is at home at the time of the interview should be interviewed for himself or herself.

## Children

Information about a child under 16 is normally obtained from one of his parents or from another related adult in the household. However:

A person usually responsible for a child's care, though unrelated to him, may give information about him. For example, the respondent should answer for his foster child or ward who lives with him.

A child or 14 or 15, though not eligible to answer for other family members, may reply entirely or partly for himself if he is present during the interview.

## Unrelated Adults

Any adult household resident (a roomer, a servant who "lives in," a "co-tenant" or "partner") must be asked all questions starting with Q6 *for himself.* However, if the household includes two unrelated family groups, any responsible adult member of each group may answer questions for all members of his or her family.

## "Incompetent" Unrelated Person

If a person is not competent to answer questions for himself and no related responsible adult can answer for him, you may ask the questions about him of someone who is responsible for his care, whether or not the latter is a household member. In such a case, write a note explaining the circumstances, with the number 45 — the number of the question asking who answered for this person.

## Return Call May Be Necessary

In some instances it may be necessary to make a second visit to interview an eligible respondent. For example:

If an otherwise acceptable respondent does not seem to be "responsible," because of extreme age, illness, etc., stop the interview and continue with another respondent even if that requires an additional call.

If an otherwise eligible respondent can answer questions for himself but does not know enough about other related adults in the household, finish the interview for him and arrange to call back for the other household members.

If no eligible respondent for unrelated persons is at home at the time of the original interview, a return call must be made to interview each of them.

## Q1,2,3. Names of All Household Members

Asking and answering these questions is usually extremely simple. Most households consist of a man and wife with their unmarried children. It is the relatively small number of households that don't fit this pattern that may be hard to handle. The following instructions, definitions, and explanations will fit virtually all situations.

## Q1. Head of Household

Begin by asking Q1. Write the name under "PERSON #1."

*Definition of Household*

A *household* is the entire group of persons who live together in an apartment, a single-family house, or a comparable unit. The household may number one or more persons. It includes a household "head" (see the next paragraph) and all of his or her relatives who live with him. Some households include other persons unrelated to the head, such as roomers or servants.

*Head of Household*

This is the person who is regarded as the head by the household members — a man or woman who is the chief breadwinner in the household, the parent of the chief earner, or the only adult household member. In any case, record the respondent's answer, not your opinion.

*Identify the Key Person*

When you list the name of the Key Person (whose name was on the face sheet), circle his Person # at the top of his column, like this: PERSON #1, or #2, etc.

## Q2,3. Other Household Members

Ask Q2 and Q3, and record the names in the appropriate columns, where possible in the order shown here:

Head of household

Wife or husband of head ("spouse")

Unmarried children of the head (or spouse), in order of their age, beginning with the oldest

Married sons and daughters, in order of their age, and their families, listed in the order: husband, wife, children

Other persons related to the head

Other persons not related to the head

If among persons not related to the head there are married couples or other persons related among themselves, list them in the order indicated for the families of married children.

Use a separate column for each person. Do not skip any column. Enter the first name and the last name in the spaces provided. If two persons in the household have the same first and last name, identify them further by a middle initial or name, or as Sr., Jr., etc. Do not assume that all members of the household have the same last name — ASK the last name of each.

286

In general, household members comprise:

Persons whose usual place of residence at the time of the interview is the sample unit (whether present or temporarily absent)

Persons staying in the sample unit who have no usual place of residence elsewhere

By "usual place of residence" we mean the place the person would normally name in reply to the question: "Where do you live?" Specifically it is the place where he usually sleeps. It must be specific living quarters held for him, to which he is free to return at any time (not, for example, just a mail address).

Count as household members persons such as the following:

Persons who consider the sample unit as their home and who are:

Living at home at the time of the interview

Temporarily absent at the time of the interview (on vacation, visiting, or on business). This includes bus drivers, railroad men, ship's crew members who consider the sample unit their home, traveling salesmen, etc.

Staying in a general hospital (i.e., where most patients remain for just a short period of time), regardless of how long they have been there

Babies newly born to household members, who have not yet left the hospital

Domestic or other employees who "live in" and sleep in the sample unit

Roomers or boarders who regularly sleep in the sample unit

Persons temporarily visiting with the household but who have no usual place of residence elsewhere

Students of any age, including student nurses, who live in the sample unit while attending school

Students who attend residential schools or colleges at which they live during the school year, but who usually live in the sample unit when on vacation from school

If the Key Person for a household turns out to be a student at a residential school or college, and is living there at the time of the interview, find out whether the address you are at or the college or school is his usual place of residence. The best way to decide is to determine whether he usually lives at this address during vacations from school.

If the Key Person's usual place of residence is *not* this address, we have no interest in members of this household. Enter the Key Person's address — his usual place of residence — with any necessary explanation on the face sheet in Item D, and return the questionnaire to your supervisor.

If this address is the Key Person's usual place of residence, but he is away at college or other school, follow the general rules for identifying an eligible respondent. If the student is married, his or her spouse (husband or wife) may be interviewed for him or her. If he is under 16, his parent may give information for him. If you cannot follow either of these rules — for example, if he is 16 or over and does not have a spouse living in this household — return the questionnaire to your supervisor with an explanation, including the Key Person's whereabouts.

If any other household member is a student away at a residential school or college, follow similar procedures.

*Whom to Exclude*

If, in addition to the household head and his immediate family, the list of persons in Q1 through Q3 includes a married child and his family, or other relatives of the head (or spouse) such as a mother, uncle or cousin, ask if they all live and eat together as one family. If they do, treat them as a single household, for which only one Form A is required. But if the respondent says that any of these persons lives separately from the others, ask if they have a separate door to their living quarters from the outside* and whether they have separate cooking equipment. If their living quarters have *either* direct access from outside* *or* separate cooking equipment *or both,* consider such persons as a separate household and exclude them by drawing an X through the name of each.

Similarly exclude:

Persons formerly household members but who are:

> Inmates of correctional or penal institutions, mental institutions, homes or hospitals for the chronically ill or handicapped, rest homes or convalescent homes or homes for the aged or needy, regardless of how long they have been there

> Living in nurses' homes, convents, monasteries or other places where they can be expected to live for long periods of time

> Working abroad if their regular place of duty is abroad

> Members of the armed services not living at home

Domestic or other employees who do *not* sleep in the sample unit. (But *do* include them if they live in quarters without cooking equipment on the same property as the sample unit — in the "main house.")

Boarders who eat with the household but usually sleep elsewhere

Persons temporarily visiting with the household who *have* a usual place of residence elsewhere to which they are free to return at any time

---

*"From the outside" means "from outside of the apartment or house."

*288*

If you are not sure whether to include a person as a household member, list him and explain the circumstances in a note.

## Q4. Relation to Household Head

Enter the relation of each person to the *head* of the household. If the respondent has already given you this information, do not ask the question; simply record the relation.

There must be one and only one head in the household. In a household consisting of two or more unrelated persons, designate one "Head" and call each of the others "Partner."

Examples of other relation entries are: wife, son, father, aunt, cousin, grandson, daughter-in-law, stepfather; roomer, maid, hired hand, partner. If there are persons unrelated to the head but related to each other, their relation to each other should also be shown. For example, list a roomer and his wife as "Roomer" and "Roomer's wife"; list a maid and her daughter as "Maid" and Maid's daughter."

## Q5. Sex

Check box for sex of each person. This can usually be told from the name or the relation. However, some names, such as Marion and Lynn, are used for both sexes. If there is any doubt, ask the person's sex.

## Q6. Race

By race we mean "color," and not a person's country of origin, not his religion, and not the language he speaks. For purposes of this survey there are three racial codes:

W White (including Cubans, Puerto Ricans, Mexicans and other Latin-Americans unless they are definitely Negro, Indian or Asian)

B/N Black or Negro

O Other (including American Indians, Eskimos and Aleuts; Chinese, Japanese, Indonesians, and other Asians; Hawaiians and other Pacific island peoples)

Code the race of each person you see; *do not* ask her or him. *Do* ask Q6 for *every* other adult household member and for *every* child whose mother does not live in this household. But for a child whose mother lives in the household, mark the mother's race for the child as well. (NOTE: THIS IS A CHANGE FROM THE INSTRUCTIONS ON THE QUESTIONNAIRE.)

## Q7. Age

Ask for and enter age of each person at his *last* birthday. For babies of less than a year enter "Under 1" in the answer space. If the respondent isn't sure of the exact age of a person, ask him to estimate it as closely as he can. If the respondent refuses to give his own age or the age of someone else, make the best estimate you can and indicate that the age is estimated by writing before it: "est." If you cannot estimate a specific year, show the range of the person's probable age; for example: "est. 10-15 years," or "est. 45-55 years." It is not enough to write "Over 21"; that will not show whether the person is a young adult, middle-aged or old.

## Q8. Marital Status

Ask the marital status of each person 14 years old or over. For persons less than 14 mark "Under 14" without asking the question. For those 14 or over, if you have been told that two household members are husband and wife, mark each of them "Married" without asking the question.

*Common-Law Marriage.* Code as "Married" a couple living together as man and wife (in a "common-law marriage").

*Separated Persons.* Accept a respondent's statement that a person is separated. If however, a respondent asks what we mean by "Separated," explain that the term refers only to married persons who have a legal separation or who live apart because they do not get along with one another.

Code as "Married" a person separated from his spouse because of circumstances of their work, service in the armed services, or similar reasons. Also code as "Married" a woman who has been deserted by her husband.

*Annulled Marriage.* Code a person whose only marriage has been annulled as "Never married."

COMPLETE Q1-8 FOR ALL PERSONS BEFORE ASKING Q9.


## Q9 Through Q18.

Ask all parts of Q9, Q10, etc., through Q18 for Person 1. Then repeat this series of questions for each related household member in turn. These questions are of major importance to this study. They will supply vital information about hearing and loss of hearing in the survey households. In addition, these questions will be used to classify household members and to let you determine which further questions each person will be asked.

## Q9, Q10.

Read the introductory sentence above Q9, and then ask Q9: "Has (he/she) ever had a hearing aid for (his/her) own use?" Mark the "Yes" or "No" box. If "Yes," ask Q10; if "No," skip to Q11.

Ask Q10, "Does (he/she) use a hearing aid now?" and enter the answer.

If the respondent says in answer to Q9 or Q10: "I have (or had) a group hearing aid in school, ask a PROBE: "Do you have one for yourself that you can take from the school?" If he only has the use of a group hearing aid, mark "No."

If the answer to Q9 *or* Q10 was "No," do not use the words: "(without a hearing aid)" in Q11, Q12 and Q13.

## Q11, Q12.

In Q11 and Q12 be sure to ask the question first, and then show the card. (If you gave the respondent the card first, he would look at it and not at you.)

Ask Q11 about the person's left ear and mark the appropriate box. Then ask Q12 about the person's right ear. Remember not to include the phrase "(without a hearing aid)" if the person does not use a hearing aid now.

If the answers to both Q11 and Q12 were "Good," ask Q11 and Q12 for the next family member. If the hearing of the last family member is "Good" in both Q11 and Q12, skip to Q19. If the hearing of all family members is "Good," end the interview.

If the person has a hearing problem but is under 1 year of age, skip to Q16.

## Q13.

Q13 consists of a series of sub-questions designed to determine the severity of the person's hearing trouble or deafness. Again add the phrase "(without a hearing aid)" only if the respondent indicates that he uses one now. Ask each sub-question, 13a through 13g, until a "No" answer is received. Then mark the "No" box and go to Q14. Otherwise, ask each part of Q13 before going to Q14.

If the respondent does not understand "usually," add: "most of the time."

After marking the answers to Q13, the instruction on the questionnaire tells you: "COPY ANSWERS TO Q11, Q12 AND Q13 INTO SPACES AT TOP OF PAGE 13." For Q11 and Q12, circle the code numbers after "Left" and "Right" that correspond to the answer boxes you marked.

For Q13, circle the letter that corresponds to the *last* "No" that you checked.

It is very important for you to circle the correct numbers. The answers to which these numbers correspond will help you decide which questions a person should be asked.

## Q14. Interviewer's Check Item

This is an instruction to you and not to be asked. Look at Q10 to determine if this person now uses a hearing aid. If he does not, check the "No" box and skip to Q16. If he uses a hearing aid now, check the "Yes" box and ask Q15.

## Q15.

Q15 a-g are parallel to Q13 a-g but ask how well a person hears *with* a hearing aid. Remember to stop asking these questions after a "No" answer is given.

## Q16, Q17, Q18.

These questions should be asked only if:

For Q11 and Q12 you circled "3,3" or "3,4" or "4,3" or "4,4"

OR

For Q13 you circled "a," "b," "c," or "d"

That is, they should be asked only for persons who are deaf or who have very poor hearing. *Do not ask* Q16, Q17 and Q18 for persons whose hearing is better than is indicated by the numbers or letters listed above.

## Q16.

For some people this may be a difficult question to answer exactly. Therefore we have provided for two kinds of answers. If the respondent can be precise ("I was born this way." "When I was seven years old."), record his answer.

If he says he does not know, ask him if it was before he was 3 years of age. If he says "Yes," mark the "Less than 3 years" box. If he says "No," ask: "Was it after he was 3, but before he was 6?" etc. Continue until you find the age before which he could probably hear and after which he could not.

Then try to get a more exact answer. For instance, if the respondent says it was before he was three years old, ask: "Was it *probably* when he was 2, or when he was 1 year old, or before that?" If he says it was after 3 but before he was 6, ask: "Was it *probably* when he was about 3, or 4 years old, or 5?" Explain that this is a very important question and that we need to come as close as possible to the exact age. If the respondent then says (for example) "4 or 5," ask if he thinks it was more likely to have been 4 or 5. If he is unable or unwilling to choose, at least you will have narrowed it down to two years — so write "4 or 5" in the "about _____ years" space.

Should the respondent be unable to fix some age, write a footnote to give us an idea of why he cannot answer this question. It is very important in any investigation of deafness to know when a person lost his hearing, so try very hard to pin down the age of loss.

## Q17.

Although Q17 resembles Q16, it is by no means the same. In Q16 we are trying to determine the age at which this person began to *have* trouble hearing or became deaf. In Q17 we try to determine the age at which his hearing problem or deafness was *discovered by his parents*. There may be an interval of as much as several years between the answers to these questions.

## Q18.

Here we can expect some "Don't knows." Occasionally, you will get a vague general answer. Some respondents may simply not know what caused their hearing loss. You should not insist on an answer. In order to help the respondent who has only partial information, we have broken the question down and provided several PROBES.

If the respondent says he was born deaf, use the first PROBE: "Do you know what caused (his/her) hearing trouble?" The first three answers refer to this question; if the answer is any other than the first two, mark "Born deaf, other" and write in the cause.

In the same way, use the second PROBE if the respondent says his hearing trouble was the result of an accidental injury. We want to know *not* what kind of *accident* (auto accident, fire, etc.) but what happened — what kind of *injury* affected his hearing.

If the respondent says his deafness is the result of a sickness, use the third PROBE to find out the name of the sickness. If you mark "Other illness" be sure to write in the name.

292

Similarly, if the respondent names any "Other cause," mark that box and show what the cause was.

If there is not enough space on the answer lines, write a note in the space below. Be sure to show the person number and the answer number with any note.

Age and cause of loss will tend to go together. That is, the person who does not know when he lost his hearing may also have difficulty telling how he lost it. If the respondent can identify the cause as a specific illness or accident, this may help make an inexact answer to Q16 more accurate.

### Q19 Through Q27. Household Information

These questions are asked only once for the family. They are designed to give us some information about the family's living conditions.

### Q19.

The answer to this question can usually be checked without asking. The terms "One-family house" and "Apartment" are self-explanatory. Some examples of other kinds of units are: boarding house, nurses' home or quarters, tent or trailer, and living quarters consisting of individual housing units, such as: Armed Forces installation; combination boarding and rooming house; convent or monastery; dormitory for students or workers; flophouse or mission; general hospital; recreational or religious camp; residential club or tourist home; or transient hotel.

Whichever answer to Q19 you mark, be sure to ask ask Q20. Disregard the instruction on the questionnaire that reads: "(SKIP TO Q21)"; that is an error.

### Q20.

"Rent" means occupied in return for money rent. If the housing is given in return for services (for example, to a janitor or to a clergyman), mark "Other" and explain.

"Own" is the proper answer even if the respondent says: "We're buying it" (i.e., it is mortgaged to a bank or other lending institution). "Own" is also the correct answer if this is part of a cooperative or condominium.

### Q21.

Ask this question for every household. Count as rooms only those that are separated by four walls. Do not count bathrooms, closets, unfinished attics or basements, garages or open porches.

### Q22 Through Q25.

Ask Q22 and mark the appropriate response. If the "No" box is marked, skip to Q26. If "Yes," ask Q23, "What is the number?" Record the telephone number in the space provided. If the household has a telephone and the number is not obtained, enter the reason.

If the respondent asks why you want the phone number, explain that:

In case you have overlooked some needed information, you could phone instead of calling back in person.

Your supervisor phones some of the people you have interviewed to be sure that your work is done properly.

Q24 and Q25 are self-explanatory. An amplifier is a device attached to a telephone for persons who are hard of hearing to increase the loudness of incoming speech. A TTY is a teletypewriter that is attached to a telephone, which enables deaf persons to use the telephone to send and receive messages.

## Q26.

Ask Q26 once for a family to obtain the total combined income for all related household members during *1971*. (NOTE: The questionnaire says 1970. That is an error.) If the respondent does not or will not answer the question for some reason, enter the reason in a footnote. Read the income question just as it appears on the questionnaire. After you ask this question, show the respondent the card; give him enough time to prepare his estimate and tell you the letter. Where necessary, help the respondent obtain the total by adding up the income of several family members or the income from several sources.

*Income of All Related Members.*

We want the money income of the household head *plus* that of all his relatives who are *currently household members*. Include the income of a member of the armed forces who is living at home with his family. If he is not living at home, include allotments and other money received by the family from him. If the head of the household is living alone or with no other relatives, include his income only.

*Income of Unrelated Persons*

On the separate Form A prepared for each roomer, servant or other person not related to the household head, mark the box for his or her individual income. If two or more such persons are related to each other (for example, a roomer and his wife), mark the box for their combined incomes.

*Include as Income.*

Wages or salary from a job, tips, net income from a business or farm, pensions, dividends, interest, rent, welfare, Social Security payments, unemployment insurance, and other money income.

*Do Not Count as Income.*

Income in kind, such as room and board, free meals in restaurants, value of crops produced by a farmer but consumed by his family, etc.

Insurance payments or lump-sum inheritances

Occasional gifts of money from persons not living in the household, or any exchange of money between relatives living in the same household

Money received from selling one's own house, car or other personal property

Withdrawals of savings from banks

Tax refunds

*Where "Zero" Income Reported.*

When no one in the family had income, or when a loss or broke even was reported as the total income for the family, mark Group "A." Before accepting an answer of "No income," be sure the respondent understands all of the things we count as income.

*Get Best Estimate.*

In difficult cases, you may have to help the respondent. Find out who worked during 1971, how much they made a week, etc.; find out who operated a business or farm, or who received any pension, dividends, etc. Add all of these to get an estimate of the total.

*Reasons for Obtaining Income.*

Information on the incomes of the deaf is important for a number of reasons, including these:

It will help us determine how the situation of deaf people compares with that of the hearing

It is of value in helping plan programs for the deaf, and to discover how well these programs are working

It is useful in comparing families in the study who have different income levels, since income obviously is related to ability to obtain education and training and health services

## Q27.

Q27 is designed to find out if anyone in the family received any *money* from welfare (or public assistance), Social Security or Vocational Rehabilitation. If the question arises, include in Welfare or public assistance: aid to families of dependent children (AFDC), old age assistance, general public assistance, and aid to the blind or totally disabled.

Exclude separate payments for hospitals or other medical care. Also exclude services paid for by welfare or rehabilitation agencies, where payment was made directly to another agency (e.g., payment made to a school by Vocational Rehabilitation on behalf of an agency's client).

## Q28 Through Q31.

These questions are not to be asked of the respondent but are to be checked by you from previous information.

## Q28.

In checking the response to this question, look at the top of this person's column. If "3" or "4" was the lowest number you checked in answer to Q11 and Q12, skip to Q30. If "1" or "2" was the lowest number you checked, go to Q29.

## Q29.

If "a," "b," "c" or "d" was checked for Q13, go to Q30; if "e," "f," "g" or "h" was checked, skip to Q36 for this person.

## Q30.

If the "Before 19" box is checked, go to Q31; if the "19 or over" box is checked, skip to Q36.

## Q31.

Look at this person's age. If he is under 65, skip to Q46, check to show who responded and check the "Yes" box to Q47. If he is 65 or older, ask Q32.

## Q32 Through Q35.

These questions are asked for deaf persons 65 or over to determine their educational achievement.

## Q32.

"A school or class for only the deaf or hard of hearing" is intended to include the following:

A public or private school that accepts:

> Only students who have impaired hearing (often with a name like "_____ School for the Deaf")

> Only students with impaired hearing or vision (often with a name like "_____ School for the Deaf and Blind")

> NOTE: Some of these schools are *residential;* that is, the students live at the school, returning to their homes only at vacation times or on weekends. Others are *day* schools; that is, students come to school each day and return to their homes daily when school is over.

A special class or series of classes for hearing-impaired students in regular schools for the hearing.

Check the appropriate answer. If you mark the "No" box, skip to Q36; if "Yes," ask Q33.

## Q33.

Ask this question to determine how many years this person went to school. If he is not sure, use the probe questions provided.

## Q34.

Circle only one number to report the answer to Q34. Thus, if the highest grade

*296*

or year a person attended is the junior year of high school, circle the "11" opposite "High school." Circle the highest grade attended regardless of skipped or repeated grades.

## Regular School

Count only grades attended in a regular school where persons are given formal education in graded public or private schools, whether day or night school and whether attendance was full-time or part-time. A "regular" school is one which advances a person toward an elementary or high school diploma or a college, university or professional school degree.

If the respondent tells you that he graduated from high school but "They only had 11 years of school back then," ask if he received a high-school diploma. If "Yes," circle the "12" opposite "High school" and mark the "Yes" box in Q35. If "No," circle the "11" opposite "High school" and mark the "No" box in Q35.

If a person volunteers that he completed college in less than four years and that he obtained a degree (graduated), circle "4" opposite "College" and mark the "Yes" box in Q35. If the person did *not* graduate or receive a college degree, the entry in Q34 should be the actual number of years he attended college, and Q35 should be asked and marked accordingly.

If a person indicates that he completed four years of college but did not get a degree because he was enrolled in a five-year program, such as engineering, circle "4" opposite "College" in Q34 and mark the "No" box in Q35. If a person completed the fifth year of a five-year degree program and received a bachelor's degree, circle "5" opposite "College" in Q34 and mark the "Yes" box in Q35.

Some persons may have entered professional schools (law, medicine, dentistry) after less than four years of college. When the respondent answers in terms of these schools, obtain the equivalent in college years. For nurses, ask to determine the exact grade attended. If a nurse received her training in a college, determine the highest grade she attended in college. However, if training was received at a nurses' school or hospital training school and did not advance the person towards a regular college degree, determine the highest grade attended at the last regular school.

## Nonregular School

Do not count education or training received in "nonregular" schools, such as vocational, trade or business schools, outside the regular school system. For example, barber colleges, beautician schools, citizenship schools, and dancing schools are not to be counted. Likewise do not count training received "on the job" or correspondence school training, unless it is given by a regular school and is credited toward a school diploma or college degree.

## Junior High School.

If the highest grade a person has attended is in a junior high school, determine the number of years attended and record the grade as if it had been in a school system with eight years of elementary school and four years of high school.

297

*Postgraduate Schooling.*

For persons who have attended postgraduate *high school* but have not attended a regular college, circle the "12" under "High school." For those with postgraduate *college* training, circle the "5+" under "College."

*Other School Systems.*

If the person attended school in a foreign country, in an ungraded school, under a tutor, or under other special circumstances, ask him to give the nearest equivalent of his highest grade attended or the number of years of attendance.

*No Schooling.*

For persons who have not attended school at all, mark the "None" box and go to Q38.

## Q35.

Ask Q35 for all persons who are shown in Q34 as having attended school. Mark the "Yes" box if the person completed the last school he attended. If he did not finish the last school or graduate from it (for example, if he completed only a half year or failed to pass the last grade), mark the "No" box and skip to Q38.

## Q36, Q37.

These questions together are parallel to Q34. While Q34 is asked for deaf persons 65 or over, Q36 and Q37 are for all other persons not in this study's target population. Note that Q34 asked for the last grade of school finished, but Q36 and Q37 ask for this information in two parts:

Q36 — the last grade attended
Q37 — whether that last grade was completed

## Q38.

This question is not to be asked of the respondent but is to be checked by you.

If this person is under 16 years of age, you have no more questions to ask about him. Mark the "Under 16" box, complete Q45 and Q46, and then go to Q28 for the next family member. If this is the last family member, fill out the required Forms B. If this person is 16 or over, ask Q39.

## Q39 Through Q44.

These questions deal with the work status and employment of persons 16 and over. After asking Q39-44 for each person, GO BACK TO Q28 FOR THE NEXT PERSON.

## Q39.

"Work at a job" refers to activity for someone else as an employee in return for wages, salary, commission or pay "in kind" (meals, living quarters or

*298*

supplies provided in place of cash wages); activity in one's own business, professional practice, or farm; and work without pay in a business or farm run by a relative.

Exclude a person's own housework chores and unpaid volunteer work for church, Red Cross, a political party, etc.

If the answer to this question is "Yes," skip to Q43. If the answer is "No," ask Q40 through Q42.

## Q40.

When questions arise, consider that a person has a job or business if he was temporarily absent from his job or business part or all of last week because of vacation, bad weather, labor dispute or illness, but expects to return when these events are ended. Also consider that he has a job if he says that he has a new job which he has not yet started. To clarify some special points:

A *job* is a definite arrangement with one or more employers to work (full-time or part-time) for pay.

A person *on call* to work only when his services are needed is not considered to have a job during weeks when he does not work. For example: a substitute teacher who did not work last week is considered not to have a job.

*Seasonal* employment is considered a job only during the season of employment and not in the off season.

*On layoff* means waiting to be called back to a job from which one has been temporarily laid off or "furloughed." A layoff may be due to a lack of work, plant retooling or remodeling, seasonal factors, etc. A person on layoff is considered to have a job.

A person not working because of a *labor dispute* (strike, lockout) at his own place of employment is not considered on layoff but as having a job from which he is absent.

If you mark "Yes, labor dispute," skip to Q43. Otherwise ask Q41.

## Q41.

Looking for work refers to any effort to get a job or to establish a business or profession. A person was looking for work if he actually tried to find work during the past four weeks or if he made such efforts within the past 60 days and was waiting for the results of these earlier efforts. Some examples of looking for work are: registering at an employment office; visiting, telephoning or writing applications to prospective employers; placing or answering advertisements for a job; and being "on call" at a personnel office or at a union hiring hall.

## Q42.

Ask the question, then show the card. If necessary, instead of "any particular reason" ask "any special reason."

We want a single answer to this question, whenever possible, and not two or more. Most respondents will choose just one answer. Follow these rules if the respondent gives more than one:

If "Retired" and *any* other answer, mark "Retired."

If "Sick" and "Going to school," mark "Going to school."

If "Sick" and "Keeping house," PROBE: "When you aren't sick, will you look for a job or will you just keep house?"

>If the answer is "Look for a job," mark Q42 "Ill."
>
>If the answer is "Just keep house," mark "Keeping house."

If "Keeping house" and "Going to school," PROBE: "When you aren't going to school, will you look for a job or just keep house?"

>If the answer is "Look for a job," mark Q42 "Going to school."
>
>If the answer is "Just keep house," mark "Keeping house."

If you mark "Retired" or "No" in Q42, skip to Q45. Otherwise, ask Q43.

## Q43.

It is important to give a clear and exact description of the industry. To do this, the entry must indicate both a general and a specific function for the employer; for example, cattle ranch, copper mine, fountain-pen manufacturer, wholesale grocery, retail bookstore, road construction, shoe-repair service. The words ranch, mine, manufacturer, wholesale, retail, construction, and repair service show the general function. The words cattle, fountain-pen, grocery, bookstore, road, and shoe indicate the specific function.

*Distinguish Among Manufacturing,*
*Wholesale, Retail and Services.*

It is essential to distinguish among manufacturing, wholesale, retail and service companies. Even though a manufacturing plant sells its products in large lots to other manufacturers, wholesalers, or retailers, it should be reported as a manufacturing company. Use the following as a guide:

A *wholesale* establishment buys (rather than makes) goods in large quantities for resale to retailers, industrial users or other wholesalers.

A *retailer* sells primarily to individual consumers or users but seldom makes products.

Establishments which render *services* to individuals and to organizations, such as hotels, laundries, hospitals, law firms, cleaning and dyeing shops, advertising agencies, and automobile repair shops, are not in manufacturing, wholesale trade or retail trade. Note that repair and similar service shops are not in retail trade, since what they sell is primarily their services, rather than goods. Show the kind of service, such as shoe repair shop, cleaning and dyeing shop, TV and radio repair service.

*Avoid Use of the Word "Company."*

Do *not* use the word "company" in this entry. It does not give useful information. If the respondent reports that he works for a furniture company, use the PROBE shown. If the respondent can not answer that, ask: "Do they manufacture (or make) things or do they just buy and sell them?'' If they just buy and sell, ask: ''Do they sell to other stores or to individuals?'' You would record the replies respectively as: ''Furniture manufacturer,'' ''Furniture wholesaler'' or ''Furniture retailer.''

*Multiple-Activity Businesses.*

Some firms carry on more than one kind of business or industrial activity. If the activities are carried on *at the same location,* describe only the *major* activity *at that location.* For example, employees in a retail salesroom, located at the factory of a company primarily engaged in the manufacturing of men's clothing, should be reported as working in ''Men's clothing manufacturing.''

If the different activities are carried on at *separate locations,* describe the *activity where the person works.* For example, a coal mine owned by a large steel manufacturer should be reported as ''Coal mine''; the *separate* paint factory of a large chemical manufacturer should be reported as ''Paint manufacturing.''

A few specified activities, when carried on at separate locations, are exceptions to the above. The activity of the parent organization should be recorded for research laboratories, warehouses, repair shops, and storage garages, when these kinds of establishments exist primarily to serve their own parent organizations rather than the public or other organizations. For example, if a retail department store has a separate warehouse for its own use, the entry for the warehouse employees should be ''retail department store'' rather than ''warehouse.''

A separate sales office set up by a manufacturing firm to sell to other business organizations and located away from the factory or headquarters of the firm is recorded as ''(Product) manufacturer's sales office.'' For example, a St. Louis shoe factory has a sales office in Chicago; ''Shoe manufacturer's sales office'' is the correct entry for workers in the Chicago office.

*Government Agency.*

Record the specific name of the agency and indicate whether it is Federal (U.S.), State, County, City, etc. For example: *U.S.* Treasury Department, *State* Highway Police, *City* Tax Office. It is not sufficient to report ''U.S. Government'' or ''Police Department.''

Remember that ''Government agencies'' as used here includes *all* branches of government, whether U.S., those of foreign countries, or international agencies (such as the U.N.). It includes all levels, from Federal to village, and all activities: for example, government-owned utilities, Federally-owned railroads, city-owned bus lines, public school systems. Government employees include civilian employees of the armed forces and persons elected to paid public office.

Usually the name of the government agency is adequate; for example, U.S. Census Bureau, State Department of Vocational Rehabilitation. This will be enough if the activity of the agency is absolutely clear from its name. However, sometimes an agency has a great many activities or functions. In that case ask in what part of the agency the person works and report that activity. For example, for a City Department of Public Works a correct entry might be one of the following: "City street repair," "City garbage collection," "City sewage disposal," or "City water supply."

*Business in Own Home.*

Some people carry on businesses in their own homes. Report these businesses as if they were carried on in regular stores or shops; for example, dressmaking shop, lending library, retail antique furniture store, insurance agency, piano teaching, boardinghouse, rest home, boarding children (for a foster home).

*Domestic and Other Private Household Workers.*

When the name of a single individual is given as the employer, find out whether the person works at a place of business or in a private home. The proper industry entry for a domestic worker employed in the home of another person is "private home."

*Examples of Adequate Entries for Q43.*

Following are some examples of adequate and inadequate entries for kind of business and industry. Study them carefully and refer to them periodically to familiarize yourself with the types of entries that are proper and adequate.

| Inadequate | Adequate |
|---|---|
| Agency | Collection agency, advertising agency, real-estate agency, employment agency, travel agency, insurance agency |
| Bakery | Wholesale bakery (sells to grocers, restaurants, hotels, etc.), retail bakery (sells only to private individuals) |
| Box factory | Paper-box factory, wooden-box factory, metal-box factory |
| Club, private club | Golf club, fraternal club, night club, residence club, boardinghouse |
| Coal | Coal mine, retail coal yard, wholesale coal yard |
| Credit company | Credit rating service, loan service, retail clothing store (sometimes called a credit company) |
| Dairy | Dairy farm, dairy depot, dairy bar, dairy products — wholesale, dairy products — manufacturing |
| Engineering company | Engineering consulting firm, general contracting, wholesale heating equipment, construction machinery factory |
| Express company | Motor freight, railway express agency, railroad car rental, armored car service |

| Inadequate | Adequate |
|---|---|
| Factory, mill or plant | Steel rolling mill, hardware factory, aircraft factory, flour mill, hosiery mill, commercial printing plant |
| Foundry | Iron foundry, brass foundry, aluminum foundry |
| Fur company | Fur dressing plant, fur garment factory, retail fur store, fur wholesaler, fur repair shop |
| Laundry | Own home laundry (for a person doing laundry for pay in her own home) |
| | Laundering for private family (for a person working in the home of a private family) |
| | Commercial laundry (for a person working in a steam laundry, hand laundry, Chinese laundry, French laundry or similar establishment) |
| | Self-service laundry (for a person working in an establishment where the customer brings her own laundry and pays a fee to use the washing machines or other equipment) |
| Lumber company | Sawmill, retail lumber yard, planing mill, logging camp, lumber manufacturer |
| Mine | Coal mine, gold mine, bauxite mine, iron mine, copper mine, lead mine, marble quarry, sand and gravel pit |
| Nylon factory | Nylon chemical factory (where chemicals are made into fibers), nylon textile mill (where fibers are made into yarn or woven into cloth), women's nylon hosiery factory (where yarn is made into hosiery) |
| Office | Dentist's office, physician's office, public stenographer's office, life insurance agency |
| Oil company | Oil drilling, petroleum refinery, retail gasoline station, petroleum pipeline, wholesale oil distributor |
| Packinghouse | Meat-packing plant, fruit cannery, fruit-packing shed (wholesale packers and shippers) |
| Pipeline | Natural-gas pipeline, gasoline pipeline, petroleum pipeline, pipeline construction |
| Plastics factory | Plastic materials factory (where plastic materials are made), plastic products plant (where articles are actually manufactured from plastic materials) |
| Public utility | Electric light and power utility, gas utility, telephone utility, water-supply utility |
| Railroad car shop | Railroad-car factory, railroad repair shop |
| Repair shop | Shoe-repair shop, radio-repair shop, blacksmith shop, welding shop, auto-repair shop, machine-repair shop |

| Inadequate | Adequate |
|---|---|
| School | City elementary school, private kindergarten, private college, state university. (Distinguish between public and private, including parochial, and identify the highest level of instruction provided such as junior college, senior high school) |
| Tailor shop | Tailoring and cleaning shop (provides a valet service) custom tailor shop (makes clothes to customer's order) men's retail clothing store |
| Terminal | Bus terminal, railroad terminal, boat terminal, truck terminal, airport |
| Textile mill | Cotton cloth mill, woolen cloth mill, cotton yarn mill, rayon thread mill |
| Transportation | Motor trucking, moving and storage, water transportation, airline, street railway, taxicab service, subway or elevated railway, railroad, petroleum pipeline, carloading service |
| Water company | Water supply, irrigation system, water filtration plant |
| Well | Oil drilling, oil well, salt well, water well |

## Q44.

The entry in Q44 should describe the kind of work the person himself does in enough detail for us to be able to classify his occupation accurately. For example: "Janitor," "Salesclerk," "TV serviceman," "Auto mechanic."

If the answer you receive is not an adequate description, use one or both of the PROBES provided under Q44 to find out what the person does. Enter this information in Q44. For example, "Nails heels on shoes," "Operates dough-cutting machine." When more space is needed, continue the entry in a footnote.

Observe the following special cases:

| Apprentice versus Trainee | An "apprentice" is under a contract during his training period but a "trainee" is not. Include both the occupation and the word "apprentice" or "trainee" in the description; for example, "Apprentice plumber," "Plumber trainee." |
|---|---|
| Contractor versus Skilled Worker | A contractor is engaged principally in obtaining building or other contracts and supervising the work. A skilled worker who works with his own tools should be described as a "Carpenter," "Plasterer," "Electrician," etc., even though he hires others to work for him. |

| | |
|---|---|
| Nurse | Registered nurse, nursemaid, practical nurse, nurse's aide, nursing student, professional nurse |
| Office worker | Typist, secretary, receptionist, comptometer operator, file clerk, bookkeeper, physician's attendant |
| Salesman | Advertising salesman, insurance salesman, bond salesman, canvasser, driver-salesman (routeman), fruit peddler, newsboy |
| Supervisor | Typing supervisor, chief bookkeeper, steward, kitchen supervisor, buyer, cutting and sewing forelady, sales instructor, route foreman |
| Teacher | College teachers should be recorded by subject and title, for example, "English instructor" or "History professor." For high school and elementary school teachers, grade or level is adequate; for example, "fourth grade teacher" or "junior high school teacher." |
| Technician | Medical laboratory technician, dental laboratory technician, X-ray technician |
| Tester | Cement tester, instrument tester, engine tester, battery tester |
| Trucker | Truck driver, trucking contractor, electric trucker, hand trucker |

## Q45.

These items must be checked by you.

Show who responded to questions 1-44 for each person in the household. If a person answered all questions for himself, mark the "Self entirely" box. If a person answered some questions for himself and some other family member answered the others for him, mark the "self partially" box and enter the other family member's number on the line labelled "person number." If a person answered no questions for himself, enter the person number of whoever responded.

## Q46.

This again is directed to you and not the respondent.

Mark the "Yes" box for persons who must receive Form B and the "No" box for all others. If you are in doubt as to who should receive Form B, refer to Q31. If the "Under 65" box is marked, Q46 should be checked "Yes." If this is the last family member, add up the number of Forms B required and enter this number on the front of this questionnaire.

## Summary of Procedure for Asking Questions on Form A

| Question Number | Ask as a block once for the whole household | Ask for each person in turn | Ask as a block for each person in turn |
|---|---|---|---|
| 1-5 | X | | |
| 6 | | X | |
| 7 | | X | |
| 8 | | X | |
| 9-18 | | | X |
| 19-27 | X | | |
| 28-46 | | | X |

# PART 4

# Completing the Personal Interview Form

Complete one copy of Form B for each person in the household who meets these criteria:
1.  Has severely impaired hearing (as defined by Q28 and Q29 on Form A)
2.  Was less than 19 years old at the onset of the impairment
3.  Is now less than 65 years old

Such persons were identified by Form A Q28 through Q31. Before completing Form B for a household member be sure that he does meet the above criteria.

Copy on to the blank Form B the household identification number from the face sheet of Form A. Enter the person number and person's age from the top of page 13, Form A, and the age at onset of deafness from question 16, Form A. You will need to refer to age and age at onset of deafness several times in Form B.

## Education

Questions B-1 through B-22 deal with education. These questions are designed to make it possible for us to describe the extent and type of education received by the deaf persons in the survey.

## B-1.

This question refers to the first attendance at school, and therefore excludes education at home (for example, by a tutor). It refers to attendance at any school, whether for the deaf alone or for the hearing.

If the respondent does not know the exact age at which he started school, probe for his best estimate (e.g., "About how old were you ...") If this person gives an age, record that age in the answer space to the right of the question and skip to B-3. If this person has never attended school, mark that box and go to B-2.

## B-2 and B-3.

These questions are not to be asked of the respondent but are to be checked by you from previous information.

## B-2.

This question is not to be read to the respondent. It asks you to check the age of the person for whom this form is being completed (refer to face sheet of Form B). If he is under 16, skip over the questions dealing with work experience to B-79, which starts the series on communication. If he is 16 or over, skip to B-23, which starts the section on work.

## B-3.

Check B-3 to determine if the respondent became deaf before or after starting school. If the age in response to B-1 is less than the age of onset of deafness, which you will have entered on the Face Sheet of Form B, mark the "Before" box. If the age in response to B-1 is equal to or greater than the age of onset of deafness, mark the "After" box.

### B-4 Through B-8.

These question numbers were not used. Turn to page 2 and ask B-9.

### B-9 Through B-19.

These questions are for persons who have attended school. Questions in this series seek to obtain a short educational history of the persons covered.

### B-9 Through B-12.

These questions obtain the educational history. Answers to them are recorded in the table below the questions. Record information for the first school attended on line 1. For *each* school *of any kind* attended after that, use the available line. (Do not skip any line.) Usually only three entries are required on each line:

The name of the school
The number of years attended (under the appropriate "Kind of School")
A check under "Yes" or "No" for the answer to B-12.

The only time a fourth entry is needed for a school is when it is a kind other than those listed. Then write in "What Kind" in the appropriate column and the number of years attended.

Ask B-9, adding the phrase "after you became deaf" for persons who became deaf after starting school. Record the name of the school on line 1 of the table and ask B-10.

As soon as you have asked B-10, show the respondent the card with its list of "Kinds of Schools." When the respondent has answered, make no entry in the table, but ask B-11. Enter *that* answer under the kind of school. Then ask B-12 and check the answer. If it is "No," go to B-13. If the answer to B-12, however, was "Yes," repeat B-9 through B-12, recording the answers, until a negative answer is given to B-12. Then go on to B-13.

The first time you ask B-9 you may use the parenthetical "After you became deaf." You will not need to add these words when you repeat the question.

The kinds of schools are defined as follows:

| | |
|---|---|
| Residential School for the Deaf | A school for the deaf (or the deaf and blind) at which the students live, returning to their homes on weekends, at vacation periods, or at the end of school terms or school years. |
| Day School for the Deaf | A school for the deaf to which the students go each day, returning to their homes each night |
| Classes for the Deaf in Regular School | A class for deaf and/or hard of hearing students in a school with hearing students |
| Other | Any school with no special class for hearing-impaired students |

Note that only "regular schools" are to be listed (see Form A, Q34) — those in the usual progression from elementary through junior and senior high schools, colleges, and universities, awarding academic diplomas and academic or professional degrees. *Exclude* here education or training received in vocational, trade, or business schools outside of that progression. For example, do not count barber colleges, beautician schools, citizenship schools, dancing schools, auto mechanics institutes; or on-the-job training; or correspondence school training, unless it is given by a regular school and credited toward a school diploma or college degree.

## B-13 and B-14.

These questions are the same as those in Form A (Q36 and Q35), which were asked for other household members. After you ask B-13, show the respondent the card for this question and circle the appropriate year (grade). Then ask B-14 to determine whether that grade was completed. If it was, skip to B-16. Otherwise ask B-15.

## B-15.

This question will permit us to identify all persons in the study who are still attending school. Remember that "school" in these questions refers only to academic schools (not business and trade schools).

## B-16.

Not all schools for the deaf have had the same number of grades as ordinary schools. Although the previous questions will show the last grade completed,

*311*

B-16 is needed to learn whether the person finished the education offered by the last school he attended.

**B-17.**

This is an Interviewer Check question, addressed to you. Check the age by referring to the face sheet of Form B. If the age is 21 or over, skip to B-23; otherwise, ask B-18.

**B-18.**

This question permits us to identify persons in whom this study has a particular interest — those who were enrolled in special education for the hearing-impaired during the academic years 1970-1971 and 1971-1972.

**B-19.**

Again an Interviewer Check question, the same as B-8. For those under 16, skip past the questions on work to B-79. For those 16 or over, skip to B-23.

**B-20.**

B-20 is the one to which you skipped from B-6 or B-13, for persons who had finished college. If the person finished at least two years of college, ask: "Do you have a degree from any college or university?" If the answer is "No," skip to B-23. Otherwise ask B-21 and B-22.

**B-21 and B-22.**

Space is provided to list the names of colleges or universities from which degrees are held (B-21) and to show the degrees (B-22). Show under "(A)" one college and degree(s) received from it and under "(B)" a second college and degree(s) from it. If any degree was received from more than two colleges, show the name and degree(s) in the space under B-21 and B-22.

## Work

B-23 through B-71 deal with various aspects of the person's current work, his work history, and job training he may have had. The first part of this section, B-23 through B-30, is a series of questions that indicate what the person's major activity is — that is, whether he is currently employed, or a student, or retired, or whatever may be the case.

**B-23.**

This question about employment, like several others (but not all) in this series, is similar to one that was asked for other household members on Form A. See Q39 on that Form for further discussion. If the respondent has difficulty with this question, you may change "in the last seven days" to "during the last seven days."

If the person worked during the seven days preceding the interview, check the "Yes" box and skip to B-28. Otherwise go to B-24.

*312*

**B-24.**

For explanation of the answers to this question, see Form A, Q40.

If the person has a job, even though he did not work at it during the previous week, check the appropriate answer box and skip to B-28. Otherwise go to B-25.

**B-25.**

See Form A, Q41.

**B-26.**

See Form A, Q42. As soon as you have asked B-26, show the respondent the appropriate card; then record his answer.

**B-27.**

Note that we will now break respondents into three groups, depending on when they last worked. For those who last worked before 1962, or who have never worked, skip all remaining questions on work; that is, skip to B-72. For those who last worked between 1962 and 1966, or between 1967 and 1971, skip over questions on the current jobs to B-48. For those who last worked at some time during 1972, go on to B-28.

**B-28 Through B-47.**

Various aspects of the person's job are touched on by these questions. For persons at work, or with a job but not at work ("Yes" to B-24), these questions are about the *present* job. If a person worked at or has more than one job, these questions refer to the job at which he spends the most time. If equal time is spent at each job, the questions refer to the one he considers more important or has had longer. For a person on layoff from a job, or who last worked in 1972, ask these questions about his last previous job or business.

**B-28.**

This question, concerning the business or industry in which the person works, is the same as Form A, Q43, to which you should refer for detailed instructions. If his job is with a government agency or public school system, skip over B-29 to B-30. The discussion of Form A, Q43, explains in detail what is included under "Government Agency."

**B-29.**

From the answers to this question it will be possible to see what proportion of deaf people are self-employed and what proportion work for others. When you have asked B-29, show the respondent the appropriate card and record the answer. The following notes will clarify the distinctions we want to make here and will show how you are to handle certain specific problems.

*Private Company.* Working for a private employer for wages, salary or commissions. This includes also compensation by tips, piece rates, or pay in kind, if received from a non-governmental source, regardless of whether the source is a large corporation or a single individual. Include work for wages or salary for settlement houses, churches, unions, and other nonprofit organizations, such as Red Cross and Chamber of Commerce. Also include work for private organizations doing contract work for state or local governments.

The words "Federal," "State," "County," "City," appear frequently in the names of *private* companies. Also, the names of some government agencies may appear to be private organizations. You must determine whether the employer is private or government (Federal or other) in these cases. Also, school teachers and other professional people working for pay sometimes report themselves as "self-employed," but you must report the actual kind of employer.

*Own Business*. Persons working for profit or fees in their *own business, farm, shop or office*

Include persons who have their own tools or equipment and provide services on contract, subcontract, or a job basis, such as carpenters, plumbers, taxicab drivers, or truck operators.

Exclude handymen, odd job workers, superintendents, foremen, managers, or other executives *hired* to manage a business or farm, or salesman working for commission.

*Without Pay*. Work without pay on a farm or in a business owned by a related household member. Include room and board and cash allowance. If money is received for such work, mark "Private Company."

*Special Cases*. If any of the following special cases are brought to your attention, employ the following rules:

*Domestics, etc.* A maid, laundress, cook, cleaning woman, gardener, or baby sitter working in another person's home is classified as "Private Company."

*Farm Workers*. Mark a person "Own Business" if he operates a farm for himself regardless of whether he *owns* or *rents* the land.

Also mark "Own Business" persons who have their own equipment and provide services to farmers, such as combine operator or a cotton-picking machine operator.

Farm managers, foremen, farmhands, etc., who work for wages or salary or at piece rates (for example, tomato pickers) are classified as "Private Business" or "Government" as the case may be, but not as "Own."

*Partnerships*. Two or more persons who operate a business in partnership should each be reported as self-employed in their *own* business. The word "Own" is not limited to one person.

*Clergymen*. Preachers, ministers, priests, rabbis and other clergymen attached to a particular congregation or church organization are classified as "Private Business."

Clergymen working in a civilian government position (for example, prison chaplains) are considered "Government."

Clergymen not attached to any particular church organization and who conduct religious services on a fee basis are regarded as self-employed and in their "Own" business.

*Nuns.* They receive "pay in kind" and are classified as "Private Company."

*Public Utility Employees.* Transportation, communication, electric light and power, gas, water, garbage-collection and sewage-disposal facilities may be owned by either government or private organizations. Be sure to distinguish between government-operated and private organizations for utility employees.

### .B-30.

For detailed discussion of "kind of work" see Form A, Q44.

### B-31.

This question is concerned with what the person earned *from his job or jobs* during *1971*.

Unlike the earlier question on total family income (Form A, Q26), we do not ask here about income from all sources, but only what the person received in pay from his employer or from his own business. This includes wages, salaries, tips, and all other compensation for work (See Form A, Q26, for further details on what constitutes "pay").

### B-32 Through B-36.

These questions are intended to find out about certain aspects of the process of getting a job, such as learning about a job opening, making contact with a prospective employer, and establishing one's qualifications.

### B-32.

Note that the question presents two alternatives to the respondent: "Did you ask or apply for it, or was it offered to you without you asking?" But there are three coded answers: "Applied," "Offered," and "Transferred." Others may say: "Well, I applied for a promotion and after awhile they gave it to me." In that case, mark both "Applied" and "Transferred, promoted."

If you have marked "Applied," regardless of what else has been checked, go on to Q33. If "Applied" is *not* marked as an answer, skip to B-36.

### B-33.

If the respondent says that he got the job without help from anyone else, skip to B-36. If he reports that he had some help, go on to B-34. If he had any help at all, mark the box for "Had help." B-34 and B-35 will give some indication of the kind of help received

### B-34 and B-35.

These questions should be handled in the same way. After asking the question, show the proper card for each and record the answer or answers. If the respondent mentions more than one answer, check *all* that he indicates. If the answer is not one of those listed, mark the box for "Someone else" (in B-34) or for "Something else" (in B-35) and write in the answer in the respondent's own words.

### B-36.

Read the question to the respondent and show the card. Be sure to check "Yes" or "No" for each thing the respondent may have had to do.

### B-37 Through B-46.

This series of questions is concerned with communication between the person and those with whom he has contact at work — his immediate supervisor, people whom he may supervise, and other people with whom he may work.

### B-37 and B-38.

Here we ask first how his *immediate* supervisor conveys ideas to the person, then how the latter conveys *his* ideas to the supervisor. Note that we are asking about the immediate supervisor — the one who gives orders or instructions directly to the respondent and to whom the respondent is directly responsible. Recognizing that each may use more than one mode of communication, the questions ask for the mode *most often* used. If several are mentioned, mark all that apply. If some other mode is used most, mark the box for "Some other way" and describe what it is.

If the person has no supervisor at work — for example, if he is self-employed — mark the appropriate box in B-37 and skip to B-40. Otherwise ask B-38.

### B-39.

Self-explanatory.

### B-40 through B-43.

This set of questions, parallel to B-37 through B-39, is concerned with communication between the person and others whom he may supervise. If the person does not supervise anyone at work, mark the "No" box in B-40 and skip to B-44. If he *does* supervise any others, ask B-41 and B-43.

B-41 and B-42 are similar to B-37 and B-38, and the same instructions apply. B-43, like B-39, is self-explanatory.

### B-44 Through B-46.

These questions concern communication with "other people at work" — "fellow workers" or "colleagues" who neither supervise nor are supervised by the person. This is intended to apply *not* to anyone he may happen to know who works in the same organization (especially if it is a factory or office with numerous departments and employees), but only to those persons with whom he has regular face-to-face relations in the ordinary course of this work. If in answer to B-44 the respondent says there are no other people at work, mark the appropriate box and skip to B-47. Otherwise go on to B-45.

Otherwise, the instructions for B-37 through B-39 apply to B-44 through B-46.

## B-47.

This is another Interviewer Check question, not for the respondent but for you to complete. B-28 through B-46 were asked, you will remember, not only for those who are currently employed, but also for those who do not have a job but did have a job at some time during 1972. B-44 now asks you to separate those who do have a job from those who do not.

Refer back to B-27. If you marked the "1972" box, this person did not have a job. All others for whom you asked B-28 and the following questions should be persons who had jobs. If you have followed your previous instructions correctly, the following will apply:

If the answer in B-27 is "1972," mark "No" in B-47 and go on to B-48.

If there is no answer checked in B-27, mark "Yes" in B-47 and skip to B-54.

## B-48 Through B-61.

These questions seek information on the person's major activity, including his work history, for the ten years since 1962. B-48 through B-53 are for those who are not now employed. You will ask these questions for persons marked "No" in B-47 and also for those who last worked between 1962 and 1971 (as shown in B-27) and for whom you skipped directly from B-27 to B-48. These questions, B-48 through B-53, are asked before going on to B-54 through B-61. The latter eight questions provide a short work history.

## B-48 and B-49.

These questions provide a baseline date for the beginning of the present major activity (keeping house, going to school, looking for work, etc.). If the answer to B-48 is "Yes," mark the box and skip to B-50. Otherwise, ask B-49 and enter the answer.

## B-50 Through B-53.

Since these questions are parallel to the job-history series B-54 through B-61, the answers to questions beginning with B-50 are recorded in the table on page 9.

B-50 (occupation or "kind of work") and B-51 (business or industry) are comparable to Q44 and Q43, respectively, on Form A, to which you should refer for detailed instructions.

## B-52.

This question is in two parts. First it asks:

"Why did you leave that job?"

This is followed by a PROBE:

"Why was that?"

Be sure to ask both parts. The PROBE is the most important part of the question. Do not accept a vague answer like: "It wasn't a good job." If necessary, probe a second time to get a complete answer. Here are some examples of how to proceed:

| If the respondent says: | Ask: | If the respondent then says: | Ask: |
|---|---|---|---|
| "I was fired" "I was laid off" "I was transferred" | "Why was that?" or "Why were you (fired/laid off/ trans- ferred)?" | "Because they didn't like me" or "Because I couldn't do the work" | "What didn't they like about you?" or "Why didn't they like you?" or "Why couldn't you do the work?" |
| "I retired" "I quit" | "Why was that?" or "Why did you (retire/quit)? | "Because I didn't like the job" "Because they didn't treat me right." "Because I couldn't do the work" | "What didn't you like about the job?" "Why didn't they treat you right?" "Why couldn't you do the work?" |

Mark one box for the answer to the first part of the question. Write the answer to the PROBE in the respondent's words. If there is not enough room of the answer, write a footnote including the answer with the number of the question (B-52) and the person number.

## B-53.

The question itself is self-explanatory. If the answer is any year before 1962, you have obtained a ten-year history; skip to B-62. Otherwise skip to B-55.

## B-54.

This begins the job history *for those currently employed*. Note that the answer to B-54 is to be recorded *not* in the table on page 9 but on page 8 with the question. As in B-53, if the answer is any year before 1962, you have completed a ten-year history, so skip to B-62. Otherwise, go to B-55.

## B-55.

Answers to this question and those through B-61 are recorded in the table on page 9. The question identifies the person's major activity. Two forms of the question are provided—the first for females, the second for males. If the answer "Something else" is given, PROBE to identify the activity. Mark the box for the correct answer in the table. If any activity other than "Working" is marked, skip to B-61. If the answer was "Working," go on to B-56.

## B-56, B-57 and B-58

B-56 ("kind of work" or occupation) and B-55 (industry) are the same as those asked for other household members. See Form A, Q44 and Q 43, for detailed instructions. Record answers in the table as indicated.

B-57 is self-explanatory. If the job was "with the same employer," mark the "Yes" box in the table and skip to B-59. If "No," mark the appropriate box and go on to B-58.

## B-59 and B-60.

See B-52 for instructions. B-60 corresponds to the PROBE in B-52.

## B-61.

Select the appropriate form of this question, depending on the answers to B-55.

If the answer is any year before 1962, go on to B-62. Otherwise repeat B-55 through B-61. Continue repeating these questions until you reach an activity that began in 1961 or earlier. Then go to B-62.

## B-62 Through B-69.

These questions ask about training in vocational or job skills received either in school or after leaving school and whether the training was ever utilized. B-62 through B-64 refer to training in school, B-65 through B-69 to subsequent training.

## B-62 and B-63.

B-62 and B-63 ask about trades taught or job training received in school. If there were none, mark the "No" box in B-62 and skip to B-65. Otherwise ask B-63. Since many schools for the deaf have given their students training in several manual trades, be sure to PROBE for more than one "kind of work . . . trained for." Since the "kind of work" is essentially the same information as asked for in Form A, Q44, review the instructions for that question.

## B-64.

Since we have asked whether any of the training was used in *any* job, the answer could logically be expected to be "Yes" in a large proportion of cases. However, many respondents may be inclined to say "No" if they've never held a job in the trade they were taught. Since we are asking the respondent for his opinion here, we will not argue about the accuracy of his answer.

## B-65 Through B-69.

Do not omit the "bridge" sentence: "Now let's talk about after you left school." Without this, some respondents in earlier pre-tests were confused by the unannounced transition. All answers to this series are to be entered in the table on page 11.

**B-65.**

Listed on the card for this question are various types of training or training situations. Use *one column* for each kind of training the person has had, up to a total of three types. If the answer to B-62 is "None," mark the "No" box for B-65 in the first column and skip to B-70.

A *course or program in a trade or business school* refers to a separate course, or a series of courses, in a school which is not a regular academic elementary school, junior high school, high school, or college.

A *correspondence course* is one in which the instruction is given by mail; there are no classes to attend.

*Apprenticeship training* is usually in a skilled manual occupation, such as the various building trades (carpenter, plumber, electrician). It is usually covered by a contract between the trainee and the employer. It is often sponsored by an employers' association, a labor union, or both jointly. It lasts for a relatively long period of time—often for several years.

*On-the-job-training* is generally not covered by a contract specifying length of the training period, etc. It is ordinarily a less formal training program, intended to teach the trainee to do the particular job rather than to teach him a trade. It thus provides training that ends when the person can do the job. It therefore is usually of relatively short duration (from a few weeks to a few months) and provides training in jobs less skilled than those for which there is an apprenticeship system.

*Orientation.* In most places of work there is some short period ranging from a few minutes' talk to a week or two of formal meetings, lectures, or movies, designed to tell a new employee about the company, its organization and rules, and (sometimes) his place in the organization. This is *orientation. Ordinarily it does not try to teach work skills,* and we are therefore not concerned with it here. We mention orientation only to emphasize the distinction between it and training.

A *special workshop for handicapped workers* is what is sometimes called a "sheltered workshop." It is operated by a government agency or by a private social-welfare agency, such as Goodwill Industries. Such a workshop provides training for handicapped workers and jobs for some who cannot hold regular jobs.

**B-66.**

See the instructions for Form A, Q44.

**B-67.**

This question is designed to find out whether or not the person completed the course or training. If he is not sure, try to learn whether he received some kind of diploma or certificate for finishing the course. If he finished, skip to B-69; if not, go on to B-68.

**B-68.**

Self-explanatory.

**B-69.**

Self-explanatory.

**B-70 and B-71.**

These questions deal with labor union membership. Ask B-70 and check the appropriate answer box. If the answer was "Yes," skip to B-72; if "No," ask B-71.

## Communication

### B-72 Through B-87.

These questions inquire about the ways in which the respondent communicates in various situations away from work, his judgment of his own ability to communicate by various modes of communication, and related matters.

### B-72 Through B-77

These questions refer to the ways the person most often uses to tell things to various people and the ways others use most often to tell things to the person.

### B-72.

Mark all of the alternatives that apply. Try to eliminate rare or frivolous responses. For example, a person may say that his parents wrote to him, by which he means that when he was away from home his parents wrote letters to him. It is obvious that that is not what we wish to know. If the respondent indicates that his parents signed to him, be sure to clarify whether this means that they gestured, fingerspelled, signed, or used any combination of these.

If the respondent asks: "What do you mean, 'When I was a little child?' " say: "When you were very young." We do not have a specific age in mind; it might be, for example, before the age of eight years. Certain problems may come up; for example:

> The respondent says: "Before I became deaf at the age of 6, they spoke to me. After I became deaf, they learned to fingerspell and then that's the way they used most." For such an answer leave a footnote marked with the question number, B-72.

> The respondent says: "My mother signed; my father talked." In such a case, write "Father" under "Speak" and "Mother" under "Sign."

### B-73 and B-74.

Ask these questions only if the respondent is married. For a married woman, ask how she communicates with her husband; for a man, how he communicates with his wife.

### B-75 and B-76.

These questions apply only if the respondent has children. If the respondent says: "I talk to the hearing children, but sign to the deaf ones;" follow the procedure explained for B-72.

### B-77.

This refers to general experience with store clerks. If the respondent says it depends on the store, explain that we mean in stores where he doesn't usually shop. We are interested in what he does with strangers—clerks who do not know him.

### B-78.

This question is asked to determine if the respondent had any training in speaking, lipreading, signing or fingerspelling after he left school. Since a person may have been trained in more than one of these methods, check as many as apply.

### B-79 and B-80.

These questions are only asked if the respondent in under 16 years of age.
In asking these questions, proceed as in B-72.

### B-81 Through B-86.

Notice that with each kind of communication we ask the respondent to rate his ability to "send" and his ability to "receive." As you are aware, it is one thing to be able to fingerspell and another to be able to read fingerspelling.

If the respondent says that he cannot do one of these things, mark the box for "Not at all."

If he says: "I don't know; you tell me," answer: "What I want is your own idea about how well you can do this. How good is your (speaking, lipreading, etc.) good, fair, poor, or not at all?"

Record any comments that the respondent makes about these questions in the space following B-86.

### B-87.

This question is for each respondent who has been communicating manually in the interview or who said that he can in answer to B-83 or B-84.

Do not accept only the name of a person in response to this question. If the respondent answers with a name, PROBE to identify its bearer as being, for example, a teacher, a counsellor or a school-mate in elementary school.

## Other Health Problems

### B-88 Through B-97.

These questions are concerned with selected impairments that frequently accompany deafness and with the care that persons having these impairments may need and be obtaining.

### B-88 Through B-90.

These questions ask how well the respondent sees. Ask B-88 and mark the appropriate box. If the "No" box is marked, skip to B-91; if "Yes," ask B-89 and mark the appropriate box.

If the response to B-89 is "Blind," mark the proper box and ask B-90. If the answer to B-89 is any other than "Blind," mark the answer box and skip to B-91.

For those who have said they are blind, ask B-90. Each state defines blindness in its laws; the exact definition is not the same in all states. A person who is legally blind may have some vision—he need not be *totally* blind. Usually a legally blind person knows that he falls within this category because he is eligible for a Federal (and state) income tax exemption.

## B-91.

Ask B-91 and show the respondent the card. Mark the "Yes" or "No" box for each condition according to the respondent's answer. If the respondent says "No" and you think that he has the condition, remember: You are to record what the respondent says and not to try to make a diagnosis. If you don't agree that his answer is correct, mark the box for his answer and then write a footnote explaining your opinion.

Here, as elsewhere in the interview, you should not attempt to explain to the respondent conditions he has never heard about. If the respondent was born with a harelip, we will have to hope that he knows that that is the name of the condition. (If you are interviewing a parent about his or her child, the parent is more likely to know if the child has one of these conditions.) For your own clarification, we may note the following:

*Harelip or cleft palate.* These are conditions with which a child may be born. A harelip is a vertical fissure (cleft, or crack) in the upper lip, due to the failure of the bones and flesh to unite prior to birth. A similar fissure in the palate (roof of the mouth) results in a cleft palate. Our question is intended to identify persons *born with* these conditions. Frequently they are repaired by plastic surgery. If the respondent says: "I was born with a harelip but it was stitched up," write a note like this: "Born with/repaired with the arrow pointing to "Cleft palate."

*Cerebral palsy.* This is a name for a group of conditions that affect a person's ability to control his bodily movements, especially his head and limbs. These conditions are due to brain damage resulting from birth injuries or to prenatal birth defects.

## B-92.

Ask B-92 and report in the respondent's own words whatever condition(s) he mentions. PROBE to obtain as complete an identification of the condition(s) as possible.

## B-93.

Do not ask this question of the respondent, but mark the appropriate box. If there are no conditions reported in B-89, B-91 or B-92, skip to B-98. If one or more conditions are reported, ask B-94.

### B-94 Through B-97.

These questions are asked for each person reporting any seeing or blindness in B-89, or some other condition in B-91 or B-92. They deal with the possible need to reduce one's activities due to such conditions and with the receipt of special care or treatment for those conditions.

### B-94.

This question is asked to learn whether this person has to cut down on the things people his age normally do.

Choose the proper wording; for example:

"Does your eye trouble keep you from doing the things . . . "
"Does your diabetes keep you from doing the things . . . "

or whatever condition may have been mentioned.

For an adult male, end the question with:

" . . . other people your age do, like working?"

For an adult woman, ask:

" . . . other people your age do, like working or keeping house?"

For a child, ask:

" . . . other children his age do, like going to school?"

If the respondent wants to explain, write down the explanation in the blank space.

### B-95 Through B-97.

These questions, concerned with treatment or care for the conditions mentioned, are self-explanatory.

### B-98 Through B-117.

These questions cover three topics: services the person may need; why he hasn't obtained them; whether he knows of an agency in his state that offers such services.

### B-98 Through B-101.

Ask each question individually and wait for a response. Mark either the "Yes" or "No" box before going to the next question. If you have checked "No" for all of these, skip to B-103; otherwise, ask B-102.

### B-102.

Ask this question for each kind of help the respondent says he needs and record the answer in the respondent's own words. For the phrase "(kind of help needed)," substitute the kind of help, such as: "an ear examination" or "a hearing aid." In recording answers for more than one kind of help, identify each kind by placing the question number before the response.

### B-103.

This question is to determine whether the respondent knows where to turn for help to obtain health, rehabilitation or related services. If he says "Yes," PROBE to find out the name of the agency.

### B-104 Through B-109.

These questions are parallel to B-98 through B-101, but deal with educational and vocational services. Apply the same procedure for these questions as for B-98 through B-101.

### B-110.

This question is the same as B-102, except that it refers to B-104 through B-108. Follow the same procedure for this question as for B-103.

### B-111.

This question is parallel to B-103, except that it asks about education or training and counseling about work. Follow the same procedure for B-111 as for B-103.

### B-112 Through B-114.

Follow the same procedure for asking these questions as for B-98 through B-103 (or B-104 through B-111).

### B-115 Through B-117.

These questions refer to difficulties the respondent may have had in obtaining needed insurance. Ask each of these questions and record the kind of insurance in column A and the reason for the trouble in column B.

### B-118 Through B-127.

These questions are about the respondent's knowledge of or experience with the state Vocational Rehabilitation agency. Because the names of such agencies are not the same in every state, a blank space has been left for the name. The correct name will be inserted by the NCD office.

### B-118.

This question asks if the respondent has ever heard of the state Vocational Rehabilitation agency. If his answer is "No," mark the "No" box and skip to B-128; if "Yes," mark that box and ask B-119.

### B-119.

Ask the question and record the answer in the respondent's own words. If he says he doesn't know, ask his whether he can mention anything that the agency does. Only if he can give no answer, write "DK" (for "don't know").

**B-120.**

Ask the question and record the answer. If "No," skip to B-128; if "Yes," ask B-121.

**B-121 Through 124.**

These questions are asked of every respondent who indicated in B-120 that he had requested service from the state Vocational Rehabilitation agency.

B-121 asks what kind of help was sought
B-122 asks how long ago that help was sought
B-123 asks if the respondent got the help he wanted
B-124 asks, for those who did not get what they wanted: "Why not?"

The respondent may have asked for more than one type of service from the agency. In such cases, be sure to label the type of service to which the respondent refers. Ask these questions for each type of help the respondent says he asked the agency to provide. Be sure to follow the "SKIP" instructions in B-123 and B-124.

**B-125.**

Ask of each respondent who indicated in B-123 that he got the help he requested, to find out whether he was satisfied with the service. If "Yes," check the "Satisfied" box and skip to B-127; if "No," check that box and ask B-126.

**B-126.**

Ask the question for respondents who were not satisfied with the agency's service to find out the reason for the dissatisfaction. Enter the answer in the respondent's words.

**B-127.**

Ask the question and show the respondent the card. Check "Yes" for each mode of communication he mentions. Be sure to PROBE ("Any other way?") and add any other "ways" mentioned. Mark the "No" box for those not mentioned. If more than one counselor helped the respondent, mark all of the ways used by all counselors involved.

**B-128 Through B-136.**

These questions deal with the respondent's childhood background and provide some information about his parents. Some respondents may not be sure of some of the answers. Remember that the respondent's best estimate of the probable answer is worth much more than a "Don't know." If the respondent is unsure, explain that we want whatever he can tell us, even if it's only *probably* correct.

## B-128.

"Country" means: United States or the name of a foreign country. If born in the United States, mark that box and ask question B-129. If born in a foreign country, mark the "other" box and record the name of the country in the space provided. Then skip to B-130A.

## B-129.

Ask this question only of respondents who say they were born in the United States in response to B-128. Here we want the name of the city or town and the state where the respondent was born. After recording this information, skip to B-131.

## B-130A.

If the respondent says he made several trips between another country and the United States, we want the last date when he came to this country to live permanently. (Ignore short vacation trips, etc.)

## B-130B.

This question is asked to determine if the respondent is now a citizen of the United States.

## B-131 and B-132.

These questions asked about the hearing of the respondent's parents when he was a child. PROBE to get the most accurate response possible.

## B-133.

Ask this question to find out what language other than English was spoken in the respondent's home when he was a child. If "No," mark the "None" box. If "Yes," PROBE to find out which language.

## B-134.

This question is asked about the respondent's father only. In recording the information, use the same procedure as was used to cover education of the respondent. (See Form A, Q34, and B-13 and B-14.)

## B-135 and B-136.

These questions are about the kind of work the respondent's father did for most of the years the respondent was in school. The answers to these questions must show the same kind of detail as the answers to B-28 and B-30. See instructions for those questions. Apply the same procedure for B-135 and B-136 as for B-28 and B-30.

## B-137 Through B-140.

Ask or check these questions for every female respondent who is 14 years of age or older. Do not count any stillbirths, step-children or children she has adopted.

## B-141.

At this point, thank the respondent and end the interview.

## B-142.

Same as Q46 on Form A. Refer to the instruction for Q46 in completing this item.

## B-143.

Before leaving the household, rate the respondent's ability to communicate by each mode of communication listed.

# References

Beasley, W. C. Characteristics and distribution of impaired hearing in the population of the United States. *Journal of the Acoustical Society of America,* 12, 1940, 114-121.

Berger, D.G., Holdt, T. J. and La Forge, R. A. (Eds.) *Effective vocational guidance of the adult deaf.* Eugene, Oregon: Oregon State Board of Control, Special Schools Division, 1972. (Grant No. RD-2018-S. Rehabilitation Services Administration, Social and Rehabilitation Service, Department of Health, Education and Welfare).

Best, H. *Deafness and the Deaf in the United States.* New York: Macmillan, 1943.

Boatner, E. B., Stuckless, E. R., and Moores, D. F. *Occupational status of the young adult deaf of New England and the need and demand for a regional technical-vocational training center.* West Hartford, Connecticut: American School for the Deaf, 1964. (Grant NO. RD-1295-S-64. Vocational Rehabilitation Administration, Department of Health, Education and Welfare).

Bowe, F. G., Delk, M. T., and Schein, J. D. Barriers to the full employment of deaf people in federal government. *Journal of Rehabilitation of the Deaf,* 6, 1973, 1-15.

Brill, R. G. *Administrative and professional developments in the education of the deaf.* Washington, D.C.: Gallaudet College Press, 1971.

Bureau of Labor Statistics, U. S. Department of Labor. *Employment and earnings,* 20 (9), 1974.

Campanelli, P. A. and Schein, J. D. Inter-observer agreement in judging auditory responses in neonates. *Eye Ear Nose Throat Monthly,* 48, 1969, 697-702.

Craig, W. N. Post secondary education: research implications. *Deafness Annual,* 3, 1973, 175-181.

Craig, W. N. and Silver, N. H. Examination of selected employment problems of the deaf. *American Annals of the Deaf,* 111, 1966.

Crammatte, A. B. *Deaf persons in professional employment.* Springfield, Illinois: Charles C. Thomas, 1968.

Crammatte, A. B. Insurance problems of deaf people. In R. L. Meyer (Ed.), *The deaf man and the law.* Washington, D.C.: Council of Organizations Serving the Deaf, 1970.

DiFrancesca, S. *Academic achievement test results of a national testing program for hearing impaired students. United States: Spring 1971.* Washington, D.C.: Office of Demographic Studies, Gallaudet College, 1972.

Fraser, G. R. Profound childhood deafness. *Journal of Medical Genetics,* 1, 1964, 118-151.

Freebairn, T. *Television for deaf people: selected projects.* New York: Deafness Research & Training Center, New York University, 1974.

Friedman, M. and Hall, M. *Workshop on continuing education for deaf adults.* New York: Deafness Research & Training Center, New York University, 1971.

Gentile, A. and DiFrancesca, S. *Academic achievement test performance of hearing impaired students. United States: Spring, 1969.* Washington, D.C.: Office of Demographic Studies, Gallaudet College, 1969.

Gentile, A. and Rambin, J. B. *Reported causes of hearing loss for hearing impaired students, United States: 1970-71.* Washington, D.C.: Office of Demographic Research, Gallaudet College, 1973.

Gentile, A., Schein, J. D., and Haase, K. Characteristics of persons with impaired hearing. *Vital and Health Statistics,* Series 10, No. 35, 1967.

*Georgia's Deaf.* Atlanta, Georgia: Works Project Administration of Georgia (Official Project Number 665-34-3-90), 1942, 19.

Glorig, A. and Roberts, J. Hearing Levels of Adults by Age and Sex. *Vital and Health Statistics,* Series 11 No. 11, 1965.

Guttman, L. The Cornell technique for scale and intensity analysis. *Educational and Psychological Measurement,* 7, 1957, 247-279.

Hansen, M. H., Hurwitz, W. N. and Madow, W. G. *Sample survey methods and theory. Volume I.* New York: John Wiley & Sons, 1953.

Hatfield, E. M. Estimates of blindness in the United States. *The Sight-Saving Review,* 43, 1973, 69-80.

Hull, F. M., Mielke, P. W., Timmons, R. J., and Willeford, J. A. The National Speech and Hearing Survey: preliminary results. *Asha,* 13, 1971, 501-509.

Kish, L. *Survey sampling*. New York: John Wiley & Sons, 1965.

Kroneberg, H. H. and Blake, G. D. *A study of the occupational status of the young adult deaf of the Southwest and their need for specialized vocational rehabilitation facilities.* Little Rock, Arkansas: Arkansas Rehabilitation Service, 1966. (Grant No. RD-1652. Vocational Rehabilitation Administration, Department of Health, Education & Welfare).

Lauritsen, R. R. Vocational education of the deaf—1973. *Deafness Annual*, 3, 1973, 103-104.

Lloyd, G. T. (Ed.) *Planning for deaf community development*. New York: New York University, Deafness Research & Training Center, 1973.

Lunde, A. S. and Bigman, S. K. *Occupational conditions among the deaf*. Washington, D.C.: Gallaudet College, 1959.

Miller, H. W. Plan and operation of the health and nutrition examination survey. *Vital and Health Statistics*, Series 1 No. 10 abb, 1973.

Mindel, E. D. and Vernon, M. *They grow in silence*. Silver Spring, Md.: National Association of the Deaf, 1971.

Murray, N. E. Deafness following maternal rubella. *Medical Journal of Australia*, 1, 1949, 126-130.

National Center for Health Statistics. Origin, Program, and Operation of the U.S. National Health Survey. *Vital and Health Statistics*, Series 1, No. 1, 1965.

National Center for Health Statistics: Estimation and sampling variance in the Health Interview Survey. *Vital and Health Statistics*. PHS Pub. No. 1000 — Series 2 — No. 38. Public Health Service. Washington. U.S. Government Printing Office, June, 1970.

National Center for Health Statistics: Health Survey Procedure: concepts, questionnaire development, and definitions in the Health Interview Survey, *Vital and Health Statistics*. PHS Pub. No. 1000 — Series 1 — No. 2. Public Health Service. Washington. U.S. Government Printing Office, May, 1964.

National Center for Health Statistics: *Vital and Health Statistics*. PHS Pub. No. 1000 — Series 10. Public Health Service. Washington. U.S. Government Printing Office.

Phillips, G. B. *A survey of career opportunities for the deaf*. Rochester, N.Y.: University of Rochester, M.Ed. dissertation. June, 1973.

Post, R. H. Hearing acuity variation among negroes and whites. *Eugenics Quarterly*, 11, 1964, 65-81.

Rainer, J. D., Altshuler, K. Z., and Kallman, F. J. (Eds.) *Family and mental health problems in a deaf population*. New York: New York State Psychiatric Institute, 1963.

Rawlings, B. *Summary of selected characteristics of hearing impaired students. United States: 1969-70*. Washington, D.C.: Office of Demographic Studies, Gallaudet College, 1971.

Rawlings, B. *Characteristics of hearing impaired students by hearing status, United States: 1970-71*. Washington, D.C.: Office of Demographic Studies, Gallaudet College, 1973.

Rawlings, B. and Gentile, A. *Additional handicapping conditions, age at onset of hearing loss, and other characteristics of hearing impaired students, United States: 1968-69*. Washington, D.C.: Office of Demographic Studies, Gallaudet College, 1970.

Rickard, T. E., Triandis, H. C., and Patterson, C. H. Indices of employer prejudice toward disabled applicants. *Journal of Applied Psychology*, 47, 1963, 52-55.

Roberts, J. and Bayliss, D. Hearing levels of adults by race, region, and area of residence. *Vital and Health Statistics*, Series 11, No. 26, 1967.

Roberts, J. and Federico, J. V. Hearing sensitivity and related medical findings among children. *Vital and Health Statistics*, Series 11, No. 114, 1972. pp 72.

Rodda, M. *The hearing-impaired school leaver*. London, England: University of London Press, 1970.

Rosen, S., Plester D., El-Mofly, A. and Rosen, H. V. Relation of Hearing Loss to Cardiovascular Disease. *Transactions of the American Academy of Ophthalmology and Otolaryngology*, 68, 1964, 433-444.

Rosenstein, J. and Lerman, A. *Vocational status and adjustment of deaf women*. New York: Lexington School for the Deaf, 1963.

*330*

Schein, J. D. Factors in the definition of deafness as they relate to incidence and prevalence. In *Proceedings of the Conference on the Collection of Statistics of Severe Hearing Impairments and Deafness in the United States, 1964.* Public Health Service Publication No. 1227, Washington, D.C.: U. S. Government Printing Office, 1964.

Schein, J. D. *The deaf community.* Washington, D.C.: Gallaudet College Press, 1968.

Schein, J. D. *Analysis of factors affecting undergraduate enrollments at Gallaudet College.* New York: Deafness Research & Training Center, New York University, 1972. Also in *Program master plan summary Gallaudet College including pre-college programs.* Washington, D.C.: Gallaudet College, Office of the Vice President for Planning and Public Service, 1973. pp N1-N30.

Schein, J. D. Hearing disorders. In *Epidemiology of neurologic and sense organ disorders,* L. T. Kurland, J. F. Kurtzke, and I. D. Goldberg (Eds.) Cambridge, Massachusetts: Harvard University Press, 1973 A. pp. 276-304.

Schein, J. D. (Ed.) Model for a state plan for vocational rehabilitation of deaf clients. *Journal of Rehabilitation of the Deaf,* Monograph No. 3, 1973 B.

Schein, J. D. (Ed.) *Education and rehabilitation of deaf persons with other disabilities.* New York: Deafness Research & Training Center, New York University, 1974.

Schein, J. D. and Bushnaq, S. M. Higher education for the deaf in the United States: a retrospective investigation. *American Annals of the Deaf,* 107, 1962, 416-420.

Schein, J. D. and Delk, M. How many deaf people? *Rehabilitation Record,* 14, (4), 1973, 36-38.

Schein, J. D. and Delk, M. The National Census of the Deaf Population. *Deafness Annual,* 3, 1973, 183-193.

Schein, J. D., Freebairn, T., Sund, B. and Hooker, S. Television for deaf audiences. *Deafness Annual,* 2, 1972, 71-80.

Schein, J. D., Gentile, A., and Haase, K. Methodological aspects of a hearing ability interview survey. *Vital and Health Statistics,* Series 2, No. 12, 1965.

Schein, J. D., Gentile, A., and Haase, K. W. Development and evaluation of an expanding hearing loss scale questionnaire. *Vital and Health Statistics,* Series 2, No. 37, 1970.

Schein, J. D. and Ries, P. W. *Special meeting on the identification of black deaf persons.* Silver Spring, Md.: National Association of the Deaf, 1970.

Schein, J. D. and Roy, H. L. Some physical characteristics of the deaf college student. Washington, D.C.: Office of Psychological Research, Gallaudet College, 1961.

Schlesinger, H. S. and Meadow, K. P. *Sound and sign.* Berkeley, Cal.: University of California Press, 1972.

Silver, N. H. Employment practices and trends in industry. *Journal of Rehabilitation of the Deaf,* Monograph No. 2, 1970. pp 10-14.

Stahler, A. Underemployment. In R. L. Jones and K. Stevenson (Eds.) *The deaf man and the world.* Council of Organizations Serving the Deaf, National Forum II, 1969. pp 33-40.

Stewart, M. G. The U. S. economy in 1980: a preview of BLS projections. *Monthly Labor Review,* April, 1970, 3-34.

Texas School for the Deaf and Texas Education Agency. *An employment analysis of deaf workers in Texas.* Austin, Texas: Authors, 1972.

U. S. Bureau of the Census. *The blind and deaf-mutes in the United States: 1930.* Washington, D.C.: U. S. Government Printing Office, 1931.

U. S. Bureau of the Census. *Census of Population 1970. General Social and Economic Characteristics, Final Report.* PC (1) — C1, U. S Summary. Washington, D.C.: U. S. Government Printing Office, 1970.

U. S. Bureau of the Census. *Current population reports,* Series P-60, No. 85, 1972.

U.S. National Health Survey: The statistical design of the health household interview survey. *Health Statistics.* PHS Pub. No. 584-A2. Public Health Service. Washington, D.C., July, 1958.

Waksberg, J. *The deaf community study of a metropolitan area: sample design for household survey.* Washington, D.C.: Office of Psychological Research, Gallaudet College, 1961.

*331*

Webb, C., Kinde, S., Weber, B., and Beedle, R. Incidence of hearing loss in institutionalized mental retardates. *American Journal of Mental Deficiency,* 70, 1966, 563-568.

Williams, B. R. and Sussman, A. E. Social and psychological problems of deaf people. In A. E. Sussman and L. G. Stewart (Eds.) *Counseling with deaf people.* New York: Deafness Research & Training Center, New York University, 1971.

Williams, C. A. Is hiring the handicapped good business? *Journal of Rehabilitation,* March-April, 1972, 30-34.

# Index

*335*